FASHIONING MASCULINITY

'Original, thought-provoking, and argued with tremendous rigor and clarity'

John Brewer, *European University Institute*

The fashioning of English gentlemen in the eighteenth century was modelled on French practices of sociability and conversation. Michèle Cohen shows how, at the same time, the English constructed their cultural relations with the French as relations of seduction and desire. She argues that this produced anxiety on the part of the English over the effect of French practices on English masculinity and the virtue of English women.

By the end of the century, representing the French as an effeminate other was integral to the forging of English, masculine, national identity. Michèle Cohen examines the derogation of women and the French which accompanied the emergent 'masculine' English identity. While taciturnity became emblematic of the English gentleman's depth of mind and masculinity, sprightly conversation was seen as representing the shallow and inferior intellect of English women and the French of both sexes.

Michèle Cohen also demonstrates how visible evidence of girls' verbal and language learning skills served only to construe the female mind as inferior. She argues that this perception still has currency today.

Michèle Cohen is Senior Lecturer in Languages and Linguistics at Richmond College, the American International University in London.

FASHIONING MASCULINITY:

national identity and language in the eighteenth century

Michèle Cohen

London and New York

First published 1996
by Routledge
2 Park Square, Milton Park, Abingdon, Oxon, OX14 4RN

Simultaneously published in the USA and Canada
by Routledge
270 Madison Ave, New York NY 10016

Transferred to Digital Printing 2005

© 1996 Michèle Cohen

Typeset in Palatino by
Florencetype Ltd, Stoodleigh, Devon

British Library Cataloguing in Publication Data
A catalogue record for this book is available from the British Library.

Library of Congress Cataloguing in Publication Data
Cohen, Michèle, 1944–
Fashioning Masculinity / national identity and language in the
eighteenth century / Michèle Cohen
p. cm
Includes bibliographical references and index.
1. English literature – 18th century – History and criticism.
2. National characteristics, English, in literature.
3. Nationalism – Great Britain – History – 18th century.
4. Masculinity (Psychology) in literature. 5. English literature –
French influences. 6. Women and literature – Great Britain.
7. Nationalism in literature. 8. Sex role in literature.
9. France – in literature.
10. Men in literature I. Title
PR448.N38C64 1996
155.3′32′0941–dc20   96-7553
CIP

ISBN 0–415–10736–9

For my son Daniel

CONTENTS

PREFACE

On 6 May 1994, Queen Elizabeth II of England and President François Mitterand of France officially inaugurated the Channel Tunnel. For Britain, this momentous event ended centuries of insularity from the Continent, an insularity that implied protection and proud difference. Symbolically, to 'mark the official joining of England and France', two newspapers, *The Guardian* and *Libération* exchanged format and layout for the day. The features advertised in *The Guardian* were practical, if conventional: 'fares, phobias and food'.[1] Having recently heard on BBC Radio 4 that only 4 per cent of English people speak French, I was struck by the absence of any mention of practicalities relating to the French *language*, except for one. This was an article entitled 'Thomas the trans-Europe TGV seeks superman – or woman' describing the search for drivers for the 'Eurostar Trans-Manche Super Train'. As only experienced drivers could apply, the sole criterion for selection was the candidates' language learning aptitude, something the European Passenger Services company took seriously enough to commission its own 'tailor-made, 600 hour, multi-media language learning pack – aptly called En Train de Parler'. But it is the following comment that caught my attention.

> Staff who joined British Rail simply to drive trains and who had never envisaged learning *another language* have shown great enthusiasm, motivation and proficiency in learning French . . . 'Our drivers have shown that the old cliché that the British can't learn foreign languages simply is not true', concluded Kate Pearce, project manager of languages at European Passenger Services.[2]

This excerpt should raise a few eyebrows, although it probably also confirms popular prejudices about language learning in England. Since the study of one foreign language is compulsory in English secondary schools and French is commonly that one, had not these British drivers been exposed to *some* French already?[3] Of most interest, however, was Ms Pearce's conclusion that since drivers had been successful, enthusiastic and motivated language learners, 'the old cliché that the British *can't* learn foreign languages simply is not true'. How can the (in)ability to learn foreign languages, an individual psycholinguistic trait,[4] be said to be a *national* characteristic?[5] And how can a trait be said to be 'national' when it describes mostly the male section of the population, not the female?

Recent figures reveal that at least twice as many girls as boys take French at school in England, a situation that has worried the modern language establishment for a number of years. Among the reasons adduced to explain why boys don't take French, one recurs: boys perceive French to be a 'girls' subject', a 'female' language.[6] This was particularly intriguing to me, a French national. It had never occurred to me that my native tongue might have a gender. But the gender of French is not just a linguistic or academic curiosity, the product of a national quirk. It has serious implications not only for language classrooms today but, ultimately, for relations between England and France, as the 'linguistically challenged' English stand poised on Europe's doorstep.

When was the statement that French is a female language made, and why was it made at all? When I started researching this question, I expected it would lead me to investigate the historical construction of femininity. But no. Tracing the emergence of the notion that French is a female language led me to explore not femininity, but the fashioning of the *gentleman* in eighteenth-century England, and the role of representations of French manners and language in the formation of an English masculine national identity.

ACKNOWLEDGEMENTS

This book owes a great deal to individuals and institutions, and could not have been written without their generosity. I would first like to thank the European University Institute in Florence, Italy, for the award of a Jean Monnet Fellowship in 1994–5 which enabled me to spend a year reflecting and writing in beautiful Florence. I also want to thank Richmond College for supporting my leave. In particular, I am grateful to Edna Clark who took care of the details, and to Jim Madden and Sara Chetin who taught my courses so that I had a stress-free year away.

None of it would have happened without John Brewer. He encouraged me to consider publishing the thesis upon which this book is based, supported my application for the Jean Monnet Fellowship, read and commented on my work while in Florence, and always gave me the most generous intellectual support. My gratitude to him goes beyond anything words can express.

I thank my friends who listened patiently and made constructive criticisms which I tried to implement. I am particularly indebted to Bob Batchelor, Phil Bevis and Anne Goldgar, who made me think further and more clearly. I also thank Nels Johnson, Luisa Passerini and Stella Tillyard for reading work in progress rigorously and making useful comments, and Sandy Brewer, Patricia Fara, Sara Graham-Brown, Tim Hitchcock, Olwen Hufton, Nels Johnson, Peter Leuner and Kathryn Lovering for their time and support. I am especially grateful to Lawrence Klein, whose work has been so important to the development of mine, for his sympathy and support of my ideas.

My thanks also go to my editors, Claire L'Enfant, for her vision, her insight into my work and her kindness; and Heather McCallum, for her enthusiasm and her encouragement.

ACKNOWLEDGEMENTS

Thanks are also due to libraries and their staff. The British Library, the library of the European University Institute and above all, the Richmond College library, whose staff obtained, throughout the years, the myriads of inter-library loans without which research would have been very difficult. I thank in particular Jean Challender, Julie Ellin, Tracy Goodfellow and Frank Trew for their patience and efficiency. I also thank Michael Goerke at the European University Institute and Sahan Deb and Simin Foster at Richmond College for demystifying computer programmes. Many thanks, too, to Paula Stahley for help with printing the manuscript.

I am also grateful to my friends, in London and in Florence, for providing emotional support and distraction from my obsessive labour. I thank Grace Tillyard and Luigina Toscano for being who they are and being there for me. I am also grateful for the friendship and support of Carrie Alyea, Phil Bevis, Diemut Bubeck, Sara Graham-Brown, Nels Johnson, Anne Goldgar, Deniz and Rifat Kandiyoti, Maurice Milne, Filippo Misanelli, Federico Marotta, Angela Schenk and Tessa Storey.

My parents have been enthusiatic supporters of my work since the beginning, and I thank them for their belief in me. Above all, I thank my son, Daniel, for his love, for taking care of everything while I was writing, for making me laugh, and for his constancy.

TEXTUAL NOTE

All French texts quoted in the text have been translated by me. All French spellings have been modernized.

INTRODUCTION

THE ENGLISH TONGUE

This book is about the construction of the gentleman. 'Self-fashioning', Stephen Greenblatt has noted, 'is always ... in language'.[7] Language, defined not as an abstract but as an historically specific system 'through which meaning is constructed and cultural practices organised', is central to the construction of subjectivity.[8] However, when the connection between linguistic practice and identity is discussed, the language concerned is usually the mother tongue.

In this study I explore how the play of tongues – English, French and Latin – was implicated in the shaping of the English gentleman.[9] The following chapters will trace why cultivation of the tongue was essential to politeness and to the construction of the gentleman, and why tongues (languages) and the tongue (of the speaking subject) came to be critical sites for the representation, articulation and production of national and gender identities. My use of the word 'tongue' is deliberate. My intent is to impart to my text the eighteenth-century slippage between the tongue as language and the tongue as organ of speech, a slippage central to the belief that language and national character were indissolubly linked.[10]

The tongue, then, was pivotal throughout the eighteenth century. Yet, it is hard to find the word in nineteenth-century discourses, even those relating to conversation – this is still true today.[11] Why is it that whereas both Italian and French have retained the term *lingua* and *langue* to refer both to their national language and to the organ of speech, this usage has virtually disappeared in English?[12] In seventeenth- and eighteenth-century

1

England, tongue and language were synonymous and used inter-changeably. Johnson defined 'tongue' as 'a nation distinguished by their language', and explained his attitude to change in language with the comment that 'tongues, like governments, have a natural tendency to degeneration'.[13] At the same time, the tongue was also that 'slippery member' which both men and women found difficult to control, and caution was often made that it should not be loosed, lest it wreak havoc. But it was also reckoned to be the 'glory of man'.[14] The English (the Americans perhaps as well) now have an ambivalent relation to the tongue and the very use of the word is uncomfortable. Could this be a consequence of the association not only between tongues and women but between the tongue and effeminacy? Since the more abstract 'language' has become the dominant term, the tongue is inescapably embedded in its materiality, with all the ambiguities – especially sexual – this entails. It is perhaps no coincidence that the essays I found addressing the tongue and its ambiguities consider mainly *women's* tongues.[15]

A major eighteenth-century preoccupation was the concern over the regulation of the English language.[16] This concern was rooted in part in the belief that whereas Italian and French had long been regulated and fixed by their academies, English, 'neglected . . . by *English* grammarians', was 'without order' and 'without rules'. And while it was generally felt, as Thomas Wilson put it in 1729, that 'a good language' was an 'Honour' to a nation and 'an unimproved Tongue' a 'Mark either of care-lessness or a low Genius of the People', the English alone, complained Sheridan in 1781, had 'left theirs to the power of chance and caprice'.[17]

The concern over the English tongue involved not only the language that the gentleman was supposed to speak,[18] but the speaker himself. The English gentleman's tongue was implicated, from the late seventeenth century in 'The rise of politeness', because fluent and polished discourse was a fundamental condi-tion of politeness, and conversation, as Lawrence Klein has put it, its 'master metaphor'.[19] The art of conversation, treatises and manuals on the subject stressed again and again, was premised on the discipline and cultivation of the tongue.[20] One way to achieve the necessary polish was to converse with women. Another was the Grand Tour, which provided the opportunity for young men of rank not just to perfect their French accent but to polish their conversation in the company of the French, whose refined language and brilliant conversational skills the English admired – though not always unequivocally.

The French tongue was held to be soft, harmonious and elegant, and the 'vivacity' of discourse the French displayed deemed very pleasing.[21] However, as Addison observed, that 'light talkative humour' had not a little 'infected their tongue'; John Andrews, at the end of the century, was more caustic: French may be elegant and refined but it had 'lost in strength what it had gained in politeness'. And if it was a language 'most admirably calculated to express verbal civilities', these ' "unmeaning terms" ' just made people 'substitute politeness in the place of truth.'[22] Strength and sincerity, on the other hand, were the distinguishing characteristics of the English tongue. And although practices of sociability central to the fashioning of the English gentleman required the mastery of verbal arts evinced by the French, not only was the monosyllabic English tongue lacking in polish but the English as a nation were said to 'delight in Silence'.[23]

How did these major obstacles to the achievement of polite conversation come to be, by the end of the eighteenth century, the building blocks, so to speak, not only of the national character, but of its masculinity? How did the English come to value their blunt but 'sincere and manly' language? Why did the reticent tongue of the Englishman stand as the testimony of his depth of mind, while their sprightly conversation represented the shallow and inferior intellect of English women and of the French of both sexes? How did conversation, central to the shaping of the gentleman for a century, get to be relegated to a frivolous and mainly female social accomplishment while taciturnity became emblematic of English masculinity? And why, finally, did it become a matter of pride *not* to *speak* foreign languages? By the early twentieth century, the typical English gentleman was one who

> declares, with a tone savouring of pride and disdain, that the sounds of [French] have no interest for him, who skips every chapter on pronunciation ... [but who] will blush with shame if he so much as omits to dot an *i* when writing the language of which he claims to be master.[24]

3

The trajectory of the tongue since the early eighteenth century frames the story I tell in this book, and the tongue is a main character in that story.

CONVERSATION AND POLITENESS

The mutual conversation of the sexes, it was generally agreed, was the best way to achieve politeness. As Addison put it, it is 'the Male that gives Charms to Womankind, that produces an Air in their Faces, a Grace in their Motions, a Softness in their Voices, and a Delicacy in their Complexions'. Without women,

> Men would be quite different creatures from what they are at present; their Endeavours to please the opposite Sex, polishes and refines them out of those Manners most natural to them ... Man would not only be an unhappy, but a rude unfinished Creature, were he conversant with none but those of his own Make.[25]

The conviction that conversation between men and women 'improved' and refined them both was so abiding that by the end of the century, it had become a virtual commonplace that 'free communication between the sexes' was an index of the refinement and polish of a nation.[26]

Polite society, the most civilized type of society was, however, fraught with danger. While mixed social intercourse and conversation were indispensable to the fashioning of the gentleman, they were, paradoxically, also the site for the greatest anxiety. 'Refinement should only go so far or it would become effeminacy', Shaftesbury had declared early in the century, and Joseph Spence, writing in the 1730s, cautioned that 'some conversation with the ladies is necessary to smooth the temper as well as the manners of men, but too much of it is apt to effeminate or debilitate both'.[27] If the presence of men made women more feminine, women, in polishing men out of rude nature, did not necessarily make them more *manly*. The question that exercised moralists, essayists and educationists alike throughout the century was whether the distinction between 'manly politeness and luxurious effeminacy' could be sustained.[28]

It would appear that for Shaftesbury and Spence, the difference between them was principally a matter of 'excess'. With its connotations of luxury and self-indulgence, excess was in total contrast to frugality, simplicity and self-discipline, characteristics of the virtuous citizen imagined by classical republicanism, what John Barrell has called 'the most authoritative fantasy of masculinity in early eighteenth-century Britain'.[29] Excess positioned the gentleman as effeminate, 'self-control' positioned him as manly.[30] Even an article of apparel like the wig could denote status and 'masculine authority' and at the same time pose 'the threat of excess and ... effeminacy'. The 'dilemma of masculinity' is aptly summarized by Marcia Pointon. While the 'artificial covering of the head' was required as a sign of 'virility, station and decency', it was 'simultaneously threatened by the connotations – religious, moral and sexual – of the only item that could secure that signification'.[31] But how much constituted 'excess'? And how could effeminacy be found in 'excess' and at the same time, be conceived of as not 'enough' manliness?[32] What was meant by 'effeminacy'?

It could be said that in many ways, the discursive domains of effeminacy mirrored those which John Sekora identified for 'the greatest single social issue and the greatest single commonplace' in the eighteenth century: luxury.[33] Often either conflated with luxury or held to be its inevitable consequence,[34] the effects of effeminacy, like those of luxury, ranged from the individual to the nation, from 'an index of human sinfulness' to 'sapping a nation's economic and military strength'.[35] The pervasiveness of the concept as well as its ambiguities and shifts are also highlighted by George Barker-Benfield, one of the first historians to focus specifically on 'The Question of Effeminacy' in the eighteenth century.[36] But there is one major difference between luxury and effeminacy, a difference signalled by Sekora's own silence about effeminacy despite its insistent presence in the texts he cites. Whereas the multiple meanings of luxury in the eighteenth century 'bedevil modern students',[37] effeminacy tends to be treated with the casualness usually bred from familiarity. Its present meanings are assimilated to those of the past, it has no historicity, no strangeness, it is taken for granted. We all 'know' what effeminacy means and what it has always meant. But do we?

For G.S. Rousseau, effeminacy is unambiguously associated with homosexual tendencies; for Randolph Trumbach, it refers to the 'exclusive sodomite'.[38] Effeminacy is also associated with femininity, as when literary historian Harriet Guest for example, reads the statement '*Obscenity* itself is grown effeminate' to mean that 'the display of femininity has become obscene'.[39] On the other hand, Kathleen Wilson has shown how crucial a notion of 'effeminacy' was to arguments about the imperial project and the definition of the British nation in the eighteenth century. 'Effeminacy', she argues, 'denoted a degenerate moral, political and social state that opposed and subverted the vaunted "manly" characteristics – courage, aggression, martial valour, strength – constituting patriotic virtue.' But she also points out that while the empire 'cultivated and bolstered "manly characteristics"', it could paradoxically also foster 'an insidious and "effeminate" luxuriousness and corruption'.[40]

There is an expanding literature on effeminacy in the early modern period, and it is not my aim to get into debates about the emergence of a homosexual culture in eighteenth-century England, nor to deny that effeminacy might refer to homosexuality or to femininity. But I want to resist the attempts to make 'effeminacy' coherent and unitary by reducing it to gender, to sex or to politics. Its very ambiguity, its contradictions even, are, as Michel Foucault would say, evidence of its historicity.[41] Thus, while John Brown asserted, in 1757, that 'the true Character of the Present Times is that of a vain *luxurious*, and *selfish* Effeminacy', that an effeminate nation is 'A Nation which *resembles Women*', and that the French too were 'effeminate and vain', he also argued that they were 'brave', 'honourable', 'warlike' and, 'Heroes in the Field'.[42]

In this study, I am concerned with two expressions of effeminacy in the eighteenth century. One relates to anxieties about the effects of French seductiveness upon the English nation, the other, to anxieties about the tongue.

EFFEMINACY AND FRENCH SEDUCTION

It was not just the 'rampant Francophilia' of the upper ranks[43] and their desire for imported luxury goods that was cause for concern. For James Burgh, the danger represented by the French for *all* ranks was '*bewitching* Pleasure', not only irresistible, but unnatural, ungodly, even. It was because this enchantment produced 'inordinate and exhorbitant desires'[44] that the English became 'other', effeminated – excess is precisely the site of incommensurable desire – Frenchified, and the national fibre was weakened and enervated.[45] France's attraction was exerted not only by its fashions and luxury goods but even more insidiously by its manners and by its tongue. The 'invasion' of 'Frenchisms'[46] into English epitomized this seduction. The fear was that such 'intimacy' with French would debilitate and 'enervate' the masculine English tongue, just as consorting with women was apt to weaken and make men effeminate.

For most of the century, things French were objects of desire for the English. Thus, when John Butley declared, in 1756: 'we are at peace, it is true, with the power; but it would be well for us if we were at war with the manners of France' he was echoing an earlier comment of Addison, who, in 1711, had reflected that he wished 'a safe and honourable peace with the French', but feared 'its consequences on English manners.'[47] Though claims that cultural practices are more damaging to the nation than wars, are likely to be, at least in part, rhetorical, they convey the intensity of the concern over British vulnerability and surrender not only to France's superior military power but to the power of French seduction.

It is not enough to ask what was meant by effeminacy; the issue is also, perhaps crucially, *why* effeminacy? Why was a concept signifying problematic gender boundaries for men a dominant metaphor throughout the eighteenth century?

EFFEMINACY AND MASCULINITY

In the eighteenth century, dictionaries tell us, effeminacy meant 'admission of the qualities of a woman, softness, unmanly delicacy', but also 'addicted to women'. The term effeminate could refer either to a man who resembled women, or one who desired women.[48] Effeminacy encompassed what appears to us now at the same time a blurring of gender boundaries and an affirmation of sexual difference.

'Gender blurrings have a long pre-twentieth-century history', write Julia Epstein and Kristin Straub in the introduction to *Body Guards*, their anthology on 'the cultural politics of gender ambiguity'.[49] The eighteenth century, in particular, has been associated with an 'interest in gender ambiguity ... sexual experimentation and gender-playing'.[50] Indeed, passing women, and the transgressions authorized by masquerades and theatrical or other cross-dressing have intrigued many scholars.[51] At the same time, scholars concerned to historicize masculinity seem to imply that the eighteenth century was somehow unique: 'there can be no comprehensive definition of *manly* in Pope's day', writes Carolyn Williams, 'because no universal standard of masculinity exists'.[52] Other opinions include the suggestions that 'standards of masculinity may not have been very high', that 'masculinity was not strongly regulated', that gender boundaries were 'fluid' and even that there was a 'crisis' of masculinity.[53]

But what would a 'universal standard of sexuality' mean in the eighteenth century? And today? What does 'fluidity' mean when referring to gender boundaries? Does it signify 'bodies . . . glid[ing] in and out of varying subject positions – sometimes male, sometimes female, sometimes neuter'?[54] Does it not also evoke a 'golden age' when many 'opportunities' for transgression were made available by society in the form of cross-dressing and masquerades?[55] As for a 'crisis of masculinity', this begs more questions than it answers. Not only does it imply, as Carolyn Williams points out, that at other times, men are 'consciously serene',[56] but there seems to be little agreement among scholars as to either the circumstances or the periodization for the crises. Thus, Michael Kimmel claims that 'one ought not to be surprised to discover a gender crisis in late seventeenth- early eighteenth-century England'; the context for a 'redefinition of masculinity' was provided by changes in gender relations at the time. Reviewing the evidence for crisis theory, Arthur Brittan concludes that following the fragmentations of modernization and industrialization, men's difficulty in finding strong male figures with whom to identify may be the root cause for the crisis of masculinity, a crisis that has not yet been resolved. On the other hand, as Roper and Tosh suggest, the notion of a 'crisis of masculinity' may be 'an invention of the 1980s';[57] it might be one outcome of the historicisation of masculinity. The point is, it is not just in the eighteenth century that 'maleness [did] not automatically confer manliness'.[58] Masculinity, argue Roper and Tosh 'is never fully possessed, but must be perpetually achieved, asserted and renegotiated'. As feminist scholars have long maintained, gender is not just socially but historically constructed. Neither 'femininity' nor 'masculinity' are ever 'givens'.[59]

The question, then, is not why there was an anxiety about masculinity at a specific time, say the eighteenth century, but how the anxiety about masculinity is articulated at any particular historical moment – or geographical space.

I want to suggest that in the eighteenth century, the anxiety about masculinity was articulated in the particular way it was because the defining 'other' was neither, as is usually assumed, femininity, nor homosexuality, but *effeminacy*. As Anthony Fletcher has put it, 'the polarity of sexual difference was delineated in men's construction of it by effeminacy and manhood'.[60]

I would also dispute the suggestion that in the eighteenth century, standards of masculinity might not have been very high. There was, on the contrary, a very strong standard of masculinity, that represented in the discourse of civic humanism. But, as both Lawrence Klein and John Barrell have shown[61] – civic humanism – with its emphasis on virtuous austerity and emancipation from desire was at odds with the discourse of politeness, which stressed men's softening and refining their manners, and placed conversation with women at the heart of its practices. At the same time, there was no uncertainty about how masculinity could be achieved – it was in the company of other men.

In this book, I argue that effeminacy designated a category of meanings expressing anxiety about the *effect* women – or the feminine – on the one hand, and desire, on the other, might have on the gentleman. The figure of the fop personified this anxiety. Two of his defining traits were that he was a favourite with the ladies, whom he charmed with his empty chatter and his 'Pretences to Wit and Judgement',[62] and that he was 'Frenchified': having succumbed to the seduction of the French, he displayed French fashions, French manners and French smatterings.

By the end of the century, however, politeness and the conversation of women had ceased to be the means of shaping the gentleman. Fluency of the tongue, like the 'dilemma of masculinity' represented by the wig, had remained an unresolved tension of politeness: at the same time as it was emblematic of the gentleman's accomplishment, it called up the French and the fop, whose loquacious tongue positioned them as effeminate.[63] By 1785, however, John Andrews could write that although the English might 'gain in delicacy and refinement' by associating with women like the French did, this advantage was 'outweighed' by the threat to 'manliness of behaviour and liberty of discourse, the two pillars on which the edifice of our national character is principally supported'.[64]

The concern was now to discipline the gentleman's mental faculties and fashion him into an *English* man. This shift marked a new ordering of national and gender difference, and entailed what I call the derogation of the tongue.

GENEALOGY, DISCOURSE AND FRENCH

I began this study with questions relating to the gender and status of French in England today. It soon became clear that the issue was not to find out, once and for all, whether French had always been a female language and accomplishment, but to find a framework which would enable me to account at the same time for discontinuities in the past, problems of the present, and the centrality of language and gender. I found this framework in Michel Foucault's approach to history, archaeology and genealogy. Although most commentaries on Foucault's work point to the difficulty of deducing a clear method from either archaeology or genealogy, there is evidence that Foucault regarded them as complementary.[65] They also have different emphases. Genealogy examines process and is concerned with practices and technologies of power. It is an attempt to find in the past not 'origins', but conditions of emergence, and the traces of the present in its dispersions. Genealogy is thus a 'history of the present', in the sense that 'it finds its points of departure in problems relevant to current issues, and ... its point of arrival and its usefulness in what it can bring for the analysis of the present'. Mapping the complex landscape of discourses in which French was embedded since the late seventeenth century in England, and situating it in its historical and discursive context, have shown it to have been not the unitary, homogeneous neutral object with cohesive inner continuity described by traditional histories of language, but fragmented, dispersed over a multiplicity of discourses, and always gendered. Archaeology is 'an abandonment of the history of ideas ... an attempt to practise a different history of what men have said', and examines the "moment", however extended that moment might be'.[66] My aim has been not to uncover underlying reasons to explain the events on the surface of history, but to describe the play of discourses constituting that history. Ironically, it is because of what has been *said* about French since the nineteenth century – its association with 'frivolous' social accomplishments in the eighteenth century and with females and idle conversation in the nineteenth – that its complex role in the formation of English discourses had not really been considered.

The book has two parts, a division which can best be clarified by reference to Peter De Bolla's theoretical distinction between two aspects of discourse, what he terms the 'discourse *on*' and the 'discourse *of*'. This distinction is part of what De Bolla describes as his attempt to develop a method for mapping a 'discursive network' by distinguishing 'discrete' discourses from the network of which they are a part. More specifically, a 'discrete' discourse is one that 'can be read in a highly specific way, within a well-defined context', and constitutes a discourse *on*: in this book, the discourse *on* French describes how French was learned and by whom, and the meanings attached to its study in the eighteenth and nineteenth centuries. The discourse *of* French, on the other hand, places French in a discursive network composed of discourses 'affiliated' – to use De Bolla's term – to the discourse *on* French: the problematization of the English gentleman and his tongue, politeness, the Grand Tour, accomplishments and women's education, the construction of gendered achievement, and ultimately, the forging of an English national and gendered identity. I do not mean to imply that there were 'obvious' relations between the discourse *on* French and the discourses which make up the discourses *of* French, and that these just needed to be 'discovered'. Nor, as De Bolla is keen to stress, is there a causal relation between the discourse *on* and the discourse *of*, between a discrete discourse and the discourses affiliated with it. On the contrary, the connections between discourses 'come to light on account of the procedures and protocols' used in the historical analysis.[67]

In the first part of the book, I analyze the complex and contradictory ways in which the French language and culture were involved in a variety of English discourses. I argue that practices of sociability modelled on those of France were essential to the fashioning of the eighteenth-century gentleman, and travel to France indispensable to his accomplishment. At the same time, however, the French and their language were disparaged in discourses related to the anxiety about the effect those practices might have on the masculinity of Englishmen and the virtue of English women. In the second part, the analysis of the discourse *on* French in England illustrates how tongues and the tongue

11

eventually became critical sites for the construction of national and gender difference. This should make us rethink the stereotype of the 'xenophobic' Englishman who cannot *speak* French.[68]

This book is about the fashioning of the English gentleman, but my story begins in seventeenth-century France. It introduces one of the major themes of the study, conversation, and the positionings it produced for men and women in the social space of the aristocratic *salon*. France was regarded by contemporaries as the most civilized, the most polite nation in Europe. There is no shortage of evidence concerning its cultural influence on England, especially as regards politeness and conversation. English ambivalence towards the French has also been noted.[69] It was therefore crucial to describe *politesse* and the ideal of gentlemanliness, *honnêteté,* in their specific historical and cultural location, because of the way they were woven into English discourses and served to construct the French as an effeminate Other. I had assumed, when I started my research, that cultural patterns travelling over the Channel would not be simply translated. This assumption was to be amply justified.

1

CONVERSATION AND THE CONSTRUCTION OF THE *HONNÊTE HOMME* IN SEVENTEENTH-CENTURY FRANCE

Just as there is a specific social context for the sermon or the funeral oration, so too with conversation: it requires a context that is both historically and socially specific, thereby ordering a social space which can become its own.[1] In seventeenth-century France, the *salon* [2] was that space. Around the *ruelle* in an aristocratic lady's 'bedroom'[3] gathered not only aristocratic men but also men of letters from a variety of other backgrounds, such as Voiture, or Corneille.[4]

More importantly, though, in the *ruelles*, there were ladies of rank. The social, linguistic and aesthetic ideals which were developed in the seventeenth century centred around notions of *politesse*,[5] and the presence of aristocratic women was crucial to its elaboration. The most consummate expression of *politesse* was in conversation. Women were seen as the natural means to the achievement of this ideal because of their refined and delicate manners, their 'natural aversion to coarseness' and, according to Vaugelas, the purity of their French.[6]

Women were central to cultural and social developments of the seventeenth century, not merely because they reigned over the space of the *salon*, nor just because they were also the arbiters of taste,[7] but because polite conversation and, most crucially, *honnêteté*, could not be achieved without them. To achieve *honnêteté*, wrote Méré, it is necessary to seek the company of *honnêtes gens*,[8] and particularly women, for

> les entretiens des Dames, dont les grâces font penser aux
> bienséances sont encore plus nécessaires pour s'achever
> dans l'*honnêteté*.[9]

[the conversation of women, whose graces make us think about *bienséances*,[10] are even more necessary to perfect ourselves in *honnêteté*.]

In interpreting the positioning of the women of the *salon*, however, we need to exercise some caution if we are not to fall prey to anachronistic conclusions about their status or their 'feminism'. While they clearly had a crucial role bearing in important ways on the cultural life and manners of the nobles and the ways these were produced, we should not allow the importance of the role to obscure its nature: it was oriented not to the woman's production of her self, but to the production of the self-perfecting man, the *honnête homme*.

Similarly, while their 'freedom' may have been greater than that of noble women in Italy or Spain in the same period, whatever value we might put upon such cross-cultural comparison should not obscure the character of the practices which made up that 'greater freedom', what they were 'free' to do: these women's conversation, though securing for themselves the privilege of their class, was ultimately productive of gender difference, not power.[11] The status of *salon* women was elevated commensurably with their vital role in refining the conversation of the nobleman, but ultimately it was the noble man who benefited and achieved *honnêteté*. My primary concern, then, is with the way conversation related to gender on the one hand and to language on the other. This concern leads me directly to consider the *honnête homme*, and to examine in more detail the discourse on *honnêteté*.

HONNÊTETÉ

What was *honnêteté*? While there are many different definitions of that 'elusive concept',[12] they nevertheless share certain features. First of all, *honnêteté* entailed a notion of sociability. On *honnêteté* depended 'le plus parfait et le plus aimable commerce du monde' [the most perfect and amiable commerce of the world].[13] This sociability also maintained a complex relation to notions of urbanity[14] and *politesse*. Second, *honnêteté* was about seductiveness, about developing an *art de plaire* as part of an aesthetic of the self. The *art de plaire* itself had a number of aspects: to please, a man had to be agreeable to all, accommodate everyone's whims and moods,[15] and suffer in silence if wronged:

La colère nous porte à nous venger, et l'honnêteté s'y oppose: renonçons à la douceur de la vengeance; et pardonnons d'un visage riant et d'un coeur sincère.[16]

[Anger prompts us to revenge ourselves, but *honnêteté* opposes it; let us renounce the sweetness of vengeance and forgive with a smile and a sincere heart.]

Because *honnêteté* was an ideal of self perfection, the *honnête homme* had to excel in all the virtues of the heart, the mind and those relating to social conduct.[17] Thus, saying neither too much nor too little and cultivating an *esprit de finesse*, a penetration which allowed one to guess and preempt the secret, innermost thoughts of one's interlocutors were skills indispensable to *honnêteté*, and no conversation could take place without them.[18] However, despite all these precisions and stipulations, *honnêteté* escaped all rules and was, ultimately, a *je ne sais quoi*.[19]

The sources of *honnêteté* have been discussed in detail by Maurice Magendie, who identified Castiglione's *Il Cortegiano* as one of its most important sources.[20] One of the first major theorisations of *honnêteté*, Nicolas Faret's *L'honnête homme ou l'art de plaire à la cour*,[21] was, according to Magendie, the best-known of the French works influenced by Castiglione. Though many treatises on *honnêteté* were published in the seventeenth century, its 'foremost exponent and most profound theoretician'[22] was the Chevalier de Méré, whose work was published between 1668 and 1677. One of the most important differences between Faret and Méré is usually held to be that Faret's conception of *honnêteté* was bourgeois, and Méré's was aristocratic and *mondain*.[23] But there is a further, more crucial difference between them. Whereas Faret's *honnêteté* was aimed at constructing a code of manners and behaviour for the courtesan at Court, Méré's *honnêteté* was a means for men to perfect themselves, what Foucault called 'a technology of the self'. As Foucault explains, this concept refers to

an art of existence or, rather, a technique of life . . . a question of knowing how to govern one's own life in order to give it the most beautiful possible form (in the eyes of others, of oneself) . . . a practice of self whose aim was to constitute oneself as the worker of the beauty of one's own life.[24]

Honnêteté was not learned in books and could not be taught.[25]

Rather, it was acquired by conversing with other *honnêtes gens*, especially women, because it was in their company and in the desire to please them that men refined themselves and became *honnêtes*. Thus, one of the main ways of achieving it was love, in the tradition of courtly love established in the first decade of the seventeenth century by *L'Astrée*.[26] Women were central to this art of seduction, but not as the objects of love so much as the instruments whereby the man might produce himself as *honnête*. When the *honnête homme* Mérigène is asked who made him so accomplished, he answers that he owes everything to love:

> sans lui il ne serait point ce qu'il est, et que s'il a les qualités d'un honnête homme il les doit à une belle femme qui mit dans son coeur le désir de plaire et le dessein de mériter son affection.[27]

> [without love he would not be what he is; that if he now has the virtues of an *honnête homme*, he owes them to a beautiful woman who put in his heart the desire to please and be worthy of her affection.]

This passage is significant because of the way it positions the woman in relation to the love she elicits. Mérigène makes it clear: it is to love, not to that particular woman, that he owes his *honnêteté*. As Méré explained, love filled men's hearts and minds with noble thoughts:

> il est certain que quand on aime une personne d'un mérite exquis, cet amour remplit d'honnêteté le coeur et l'esprit et donne toujours de plus nobles pensées que l'affection qu'on a pour une personne ordinaire.[28]

> [it is certain that when we like a person of exquisite merit, this love fills the heart and the mind with *honnêteté*, and always gives nobler thoughts than the affection we feel towards an ordinary person.]

In their 'natural' state, he noted, men are usually 'all of a piece', blunt, rigid even, without manners or graces, the antithesis of *honnête*. When they are not used to women, they become tongue-tied[29] in their presence. 'Ceux qui ne sont pas faits à leur manière délicate et mystérieuse, ne savent bien souvent que leur dire'.[30] [Those who are not used to their delicate and mysterious ways often do not know what to say to them.] It is the desire to be attractive to women that changes a man, makes him 'other' and he (his tongue) becomes 'insinuant'.

Honnêteté thus appears to have an erotic character.[31] But this insinuation, which Horowitz calls a discourse of erotic domination,[32] is not concerned with possessing the object of love. Through language, love is 'de-sensualized',[33] and it represents an indispensable stage in the construction of the self-as-art, a technique for the ethical and aesthetic perfection of the (male) self. As Foucault put it,

> technologies of the self ... permit individuals to effect by their own means or with the help of others a certain number of operations on their own bodies and souls, thoughts, conduct, and ways of being, so as to transform themselves in order to attain a certain state of happiness, purity, wisdom, perfection, or immortality.[34]

The question is, where does this leave women? When Michael Moriarty, in *Taste and Ideology*, asked to what extent the discourse of *honnêteté* contributed to 'the improvement in the image, and maybe the actual condition of women',[35] he intimated that the answer would be affirmative. But, one must first ask, which women?

CONVERSATION

Most major seventeenth-century writers wrote about conversation.[36] Everyone had something to say about what conversation ought to be and how it ought to be conducted, and many of the treatises on the art were themselves written in the form of conversations. Such was its importance that in all the written portraits of the time, conduct in conversation was always included, and was often the first feature mentioned in the portrait.[37] The importance of the skill of conversation for a courtier had been described in great detail by Castiglione, and Faret also stressed its centrality as well as the difference between the conversation of men and that of women.[38] The conversation that is of interest here, however, is the verbal commerce of the *salons*, that 'most exquisite and delicate pleasure'.[39]

For Madeleine de Scudéry, whose voluminous *oeuvre* includes treatises on conversation, it represented a social and moral relation. It was 'le lien de la société de tous les hommes ... le moyen le plus ordinaire d'introduire non seulement la politesse dans le monde, mais encore la morale la plus pure.' [the link in human society . . . the simplest means of introducing not only politeness into society, but also the purest of morals.] For Vaumorière too, conversation was one of the most important aspects of social life.[40] It was Méré, however, who first theorised its principles. For Méré, conversation was primarily communication but it was not just talk. It was also about how to behave.[41] Conversation had to be easy, 'natural', free of constraints and of specialist jargon; above all, it had to please. Because women's conversation was presumed to embody these features,[42] it made men think of bienséances as well, it regulated their tongues and enabled them to achieve honnêteté. For, as Bellegarde remarked, in the company of women, men have to watch and discipline their language, and refrain from uttering uncivil words, 'de ces paroles qui blessent l'honnêteté'.[43]

The interrelation between conversation and honnêteté, and the centrality of women to the process should now be clear. Women's conversation, (as language and company), enabled men to acquire and develop the appropriate conduct of body and tongue, the politesse which was the soul of honnêteté.[44] To please in conversation was the means of achieving honnêteté, but it was the conversation of women that produced the honnête homme.[45]

How, then, did conversation position women ? Did it produce an honnête femme equivalent to the honnête homme? The way honnêteté was theorised implies that it was a social ideal which could be attained, or at least aspired to, by both men and women. Indeed, because of their 'natural' politesse, their grace and their delicate and pure language, women should have been more likely to attain this ideal than men. Yet as Furetière's definition of honnêteté reveals, there was a considerable difference between what made a man and a woman honnête. The honnêteté of women was rooted in traditional female virtues, that of men reflected their behaviour.

> L'honnêteté des femmes, c'est la chasteté, la modestie, la pudeur, la retenue. L'honnêteté des hommes est une manière d'agir juste, sincère, courtoise, obligeante, civile.[46]
>
> [Women's honnêteté is their chastity, modesty, decency, discretion. Men's honnêteté concerns their behaviour – a manner or acting justly, sincerely, courteously, obligingly, civilly.]

Indeed, one of the main functions of *honnêteté*, wrote Grenaille, was precisely to distinguish between men and women.[47] What was required of the *honnête femme* were not the virtues practised by men – although writers such as Du Bosc and Grenaille conceded that women were equally capable of practising them – but traditionally female ones: 'la sincérité, la douceur, la fidélité et la patience' [sincerity, mildness, loyalty and patience].[48] Wasn't it a remarkable coincidence, Du Bosc observed, that these virtues were also associated with humility, a primary Christian virtue for women? Thus, for women, the ideal of *honnêteté* was inextricably bound up with religion and morality, while for men it was a secular social ideal which, as Nye argued recently, was related not so much to virtue as to honour.[49]

Clearly, then, *honnêteté* was a gendered discourse, and if so, conversation too must be gendered. This issue was taken up by Scudéry. Césonie, a character in her *Conversations* asks how differently an *honnête femme* and an *honnête homme* should speak:

Mais, interrompit Césonie, encore voudrais-je bien savoir quelle doit être la différence qu'il faut qu'il y ait entre un Homme qui parle bien, et une femme qui parle bien. Car encore que je sache de certitude, qu'il doit y en avoir, je ne sais pas précisément en quoi elle consiste. On se sert des mêmes paroles; on parle quelques fois des mêmes choses; et l'on a même assez souvent des pensées qui se ressemblent. Cependant, comme je l'ai déjà dit, il ne faut pas qu'une honnête femme parle toujours comme un honnête homme: et il y a certaines expressions, dont les uns peuvent se servir à propos, et qui seraient de mauvaise grâce aux autres.[50]

[But, interrupted Césonie, I would still like to know what must be the difference between a man who speaks well and a woman who speaks well. For although I know for certain that there should be one, I do not know precisely what it is. We use the same words, we sometimes speak about the same things; and we even often have similar thoughts. Yet, as I have already said, an *honnête femme* cannot always speak like an *honnête homme*: there are certain expressions men can use which women cannot use gracefully.]

Thus, even though the difference between the conversation of an *honnête homme* and that of an *honnête femme* was elusive, it was a matter of propriety, of *bienséance*, that there should be one.

But there is a paradox. When women's conversation was deemed indispensable to the regulation of young aristocratic males entering the world,[51] the delicacy and politeness of their language were highlighted and celebrated. When women's conversation as such was discussed, it was derogated: it was always described as undisciplined, unregulated, or simply 'too much'. All of the major texts on conversation provide interesting illustrations of this paradoxical, profoundly equivocal attitude to women's talk. Du Bosc devoted a whole chapter of *L'Honneste Femme* to describing the vices of women's talk; he eventually recommended that women should model themselves on the Virgin Mary, who spoke only five times in her lifetime.[52] In *L'Art de plaire dans la conversation*, Vaumorière's chapter 'Contre les Grands Parleurs' is about women's talk, not men's. Madeleine de Scudéry was even more critical of women's conversation, which she compared unfavourably with men's: 'Je dis, à la grande honte de notre sexe, que les hommes ont un grand avantage sur nous pour la conversation'.[53] [To the shame of our sex, I would say that men have a great advantage over us as regards conversation]. Thus, Césonie claims that when women talk too much, it is much worse than when men do, because their conversation is a torrent of trifling words, tedious to any reasonable mind.[54]

How could women's conversation be praised and derogated at the same time? How could their conversation and their silence be invited simultaneously? How can these contradictory attitudes be accounted for, and what do they tell us about women's position in the society of the *salon*?

In seventeenth-century France, the discourse on women's talk produced two positionings for women: one was 'conversation' and the other was what I call 'tongue'. As 'conversation', women's talk was civilized and civilizing, polite and pleasing, even when women talked about trifling matters.[55] These qualities were necessary to, and constituted the conversation that produced the *honnête homme*. As 'tongue', women's talk was undisciplined and unregulated. This was displayed in their trivial chatter about *bagatelles*, in malicious gossip,[56] and especially in that habit women have of talking all at the same time, without listening to each other – more a vulgar contest than a civilized conversation.

C'est le défaut ordinaire des femmes ... elles crient toutes ensemble et ne veulent point s'écouter: il semble qu'elles ne parlent que pour parler. Celle qui fait le plus de bruit l'emporte toujours, et les autres sont contraintes de lui céder à la fin.[57]

[It's a common defect of women ... they all shout at the same time and refuse to listen to each other: it seems that they talk only for the sake of talking. The one that talks the loudest always wins, and the others are, in the end, obliged to give in to her.]

The significance of this criticism becomes clear when it is counterposed to the ideal conduct required for *honnêteté*: listening to one's interlocutors so as to bring them out rather than imposing oneself. Many of the virtues of *honnêteté* – such as flexibility and the ability to accommodate oneself to others by guessing their needs – all derived directly from this conduct.

CONVERSATION AND THE TONGUE

Women's conversation, then, was but a disciplined, a contained tongue. But what disciplined women's tongue? Though mixed company and conversation constituted the effective social body, men conversing on their own were said to get on better than women without men. Men, it was alleged, talk about serious matters. Women on their own are boring, and go on endlessly about insignificant domestic matters or their babies' babble.[58] Once again, Scudéry's lively pen provides the best illustration. She describes arriving in a room full of women chatting; the conversation is tedious, lacking in that indispensable quality of *divertissement* [entertainment]. A man enters and everything changes:

La conversation changea tout d'un coup, et devint plus réglée, plus spirituelle, et plus agréable, quoi qu'il n'y eut nul changement à la compagnie, sinon qu'il y était arrivé un homme qui ne parla pas même beaucoup.[59]

[The conversation changed suddenly, and became more regulated, more witty and more agreeable, even though the only change to the gathering was the arrival of a man, and he did not even say very much.]

21

And, added Scudéry, he was not even a remarkable man, 'un de ces esprits élevés qu'on trouve si rarement'[one of these elevated minds that one meets so rarely]. Yet his mere presence brought order in the conversation. Thus while women's conversation disciplined that of males, the presence of a man regulated women's talk. Women might have all the perfections necessary for conversation, even *esprit*,[60] but they did not know how to manage them. As Du Bosc put it,

> On reconnaitrait bien à la confusion et à l'inégalité de leurs discours, encore même qu'elles disent d'assez bonnes choses, que ce n'est point assez d'avoir du marbre et du porphyre pour faire des Palais, si on n'est Architecte.[61]

> [Even though women do say some good things, you can tell, from the confusion and unevenesss of their discourse, that marble and porphyry do not make a palace. You also need to be an architect.]

The architectural metaphor does not just undermine the power of women's conversation, it also suggests a way in which the 'femaleness' of the discourse on *honnêteté* could be rescued from its association with women. The beauty of the marble and the porphyry is not brought out until it is polished and ordered. If, as Stanton has noted, the principle at work in the 'system of aesthetic seductiveness' of *honnêteté* was 'female',[62] the *paraître* of the *honnête homme*, his social persona, his insinuating manners might have appeared feminine, but his *être*,[63] his profound self, was male because of his penetration and his 'boundless potential'.[64] Ultimately, what made the difference was the self-management and organization which, du Bosc implied, women 'lacked'. Women's conversational talents could be acknowledged and used by men, but it was solely in men that these talents took on the status of *honnêteté*.

THE *PRÉCIEUSES*

But there were women who, it seems, refused the verbal commerce of the *salon*. Exotic beings who had invaded the *ruelles* and spoke a strange tongue,[65] they transgressed the fundamental *politesse* of the *salon* by yawning, or worse – remaining silent until others of their 'sect' had arrived.[66] Who were these women with whom no conversation was possible? They were the *précieuses*.

Femmes savantes, (learned ladies), *femmes d'esprit* (women with literary pretensions), prudes, coquettes, old maids;[67] all could, at some time or other, earn the pejorative name of *précieuse*.[68] As *femmes savantes*, the *précieuses* were exposed as mere pedants; as *femmes d'esprit*, they were 'ridicules', betraying their lack of taste, knowledge and discernment – they could not tell the difference between good and bad verse, true and false poets, real noblemen and valets in disguise.[69] As prudes, the *précieuses* were said to either sublimate sex into the *tendre amitié* (tender friendship) pictured in Madeleine de Scudéry's *Carte de Tendre*,[70] or to reject men altogether. However, in de Pure's *La Prétieuse*, it was not gallantry but the institution of marriage that the *précieuses* found intolerable. Their rejection of sex was also said to result from being old-maids.[71] In addition, J-M. Pelous has also argued that this rejection is also related to the original definition of the term *précieuse* which, he points out, was produced by a semantic association between the idea of refusing sexual relations and valuing oneself (too) highly.[72] Not surprisingly, no women were found who willingly admitted to being a *précieuse*.[73]

Evidence for the existence of the *précieuses* has been based mostly on Baudeau de Somaize's *Grand Dictionnaire des Précieuses* and *Dictionnaire historique des Précieuses*, and on Michel de Pure's *La Prétieuse*.[74] Both authors' main claim to truth was based on their promise to disclose the real identity of the *précieuses*, an identity that was essentially related to their language. Somaize professed to provide the 'key' to their bizarre expressions in his *Grand Dictionnaire*, and de Pure alleged that having gained entry to the 'mystery' of the *ruelles*, he would provide a faithful record of their conversations.[75]

At once multifaceted and elusive, represented simultaneously as women demanding a change in marriage laws and pure spirits defying all classification,[76] the *précieuses* have, for over a century, been the object of an historiography concerned, in the main, with capturing their true essence: who they were – and who they were not [77] – what they stood for, and the nature of their dissent.[78] Some historians have attempted to absorb them into the broader discourse of *préciosité* and *le précieux*,[79] others have sought to insert them into a 'feminist' discourse, so that their (alleged) criticism of the institution of marriage and their demands for education constitute a 'movement' related to their position in the *salons*.[80] More recently, the *précieuses* have been said to represent all the learned women of the *salon* struggling together (against men) for intellectual space and for 'radical alternatives to prescribed gender roles'.[81]

There is, however, another way of telling the story of the *précieuses*. Modern historians now agree that the language attributed to the *précieuses* – the emblem of their exclusivity and extraordinary character – is a caricature and was never spoken in the *salons*;[82] and there are enough contradictions in Somaize and de Pure's texts to support Domna Stanton's contention that they were nothing other than deliberately satirical.[83] The *précieuse*, Pelous and Stanton have argued, is a representation, a figure, a composite body. For Pelous, she is the Other. For Stanton, she 'exists only through the prism of comic degradation'.[84] If so, the question is, why was she invented?

In seventeenth-century France, the discourse of conversation produced two positionings for women. One, characterized by the virtues of 'discretion, silence, modesty',[85] was idealized in the shape of the *honnête femme*; the other, the incarnation of all the female defects of the time,[86] the embodiment of the undisciplined, unregulated tongue, was the *précieuse*. Men depended on women's conversation to perfect their own *honnêteté* and politeness. What if women refused to assume that civilizing function and its precondition, the disciplining of their own tongue?

Conversation, all seventeenth-century writers insisted, is primarily an exchange, a delightful commerce in which all *agrémens* and *bienséances* converge. However, whereas the conversation of the *honnête homme* had taken on all the seductive qualities of the feminine, the talk of the *précieuses* conveyed all the aggression usually attributed to the masculine. Their 'belles conversations', de Pure 'reveals', were nothing but contests and harangues.[87] The *précieuses* could not – or would not – produce *honnêteté*.

At the same time as the *précieuses* refused the maieutic function of female conversation, they claimed to arrogate to themselves the property of males: the power of naming.[88] The possibility that women might claim the power to generate language rather than babies was a transgression of such magnitude that it threatened the social order, the 'natural order', as

Molière's *Les Femmes Savantes* brilliantly illustrated. Satire, on the other hand, could disarm them and show that the *précieuses* could only generate monstrous, incomprehensible gibberish, turning France into Babel.[89] Women who claim access to male discourse[90] are an aberration; this transgression traditionally makes them vulnerable to accusations of sexual deviancy.[91] In an age of sexual libertinism, when seduction and desire were indispensable elements in the construction of the ideal male self, it is not surprising that the *précieuses* were constructed as refusing sexuality.[92]

Though *préciosité* has been read as 'the negative pole of the ideal of *honnêteté*',[93] both were in fact produced by the discourse on conversation. It is not the case that the *précieuses* were simply counterposed to the exemplary women who 'initiated' young men into the nuances of *politesse*, gallantry and above all, conversation.[94] The *précieuse* was every woman. Women's tongue was only momentarily disciplined by conversation, in order to service men and produce them as *honnêtes*.[95] The *précieuses* served as a warning to women that their place as the initiators and regulators of social life and polite language in the *salon* did not give them the authority to control language and sexuality. A few women were exceptional: they had no need to be disciplined, they had no 'tongue'. La Marquise de Rambouillet, or Arténice, was one.[96]

In seventeenth-century French society, conversation was the measure of worth.[97] Although women's language evinced all the qualities required for the achievement of *honnêteté*, women served as instruments – albeit indispensable ones – for men to attain that ideal. These qualities were in fact highlighted only in relation to that function. Nevertheless, a space was opened up for women's voice, a space that undeniably represents a break, a shift in respect of the traditional discourse on women's talk, which enjoins them only to be silent.[98]

2

THE ENGLISH GENTLEMAN[1]
AND HIS TONGUE

There can scarce be a greater Defect in a Gentleman, than
not to express himself well either in Writing or Speaking.
But yet, I think, I may ask my Reader, whether he doth
not know a great many, who live upon their Estates, and
so, with the Name, should have the Qualities of Gentlemen,
who cannot so much as tell a Story as they should; much
less speak clearly and perswasively in any Business. This,
I think not to be so much their Fault, as the Fault of their
Education.[2]

For Locke, writing in 1693, the educational problem in question
was that young gentlemen, forced to learn the grammars
of foreign and dead languages, were 'never once told of the
Grammar of their own Tongues'. As a result, far from being
educated to 'speak well and to the purpose on any subject and
on any occasion', they 'shock[ed]' the ears 'with solicisms and
offensive irregularities'. Locke was categorical. The language
that the gentleman should 'critically study, and labour to get
a facility, clearness and elegancy to Express himself in, should
be his own'.[3] It's not that Locke opposed the learning of foreign
languages. On the contrary. Firmly rooted in the courtly tradition, which held the study of languages to be essential to the
education of young men of rank, he recommended that boys
learn French as soon as they could 'speak *English*', and regarded
Latin as 'absolutely necessary to a Gentleman'.[4]

In the late seventeenth century, however, there was growing
dissatisfaction with the way Latin was taught. Although this
was part of a general disenchantment with educational practices
and institutions,[5] there were some specific criticisms. One was

of the widespread use of corporal punishment,[6] another, of the practice of teaching boys Latin grammar in Latin, in a language which they had not yet mastered.[7] These methods were held responsible for the slow progress and meagre results achieved by boys who had spent many years on the subject. However, Locke's most severe criticism was that instruction in Latin subverted the tongue of the gentleman.[8] Given the long tradition of Latin learning in England and Locke's own position on the subject, the question that arises is why this should have become an issue. My question is, why should the tongue of the gentleman suddenly become an object of concern? Foucault's notion of 'problematization' can help clarify this. A problematization does not mean the 'representation of a pre-existing object, nor the creation by discourse of an object that doesn't exist'. It is rather that at a specific moment, 'an object is constituted for thought'.[9] The question I want to address, then, is: why was the tongue of the gentleman problematized at that specific historical moment?

THE PROBLEMATIZATION OF THE TONGUE OF THE GENTLEMAN

In the late seventeenth century, Lawrence Klein has argued, two discourses, both initially the products of Renaissance humanism, converged for the first time on the 'the same population', namely gentlemen. These two discourses were, on the one hand, the 'language of civic humanism', characterized by its emphasis on virtuous manners and on the notion of liberty, and, on the other, the language of courtly behaviour and refinement, the discourse of politeness.[10] The emergence of both these discourses had to do with the shift away from the court as a locus of both political power and status, as a result of the Glorious Revolution. It is in this context that the problematization of the gentleman and his tongue can be situated. In an absolute monarchy, the king's voice represents the sole authority.[11] The shift of political power from the Court to Parliament made unprecedented demands on the gentleman, and required him to have the ability to speak for the whole of society, with the voice of authority.[12]

However, how could the voice of the gentleman be constituted as a voice of authority when he was perceived to be inarticulate in English, and when English, as a vernacular, was

27

also the language of the 'Illiterate Vulgar'? Locke had warned
that not only were 'want of Propriety, and Grammatical
Exactness' unbecoming to the rank of the gentleman, but that
incorrect English also indicated 'Lower Breeding and worse
Company than suits with his quality'. Grammar could provide
authority, argued Lane, making the point that without it the
speaker of any language, even Latin in Roman times, is illiterate, while Locke maintained that 'To Write and Speak correctly
gives a Grace, and gains favourable Attention to what one has
to say'. To be persuasive, the tongue of the gentleman was to
be distinguished not merely by its correctness but by its graceful
manner and its polish.[13]

In France, the Académie Française had regulated and 'fixed'
the French language in a way which the English admired and
even envied.[14] In England, because of the complex relations
between the Court, the Town and the Country,[15] there was no
locus for the elaboration of such a standard. This may explain
why from the late seventeenth century, a number of scholars
and writers, among whom were Thomas Sprat – a founding
fellow of the Royal Society and author of its history – Daniel
Defoe and Jonathan Swift, called for the reform and the refinement of the English language and for the setting up of a state
supported English academy to carry it out. The concern about
the language was not purely 'linguistic', but had a moral under-
pinning, for it was believed that changes in language were
inseparable from changes in manners and morals. Thus for Swift
and Defoe, an English Academy would not only 'encourage
Polite Learning ... polish and refine the English Tongue', but
represent a place 'where all our Customs and Habits, both in
Speech and Behaviour, shou'd receive an Authority'.[16] Their
preoccupations with language coalesced on the gentleman and
on his tongue.

So far, the story of the problematization of the English tongue
shares a number of features with such standard histories of
English as Albert Baugh's *History of the English Language*.[17]
Baugh's account is worth a look because its many reprintings
attest to its enduring popularity, and because it belongs to the
tradition of the history of ideas criticized by Michel Foucault.[18]
The 'interest' in language developed when it did, Baugh explains,
because the 'adventurous individualism' of the seventeenth
century was replaced by a 'rationalist spirit' and a 'desire for

system and regularity' based on reason. Essayists, poets, theologians and grammarians all looked at their language and found it wanting. They then set out to 'standardize, refine and fix' it. In the process, they turned for inspiration to Italy and France, whose language had already been regulated and fixed by academies and dictionaries.[19] Eventually, Baugh concludes, regulation was achieved while remaining true to the 'British spirit of Freedom', without resort to the 'artificial restraints and the repressive influence of an academy'.[20] Baugh's story is unsatisfactory for a number of reasons. It is teleological, appearing like the gradual unfolding of a carefully managed programme culminating in the achievement of what gave it its initial impulse, the rationalism of the Enlightenment. Constructed within a progressive framework, it must invoke reifications such as the 'British spirit of Freedom' to ensure coherence and continuity. But it is most problematic for what it leaves out: the relation of language to the construction of the subject. This is all the more surprising because of the slippage between the tongue as national language and the tongue as organ of speech which characterizes discussions about language in the eighteenth century. In this book, I will argue that throughout the eighteenth century – and into the nineteenth – tongues and the tongue were critical sites for the self-fashioning of the gentleman and, eventually, for the forging of national and gender difference.

THE VOICE OF AUTHORITY AND WOMEN'S TONGUE

The constitution of the authoritative voice of the gentleman required that he use correct English and that he speak it eloquently and politely.[21] How was this to be achieved? As suggested in courtesy manuals since Castiglione's *The Book of the Courtier*, and as practiced in the *salon* in France, women were recruited to the task. Women's conversation, 'naturally' polite, elegant and delicate, was to discipline and polish male tongues. Swift put it most vividly: harking back to a golden age of (English) politeness when men and women met to converse on 'agreeable subjects', he declared:

> If there were no other Use in the Conversation of Ladies,
> it is sufficient that it would lay a Restraint upon those

odious Topicks of Immodesty and Indecencies, into which the Rudeness of our Northern Genius, is so apt to fall.[22]

Although Swift went so far as to attribute the present 'Degeneracy of Conversation' to the custom of excluding women from the society of men, he was not alone in suggesting this role for women's conversation. From the author of *An Essay in Defense of the Female Sex* (1697), to Hannah More's *Strictures on the Modern System of Female Education*, (1799)[23], women's conversation was held up as the best way for men to polish theirs.

It would thus appear that in eighteenth-century England, women's conversation was constructed in the same way as it had been in seventeenth-century France. But there were differences, which underline the complexity of the subject and make us aware that caution must be exercised when describing the play of cultural 'influences' between England and France. One reason why women's conversation had been so important in France was that their language had been erected into a model of purity, delicacy and *politesse*.[24] Similarly, from Locke to Hannah More, women were praised for the 'Elegancy and Politeness' of their language, all the more remarkable since it was achieved without their knowing any grammatical rules.[25] Yet, a large number of the practical English grammars published in the first half of the eighteenth century addressed women in particular. James Greenwood recommended the study of grammar to 'young Ladies, (as well as Gentlemen)', not just so they avoid the opprobrium of 'Blameable Spelling or false Syntax', but to remedy an area of neglect in the education of the 'Fair Sex'.[26] Why then, if ladies were told that they had a natural talent for speaking and writing their native tongue with 'more Grace than even the Men themselves', were they also told that they must learn the grammar of their native language? To recommend improvement in English is not as strange as it may seem, declared Mary Wray, for

> our Native Language will not come to us by Inspiration, and we shall write and speak with Rudeness and Affectation, if we know no more of it than we are bred with.[27]

Women should be better educated in general and in grammar in particular not just so they learn to express their thoughts clearly and correctly, nor because in women's language, faults were virtually equated with immorality,[28] but because they raised sons.[29] Gildon and Brightland thus enjoined women to learn English grammar because they were among the 'most numerous Teachers of it'.[30] Thomas Wilson even claimed that the improvement of the nation depended on mothers' knowledge of grammatical English. This was necessary not just because teaching their children to speak correctly would help them towards their 'Good Fortune', but, Wilson warned, if children's 'Tongues and Ears' were set wrong, this 'fundamental Error' was almost irretrievable. For Wilson, it was precisely because women's 'Voice, Ear and Tongue' were more elegant than men's that it was their moral duty to learn grammar. Women had to harness their 'natural talents to good purpose', like the mother of the Gracchi, who 'contributed very much to the forming of the eloquence of her sons'.[31]

Eloquence and an authoritative voice were necessary conditions for the gentleman's role in public service, but they were not sufficient. His voice also needed to be manly. This points to a crucial difference between England and France. In France, the *honnête homme* could model his language on that of women because it seems that masculinity was already in him. In England, I will be arguing, masculinity was not a given.[32] Because men learned their *mother tongue* at their mother's lap, it was up to women to regulate their own language through grammar and render it 'manly', to prepare their sons for service in the polis and thus ensure the future success of the nation.

Disciplining and regulating the tongue of men thus positioned French and English women completely differently. In France, it engaged women and men in an erotic discourse. In England, it positioned women first as language teachers to their sons. This role appears less dangerous because it stripped the process of its sexuality. However, it held its own perils, as will soon become clear.

CONVERSATION AND THE TONGUE

'Our sex is not able to support [politeness] without the company of women, who never fail to lead us into the right way, and there to keep us', declared Swift.[33] For the author of *An Essay in Defense of the Female Sex* too, conversing with women served as the necessary finish and polish to men's education.

> Almost all men that have had a liberal, and good education, know what is due to good Manners, and civil company. But till they have been us'd a little to our society, their Modesty fits like Constraint upon 'em, and looks like a forc'd complaisance to uneasie Rules, and forms of Civility. Conversing frequently with us makes 'em familiar, to Men, and when they are convinced of its ease and necessity they are soon reconciled to the Practice.[34]

With their conversation being ascribed such prominent importance, it is not surprising that women's conduct in conversation would attract the attention of moralists. For Mary Wray in 1722 – as for Hannah More at the end of the eighteenth century – it was precisely because women had a 'quick and pleasant Imagination', and 'fluency of Speech', that special vigilance was required. These may be qualities but, Mary Wray cautioned, because they are not usually accompanied by 'sense', they become 'contemptible'. Women must not forget that 'a Woman's Tongue should be like the imaginary Musick of the Spheres, sweet and charming, but not to be heard at a distance'.[35] Though the ideal female tongue was here conflated with the voice – the tongue cannot sound like music, only the voice can – what had to be contained was the tongue, that 'slippery Member' which both sexes found so difficult to control.[36] The incapacity to keep a secret deserved the most severe censure. This disease of the tongue, emblematic of its lack of control, was so disgusting that its diagnosis necessitated scatological terminology: it was 'a babbling Humour, being a symptom of a loose Impotent Soul, a kind of Incontinence of the Mind, that can retain nothing committed to it; but as if that also had its diabetick Passion, perpetually and insensibly evacuating all'. Although Wray affected to specify that this affliction was not due to sex but to an 'ill constitution of the Mind' and that men were also prey to it, her remedy served to highlight the problem as women's. For to have the self-control necessary to keep a secret was 'a piece of daring Manliness, which women may affect without breach of Modesty'.[37] The unrestrained tongue was inescapably female and had to be contained and controlled.

For Defoe it was education which provided that control: the conversation of a woman 'well Bred and well Taught', he wrote, is 'heavenly'. Without education, woman is all tongue: her wit makes her 'Impertinent and Talkative'; if bad-tempered, she is 'Insolent and Loud'; if 'Passionate', it makes her a 'Scold'.[38] For Wray, it was modesty. Not only did modesty prescribe the measure and manner of speaking, refine the language, 'modulate the Voice and Accent' and 'admit no unhandsome Earnestness and Lewdness of Discourse', but it restrained excessive talk. But how much talk is 'too much' talk? Even if talkativeness was not just a 'Feminine Vice', women were said to talk too much because they should talk little.[39] This ambiguity could sometimes be exploited to women's advantage, as when Bathsua Makin, promoting a new pedagogy for young ladies, had played on the image of female talkativeness to support her proposal that women should learn languages: 'It is objected against women ... that they have too much Tongue: but it's no crime that they have too many Tongues'. The problem with women's tongue was not just excess but danger. The tongue, Makin had pointed out, is the 'only weapon women have to defend themselves with, and they need to use it dextrously'.[40] Woman's tongue may be her power but that power is measured in relation not to her autonomy but to its effect on men. It is not surprising, then, to find that young ladies, instructed on the importance of restraining the passion of anger for the stability and happiness of their future married life, were told: 'First Bridle the Tongue, and seal up your Lips'.[41]

How could women be expected both to converse and to 'talk little'? Was all women's talk excessive? How could women's conversation be valued and derogated at the same time? And how can the recommendations that men *converse* with *women* have been taken up in England, when one of the dominant features of English society was the segregation of the sexes,[42] and when 'taciturnity' was, as Addison put it, an English 'national' trait?[43]

THE GENDERED SPACES OF ENGLISH SOCIABILITY

Although there were attempts to import the idea of the *salon* into England, copies of the 'Parisian prototype' in both its external aspects of lavish decoration and its function of literary discussion and patronage, the *salon* as a space for mixed conversation does not seem to have materialized in England. As Sir Nathaniel Wraxall was to remark at the end of the century, the success of mixed assemblies in Paris – 'it would be idle to contest that they altogether eclipsed ours' – must have something to do with 'the National character of the French'. Of course women such as Fanny Burney, Mrs Thrale and Mrs Montague conversed with men, but it seems that men and women mostly spent their time separately, whether in the same or in different spaces.[44] Travellers to England were struck enough to comment, as Grosley did, that when men and women met to converse, 'the women, generally speaking, place themselves near the door, and leave the upper hand and the conversation to the men'. Frenchmen were not the only ones who remarked on this. An American governor likened the separate female groupings to 'battalions on the opposite side of the room'.[45] Whereas in France, the *salon* was a feminine space for mixed conversation, the spaces for mixed conversation are more difficult to locate in England. The use of the dining room, for example, reflects this complexity. It was developed as a space for eating in England long before it was in France. Though dining was a mixed social activity, following a custom already well established by the early eighteenth century, women would retire to the drawing room soon after the meal leaving the men to drink, smoke and converse. Yet it was the dining room, where men spent a good deal of their time on their own, that was considered 'the apartment of conversation' and was lavishly decorated.[46]

TACITURNITY AND NATIONAL CHARACTER

Musing on language and national character, Addison observed:

Our Language shows the Genius and natural Temper of the English, which is modest, thoughtful and sincere, and which perhaps may recommend the People, though it has spoiled the tongue. We might perhaps carry the same Thought into other languages, and deduce a greater Part of what is peculiar to them from the Genius of the People who speak them. It is certain, the light talkative Humour of the French has not a little infected their Tongue, which might be shown by many Instances.

For Addison, it was precisely because the English language was 'abounding in Monosyllables', that it was perfectly suited not only to speakers wishing to utter their thoughts quickly and frugally, but to the taciturn English character. 'Loquacity' was the 'enemy'.[47] Even if Addison was being gently ironic, his unfashionable opinion cannot be ignored because of the way monosyllabic English was to be construed in relation to the English national character at the end of the century, as I shall discuss later. Thomas Wilson also noted English taciturnity, but unlike Addison, he was not prepared to treat what he called the 'Clog upon our Tongue' indulgently. Because 'Words come slow and with Difficulty', he argued, conversation, though enjoyed, is less pleasant to the English, they resort to solitude and silence, and the spleen gains ground. Taciturnity is no national trait, Wilson insisted, just national 'Laziness, Folly and Mismanagement' in our conduct towards our own tongue. And it is this, he warned, that would be taken to reflect the English national character: a good language is both 'an Honour' and of great use to a nation; and 'an imperfect and unimproved Tongue will for ever be a Mark either of carelessness or a low Genius of the People'.[48]

MEN AND CONVERSATION

In his 'Letter on Conversation', Samuel Parker discusses the difficulty men have in sustaining social intercourse, and wonders why they do not seek to imitate women's conversation, with its 'Vivacity of Imagination', its 'Acuteness of Wit' and its unself-conscious elegance. But, he points out, not only is women's conversation undervalued, "Tis called Effeminacy to seek it'.[49] That was the danger. The author of An Essay in Defense of the Female Sex had also been aware of it, but had unequivocally located the problem in men. After describing in detail the many intellectual pleasures and refinements afforded to men when conversing with women, she warned that not all men could benefit from women's conversation; only those who by nature have an 'Improvable Stock of wit and good sense'. The others, men who lacked the penetration and discernment to reflect upon the deeper reasons for women's 'peculiar Graces and Ornaments', just ended up aping the most visible and superficial female traits, and

> fall to licking, sprucing and dressing their Campaign Faces, and ill-contriv'd Bodies that now, like all Foolish Imitatours, they outdo the Originals, and out-powder, out-patch and out-paint the Vainest and most extravagant of our Sex at those Follies, and are perpetually Cocking, Bustling, Twiring, and making Grimaces, as if they expected we shou'd make Addresses to 'em in a short time.

It is not women's conversation that effeminates these men, argued the author: women cannot 'alter Nature', only polish it. But, while asserting that the problem was located in the men, she was aware that it was the social activity, conversation with women and, by extension, women's conversation itself that would be considered dangerous. Yet, she pointed out, travel is not brought into disrepute just because 'it is observ'd that those who go abroad Fools return Fops.'[50] This comparison is particularly relevant to this discussion, since a major aim of travel – as Grand Tour – was identical to that of female conversation: to polish the gentleman's conversation.

Mixed conversation was dangerous, Wray claimed, because men 'fall into the Effeminacy and Delicacy of Women' and women 'take up the Confidence and Boldness of Men' in their manners and their language. Men become slaves to women who have no 'scruple' about being visited and served by men 'even in their Beds'.[51] These transgressions of sexual propriety are carried out 'under a notion of Good-breeding' in imitation of the French, who have not only blurred the boundaries of sexual propriety, but perverted the meaning of Freedom. For the 'Freedom of the French' is merely sexual license; they are but 'slaves in everything else'.[52]

Not everyone was as indignant as Wray about the practice of mixed conversation. But even more measured opinions such as Joseph Spence's are indicative of a problem. 'Some conversation with the ladies', he noted, 'is necessary to smooth and sweeten the temper as well as the manners of man, but too much of it is apt to effeminate or debilitate both'.[53] In England, politeness, the antithesis of taciturnity,[54] could not be achieved without the conversation of women, just as in France. But in England, this raised profound anxieties about masculinity.[55] The nature of this anxiety is best illustrated by the character of the fop, in whom effeminacy and French manners are indissolubly linked.

THE FOP

On 19 July 1712, having just met some ladies dressed in masculine attire, Addison comments:

> I must observe that this Fashion was first of all brought to us from France, a Country which has Infected all the Nations of Europe with its Levity. I speak not this in derogation of a whole People . . . I shall therefore only Remark, that as Liveliness and Assurance are in a peculiar manner the Qualifications of the French Nation, the same Habits and Customs will not give the same Offence to that People, which they produce among those of our own Country. Modesty is our distinguishing Character, as Vivacity is theirs.[56]

What Addison was objecting to was not the French so much as the English who followed French fashions or returned 'Frenchified' from trips across the Channel. It is significant that 'Levity' and 'Vivacity', terms used here by Addison to characterize the French nation were also used by him elsewhere to differentiate English women from English men, counterposing female vivacity and airiness to male gravity and severity.[57] It is not surprising, then, that more problematic than women aping the French were the men who did so. They were the fops.[58]

'There are a sort of men', Berinthia tells her cousin Amanda, instructing her on the ways of the Town,

> that may be called the beaux' antipathy, for they agree in nothing but walking upon two legs. These have brains; the beau has none. They are in love with their mistress; the beau with himself. They take care of her reputation; he's industrious to destroy it. They are decent; he's a fop. They are sound; he's rotten. They are men; he's an ass.[59]

The gentleman who has spent a great part of his life in the nursery, knows some good remedies for colds, has acquired culinary skills and a wide vocabulary about precious fashionable stuffs, and entertains his mother every night with gossip of Town and Court, also qualifies as a fop.[60] Fondness for dress and makeup and an inordinate concern with appearance also distinguish fops from 'English' men, who 'dress in a plain uniform manner'.[61] The term 'fop' then, appears to be a category referring to a number of meanings. My concern here however is not so much with explaining who the fops were, but with discussing two of their outstanding and recurring traits: their Frenchified manners and language,[62] and their predilection for the company of women.

FOPS AND THE FRENCH CONNECTION

From Sir Fopling Flutter in Etheredge's *Man of Mode*, to Lord Foppington in Vanbrugh's *The Relapse* and young Buck in Samuel Foot's 'The ENGLISHMAN return'd from Paris',[63] fops affect French dress, French manners and French 'smatterings'. When we meet them, they have often just returned from abroad – metonymously France. The fops' French connection simply cannot be ignored. The question is, why it is there at all?

Since the fop is a figure of ridicule, he may have served to derogate the French out of concern over the invasion of foreign ideas and foreign goods, a recurring theme in the *Spectator* for example, as when Addison wishes there were an Act of Parliament for 'Prohibiting the Importation of French Fopperies'.[64] But I think something more complex is also involved. From the first decades of the century to nearly the last, all things French were thought to be so powerfully attractive and seductive to the English that they feared they might be taken over and subjugated. At the same time, not only the polish of French manners but fluency in French were held to be so indispensable to the fashioning of the gentleman that hundreds of young men from high-ranking English families were sent to France to acquire these accomplishments. Why was knowing French so important?

By the late seventeenth century, French was spoken at all European Courts and generally reckoned to be a universal language.[65] Refined and purified by the Académie Française, it had a flourishing literature and was the civilized and civilizing tongue *par excellence*. The status of French had led, inevitably, to what we would now call linguistic borrowing. English attitudes to borrowing varied, and it is important to distinguish which language was being borrowed: thus, for Addison, who had remarked elsewhere on the 'innumerable Elegancies and Improvements' that the English tongue had received from Hebrew,[66] it was not borrowing as such that was a problem, but borrowing from the French. Why was there such widespread concern about what Linda Colley calls the 'infiltration of Frenchisms'? Why the fear that the 'importation' of too many French words would 'enervate and spoil' English?[67]

While the English admired French's 'melting tone', its softness and musicality, this admiration was not unequivocal. It was also suggested that French had been so refined, purified and polished that it had lost its strength and 'sinews', in other words, its virility.[68] English, on the other hand, was said to be, and to have always been, a strong and masculine tongue.[69] French words were borrowed not because English was lacking,[70] but because it had been seduced. Borrowing was the consequence of English's illicit, immoral intimacy with French's 'Adulterous Charms', which would eventually 'Debase, not Advance, our Native and Masculine Tongue'.[71] Stackhouse even warned that the 'freedom' English had taken with French through 'too close a Commerce' with that language, might impair its 'Strength and Sinews' as if by excessive sexual indulgence.[72] The relation of English to French was thus 'sexualized', discursively constructed as a relation of seduction and desire, positioning English as male and French as female. But because desire and seduction were held to be effeminating,[73] this relation threatened the manliness of the English tongue.

The fop aped the French and had become 'Frenchified' because he too had been seduced. Fops are in fact represented as copying manners divested of meaning. They are 'all outside, no inside',[74] all show. They are an empty shell, lacking the inner virtue that constitutes the gentleman. The fop's Frenchified manners and language thus highlighted his difference from 'English' men, not because he had become *foreign* but because he had become *not-English*. He had failed at being not just a man but an *English*man.

The fops' second outstanding trait was their predilection for the company of women. Their conversation and their 'Pretences to Wit and Judgement'[75] which men (real ones, of course) rightly considered empty chatter and always ridiculed, charmed women.

If we observe the Conduct of the Fair Sex, we find that they choose rather to associate themselves with a Person who resembles them in that light and volatile humour which is natural to them, than to such as are qualified to moderate and counter-ballance it. It has been an old complaint, that the Coxcomb carries it with them before the Man of Sense. When we see a fellow loud and talkative, full of insipid Life and Laughter, we may venture to pronounce him a female Favourite.[76]

There is a further dimension to the story, that of the theatre. There are striking similarities between the fop and the *précieuses* in seventeenth-century France. Both are most famous as products of the playwright's imagination; both transgress gender boundaries in particular discourses, and are constructed as unnatural creatures; for both, questions were and have been raised about their 'reality'.[77] Yet, the point is not whether there were 'real' fops any more than 'real' *précieuses*. What is involved is not a reflection of reality, but how the social is disciplined. Thus, for John Dennis writing in 1722, the nature of comedy is not 'to set us Patterns for Imitation', but to instruct, through the fear of ridicule.

'Tis by the Ridicule that there is in the Character of Sir Fopling ... that he is so well qualify'd to please and to instruct. What true Englishman is there, but must be pleas'd to see this ridiculous Knight made the Jest and the Scorn of all the other Characters, for shewing, by his foolish aping foreign Customs and Manners, that he prefers another Country to his own? And of what important Instruction must it be to all our Youth who travel, to shew them, that if they so far forget the Love of their Country, as to declare by the espousing foreign Customs and Manners, that they prefer France or Italy to Great Britain, at their Return, they must justly expect to be the Jest and the Scorn of their Countrymen.[78]

The *précieuses* were a warning to French women: in France, the concern was over the containment and regulation of women's tongue. Fops were a warning to Englishmen about what happened to men who spent all their time in the company of women – like French men did. In England, the concern was about men and the anxiety about effeminacy.

If the French tongue was implicated in the construction of the fop, then French practices for the fashioning of the *honnête homme* must be involved as well, because of the central role of conversation. It was not just a case of the fop, or 'superfine Beau of Queen Anne's time' modelling himself on the 'messieurs of the time of Louis XIV', as Ashton suggests,[79] for if the *honnête homme* was indeed a model for the fop, he was turned upside down and inside out in crossing the channel. To fashion and perfect the self in conversation, the *honnête homme* had to cultivate the company of women and the desire to please them. To the English, this made French men effeminate. The English 'translation' and representation of French gallantry and *l'art de plaire* missed the point: the aim of the social practices around conversation was not the seduction of women so much as the fashioning and perfecting of *men*.

Fops were the products of women's company and conversation. From the cradle onwards, Englishmen were vulnerable to the power and influence of females. Unless they distanced themselves from it, they would be effeminated. Only in the company of men could masculinity be produced. But masculinity needed to be polished, otherwise it was rough-hewn and 'rustick'. Women's conversation alone could provide this polish. Could the English gentleman be at once polite and manly? How was politeness to be achieved?

3

POLITENESS

In 'The rise of "politeness" in England, 1660–1715',[1] the first major study of the subject, Lawrence Klein brilliantly mapped the ways in which politeness 'altered the landscape of discourse' in early eighteenth-century England. He argued that politeness arose as part of the spread of the courtly tradition over the English élite, something which was not unrelated to the weakness of the Court as a source of culture and as the authority on language, taste and manners that it was in France. In England it was the polite who made themselves into that authority.[2]

Klein also showed, in this and subsequent work, how politeness came to function as a 'cultural ideology' for that élite. From the start, it was 'associated with, and often identified with gentlemanliness'. Thus, as it infused increasing areas of English social and cultural life, politeness reflected what Klein describes as the 'appropriation of the world of social, intellectual and literary creation by gentlemen'. Defined at its simplest as a 'dextrous management of words and actions', the intricate play of manners, language, self-display, sociability and *je ne sais quoi* that constituted politeness became central to the self-fashioning of the gentleman. Its main expressive form, its 'master metaphor', was conversation.[3]

There is one area, however, that Klein's wide-ranging analysis does not address: the set of tensions and ambiguities to which I have already alluded in my discussion of the role of conversation in the construction of the gentleman. I am referring to the relation of politeness and conversation to France and to the anxiety over masculinity. It's not that Klein failed to acknowledge either the connection of politeness to France, or the tensions inherent in politeness. On the contrary. In 'The rise of "politeness"', he had pointed out that it was a 'vehicle for a certain view of social relations developed in France', and had examined the ways in which terms like *politesse* and *honnêteté* had been translated – or not – into English.[4]

Klein did not, however, consider the possibility that something might have been, as it were, lost in the translation, as my discussion of the fop illustrates. As for what he called the 'complex of tensions' generated by politeness, he saw them as resulting mainly from conflicts between the language of courtly behaviour and refinement and the language of civic humanism.[5]

Klein's argument is convincing, but it can be taken further, although in a slightly different direction. I want to argue that the languages of civic humanism and politeness also resonated with overtones of gender,[6] though this produced positionings not so much for masculinity and femininity but, more crucially, for manliness and effeminacy. And, I want to suggest further, these positionings also served to construct both English representations of a 'French politeness' identified with effeminacy and servility and an English politeness characterized by manliness and liberty.

To illustrate how these discourses were shaped, I have chosen to discuss two perspectives on politeness. First, that of Lord Chesterfield, an aristocrat who saw France as the model of politeness to emulate, and second, that of David Fordyce,[7] who taught at the University of Edinburgh, and for whom the association with France was one of the main problems of politeness.[8]

POLITENESS AND CHESTERFIELD'S *LETTERS TO HIS SON*

Chesterfield wrote more than 400 letters, over a period of thirty years, to his son Philip Stanhope. They begin when the boy was about five, living with his mother and educated at home, like most aristocratic boys, by a private tutor, Mr Maittaire,[9] before he was due to go to Westminster School. Chesterfield wrote to instruct his son and, as he said himself, 'never were so much pains taken for any body's education . . . and never had any body those opportunities of knowledge and improvement'.[10] The letters are about geography, the classical world and mythology, grammar and languages; they tell detailed anecdotes of the great, of history and travel. These were some of the things a gentleman ought to know.[11] At the same time as conveying 'facts',

Chesterfield continually reminded his son of the absolute necessity of good breeding, without which 'mere learning is pedantry'.
Learning is important of course, it gives 'solidity' to breeding,
but it has no charm or graces unless it is polished. Without
polish, virtues and learning, like rough diamonds, lack lustre
and despite their intrinsic value, do not shine.[12]

From the time his son approached nine years of age,
Chesterfield insisted upon his acquiring civility and good
breeding as a way of being 'welcome in conversation and
common life'. 'Remember', he admonished him,

> that to be civil, and to be civil with ease, (which is prop-
> erly called good-breeding,) is the only way to be beloved
> and well received in company; that to be ill-bred, and rude,
> is intolerable, and the way to be kicked out of company;
> and that to be bashful is ridiculous.[13]

How was good breeding acquired, since it was not learned in
books? Chesterfield saw his paternal role as transmitting the
arcana, the secret knowledge necessary to his son's 'initiation'
into that élite society, the *beau monde*.[14] One of the secrets was
to observe the French, 'whose politeness seems as easy and
natural as any other part of their conversation'. The English, on
the other hand, are not just 'awkward in their civilities', but
when they actually mean to be civil, are ashamed to 'get it out'.
This bashfulness, this *mauvaise honte*, is

> the characteristic of the British booby; who is frightened
> out of his wits when people of fashion speak to him; and
> when he is to answer them, blushes, stammers, and can
> hardly get out what he would say; and becomes really
> ridiculous, from a groundless fear of being laughed at:
> whereas a well-bred man would speak to all the kings in
> the world, with as little concern, and as much ease, as he
> would speak to you.[15]

It would not be an exaggeration to describe Chesterfield's
letters as a panegyric of French good breeding and good
manners, and an unmitigated disparagement of English ones.
The only superiority he granted the English was that of learning.
He thus exhorted his son to arrive (almost) at the 'perfection of
human nature' by practising both 'English knowledge and
French good-breeding'.[16]

Politeness and good breeding are a language of the voice and of the body, and fluency requires their simultaneous expression. 'The look, the tone of voice, the manner of speaking, the gestures, must all conspire to form that *Je ne sais quoi* that everybody feels, although nobody can exactly describe'.[17] Graceful speaking, which distinguishes 'people of fashion from the illiterate vulgar', includes accurate grammar and good pronunciation, 'according to the usage of the best companies'. Here again, the French are held up as a model. The 'measure of the well-bred man' is conversation.[18] Chesterfield therefore outlines a choreography of speaking: 'Think of your words, and of their arrangement before you speak: choose the most elegant, and place them in the best order'. Like De Vaumorière and Méré, he specifies what a man of fashion ought to say and avoid saying: it is acceptable to disagree with someone, but not to be tactless.[19] The proper conduct of conversation involves discipline of the tongue above all.

As important as polite phrases are the polite gestures and demeanour that define the gentleman: how to come into a room full of company 'with a graceful and proper assurance . . . and without embarrassment', how to eat, how not to be encumbered by one's body. Chesterfield draws a scathing portrait of the awkward fellow, whose solecisms – stumbling over his own sword, letting his coffee cup or saucer fall, coughing in his glass when drinking, not knowing what to do with his hands or where to put them – make him so ridiculous or disagreeable that he is unwelcome in society, and avoided by anyone who 'desires to please'. Just as polite conversation implies discipline of the tongue, polite demeanour entails strict discipline of the body and its gestures for a harmonious self-presentation. Not surprisingly, in the same breath as Chesterfield lectures his son on the importance of the purity, clarity and gracefulness of his diction for a Parliamentary career, he tells him that his dancing master, is 'at this time the man in all Europe of the greatest importance to you'.[20]

Chesterfield hoped to fashion a gentleman destined for the 'world of business'[21] – more precisely for diplomacy. With the education and opportunities for improvement his son had received, Chesterfield was careful to remind him, he would be far more qualified than most English ministers taking up such a post. Unlike them, not only would he speak foreign languages and thus appear to advantage in conversation, but he would possess what they all lacked: manners and breeding. A good figure in the *beau monde* and in foreign Courts could not, Chesterfield insisted, be achieved without these 'graces'.[22]

The ultimate aim of politeness and civility was to please and to make oneself agreeable. For the *honnête homme*, this was a technique for fashioning the self. For Chesterfield, as he makes ruthlessly clear, it is indispensable for another reason. Politeness and an *extérieur brillant* will make his son irresistible, especially to women, enable him to insinuate himself into people's affection, and conduct 'the principal business of a foreign minister . . . to get into the secrets'.[23] Insinuation has an altogether different meaning here than it had in seventeenth-century France:

> observe their characters, and pry, as far as you can, into both their hearts and their heads. Seek for their particular merit, their predominant passion, or their prevailing weakness; and you will know what to bait your hook with, to catch them.[24]

The seduction involved here has nothing to do with the play of gallantry, it is a cynical means to social success. That this politeness is only a mask does not worry Chesterfield unduly. He is not interested in sincerity. The deception involved in commending people, especially women, 'a little more, it may be, than [one] really thinks they deserve', is a small price to pay for the affection and goodwill of the people one converses with. Well-bred Frenchmen are 'the perfection of human nature', yet, 'what a number of sins does [their] cheerful easy good-breeding . . . frequently cover?'[25]

Chesterfield's *Letters*, which earned him Johnson's remark that they 'teach the morals of a whore, and the manners of a dancing master',[26] reveal a concept of *politesse* that narrowly meets Klein's description of the polite as 'the outer man . . . the man who was involved in the willed act of self-presentation', a figure who 'enjoyed a dubious relationship with the sphere of the ethical'.[27] It is as 'decorticated', emptied of its meaning, as the conception of *honnêteté* which produced the fop.

POLITENESS AND DAVID FORDYCE'S *DIALOGUES CONCERNING EDUCATION*

If Chesterfield was throughout his life the 'devoted servant' of the graces,[28] for David Fordyce, the question was how much –

or rather how little – to sacrifice to them. Fordyce sets up the *Dialogues* in an imaginary academy in the country, modelled on the old Academy, or Portico, at Athens, where philosophers talked philosophy in a familiar and unassuming manner. The book consists of twenty dialogues on different aspects of education, mostly comparing ancient and modern education. Simplicius, whose visit to the academy is the pretext for the *Dialogues*, is the narrator. The characters whose voices will be heard are Phylax, Philander and Euphranor and Cleora.[29] The terms of the debate are set early on. Simplicius and Cleora are discussing the contrast between the dishonesty and dissembling of polite conversation, and the 'awkward but truthful bluntness' of native English intercourse. Cleora, educated in sober virtues by Phylax,[30] argues that many of the polite forms of ordinary conversation are not just 'a more specious kind of Lies' which hinder the 'Freedom and Easiness of friendly Intercourse', but an enslavement to foreign manners, and as such, alien to the British character. She would have them 'banished out a Country, once justly celebrated for the Plainness and Bluntness of its Inhabitants'. Simplicius, who claims he would rather be called a 'scrupulous Simpleton than a polite Dissembler', nevertheless thinks Cleora too severe. Even though they are 'inferior Graces', he concedes, without the 'DECENCIES of Life, that regulate the Conversation and Practice of the Politest Part of the World', will not the English be 'reckoned awkward, antiquated Creatures, and even somewhat unsociable'? Could not the ordinary forms of civility and polite phrases just be treated as 'counters', whose value is determined and agreed upon by the well-bred who share amongst themselves the knowledge of its arbitrariness, he asks later.[31] Politeness would then just be the currency in the commerce of sociability.

For Fordyce no less than for Chesterfield, education is meant to breed up the gentleman. But, in Fordyce's view, something has gone wrong. Whereas the education of the Ancients succeeded in combining the teaching of knowledge and of manners to produce men that were at once scholars and gentlemen, there is, in modern education, a 'divorce' between 'Politeness and Learning'. The problem is that 'one kind of Knowledge has been thought necessary to furnish a learned Head, and quite another to form a Gentleman'. Parents nowadays are concerned only with their children's polite accomplishments, and think them accomplished enough when they 'talk French prettily'.[32] However, if polite education is censured for its frivolity, politeness itself is not. When Cleora asks whether there is a way of being polite and agreeable 'without polishing ourselves out of our old British Plainness and Sincerity?',[33] she expresses an implicit theme of the *Dialogues*: the attempt to create an indigenous 'British' politeness. The gentlemen who discuss these issues may be teachers and students but they are not rustics, and they want education to produce gentlemen. Like Chesterfield, they believe that 'the most perfect characters are those who have added the knowledge of the scholar to the accomplishments of the gentleman'.[34] Though the discussion is ostensibly about the ways in which learning has been brought into disrepute, it is also about the necessity of politeness. Its absence produces both Fordyce's reclusive scholar and Chesterfield's 'awkward fellow', strikingly alike in their lack of physical and verbal fluency and their transgression of the most elementary rules of polite conversation and sociability: mere scholars who know nothing about the modern world, who wear singular clothes and think a wig 'too modern an invention'; who, when they appear in polite company, look like 'the inhabitants of another world', and whose conversation is about such recondite scholarly subjects that no one can converse with them.[35]

Gentlemen they cannot be, then, unless they are polite, but French politeness – though the French are said to glory in it – is a servility, and is dishonest.[36] To suit the character of the English, politeness must be cleared of French contamination. Euphranor's 'Plan of Education' is meant to do just that. Though no explicit comparison is made with the education obtained in Dancing schools, 'those elegant nurseries of Politeness and Decorum', every single step of the plan is implicitly set in contrast to it, as can be deduced from the statements in brackets, also based on the text. First, the youth's body must be hardened by toughening exercises and a plain diet (whereas politeness entails a softening of manners). The accent is then on training an English tongue (not on learning French), on plain speaking, and perfecting the knowledge of the mother tongue by learning it 'in the grammatical way'. The youth's mind will be trained to appreciate the excellence of virtue by reading about the great characters of history (instead of becoming acquainted with 'all the Graces and Modern Decorum of Fashionable Conversation' in the company of ladies). Such an education will inevitably develop in him a 'Spirit of Patriotism', an 'invincible Love of Liberty' and a 'Contempt of Danger and Death', the seeds of 'manly Enthusiasm, the Soul and Spring of every social and political Virtue'. After attending University, the youth will go to town,

> to converse with Men of all Ranks and Characters, frequent Coffee houses, and all Places of public Resort, where Men are to be seen and practiced, go to the shops of Mechanics as well as the Clubs of the Learned, Courts of Justice and particularly the Houses of Parliament, in order to learn something of the Laws and Interests of his Country, and to inspire him with that Freedom, Intrepidity and public Spirit which does, or should, animate the Members of that August Body.[37]

It is conversing with men, not women, that will 'rub off that awkward Air and Pedantry of Manners' inevitably acquired during an academic education. Conversation polishes this gentleman too, but it is not a hot-house plant of a conversation, it roams widely, it is intrepid, above all, it is unambiguously masculine, like the education that preceded it. The sites of its production ensure that it is essentially British, free from the gilded chains of French politeness.[38] After spending up to two years in town, the youth will travel abroad, to 'bring him to the Standard of a fine Gentleman'. Not only will he be old enough by then but, Philander is careful to point out, he need not be guarded against the seduction of foreign manners, especially in those countries 'where Foppery is often mistaken for Politeness' and 'Liberty is blasphemed under the title of Licentiousness'. His education and conversation will have equipped him with the inner strength of civic and manly virtue, and constituted him as a Briton.[39] He will never be a fop.

The education Fordyce outlines, because it instils the English virtues of patriotism and love of liberty, is what will make young men able to resist French seduction: a liberal education on the classical model, not 'the Finishings of a French education',[40] can best produce an English gentle*man*. What it subverts, however, is not the necessity of politeness but its association with the French. Whereas French politeness is frivolous, English politeness is serious, and produces free men, men of civic virtue.[41] To achieve this, it is necessary to wrest politeness from its French associations.

The slavery of French politeness was a theme which became increasingly explicit as the century wore on, even while the French remained models of fashion and culture, French the language of polite learning, and France the focus of increasing numbers of English travellers. John Andrews' *A Comparative View of the English and French Nations* (1785) contains an interesting illustration of what I take to be an attempt to expose the origin of *politesse* while at the same time exculpating the French as a people, thus justifying their continuing attractiveness to the English. According to Andrews, French politeness was the product of an elaborate strategy of political tyranny feasible only in a despotic monarchy. The French aristocracy had their minds 'designedly diverted' from 'speculations of national importance' to 'affairs of little moment'. They were made passive instruments of their own fate, and, by having their freedom removed from them, were subjected, enslaved and emasculated. Richelieu and Mazarin are particularly taken to task by Andrews, the first for establishing the conditions for absolute monarchy while pretending a 'reformation of abuses', the latter for strengthening 'the establishment of slavery' while pretending to be 'restoring order and tranquillity'. In other words, they deceived their own subjects. As a result, the French nobility spend their time involved not in serious affairs of State but in that 'intercourse with the fair sex which goes under the name of gallantry'.[42] French politeness is born out of deception, subjection and emasculation, and functions to perpetuate them. One consequence is that French noblemen's conversation is frivolous and sprightly, just like that of women. Their voice has no authority.

POLITENESS AND GENDER

It is not surprising that in David Fordyce's account it is Cleora who articulates the ambiguity of politeness and is most critical of its artifice. We have seen how, to Simplicius' dismay, she condemns gallantry, the language of seduction and the tacitly sexual game of polite conversation, because it engages men in deceit and subjects women. She represents the desire to please – the main component of *politesse* – as a fraudulent way of enslaving women and taking away their liberty: 'when you see us taken with the shining Trifles, you carry us off in triumph and reduce us under the Orders of domestic Discipline'.[43] Ironically, although Cleora perhaps rightly denounces the duplicity of polite gallantry, she misses the point because she treats the game as if it were a way of seducing women to marry them. The subterfuge inherent in the polite gallantry practised by the French is not that it is a courtship, but that it has ultimately little to do with women at all.

Politeness on the French model could not be achieved without the conversation and company of women. But it is precisely fashionable conversation, with its 'Flowers of Speech' and its gallantries, which is the object of Cleora's contempt. A conversation which is about trifles and uses phrases which either signify nothing at all or 'trespass' on the truth perverts its main aim, 'to exchange sentiments with one another for mutual instruction'. Cleora prefers a conversation that 'import[s] less subjection, but more of that equality of friendship that ought to reign in society';[44] a conversation divested of artifice. Through Cleora as ideal model, Fordyce portrays a woman who knows not only that women 'excel in Conversation' and 'delight and polish the Men by their Softness and Delicacy in speaking', but that their talk – their tongue – is one of their 'instruments of power'. Gallantry and the constant desire to please, which Cleora attributes to women as well as men, eroticize verbal commerce. Her own language, on the other hand, has been regulated by grammar, and she has been taught the importance of correct and graceful pronunciation. Her voice thus has authority. Sensible men, who are 'apt to be caught by the Ear',[45] will listen to her because her conversation subdues men's passions rather than exacerbating them. The ideal conversation is unsexed, and so is Cleora, despite her alleged charms.

'The true effect of genuine politeness seems to be rather ease than pleasure', wrote Johnson in *The Rambler*.[46] From the perspective of Frenchman Abbé Le Blanc, in England the 'desire of pleasing is . . . seldom found among the Great'. They 'despise the acquisition of . . . polite and insinuating manners', especially the 'mutual attentions and regards towards each other', and consider the 'tenderness and complaisance to the Fair as something beneath them'. Nor would an English woman, he claims, be 'subdued by the insinuating softness' of the jargon of a gallant who, in France, would pass as a man of 'good fortune in Amours'. To her, these 'solicitudes and flatteries' would be 'mere trifles'.[47]

51

For Cleora, the danger of polite conversation was not only that men wanted to please women, but that 'the Ladies too generally make it their grand Aim to please the Men'.[48] Unsexing conversation and politeness removes desire and therefore danger. Dispensing with women – at least erasing or silencing their sexuality – makes it possible to find other sites for the production of politeness at the same time as it severs its French connection. English politeness must be masculine. But there is more to the story.

POLITENESS AND MOTHERS

The fact that virtuous Cleora has been brought up not by her mother but by a male guardian is not accidental. For it is mothers who, allegedly concerned only with the social advancement of their progeny, insist on their acquiring polite accomplishments at the detriment of more 'solid' ones. Diverting their children, especially their sons, from serious and proper education, they spoil them and set up the conditions for their future depravity. The representation of mothers' influence on their children, especially their sons, as pernicious, is a recurring theme which appears in a variety of guises, as we shall see later. In *The Rambler*,[49] Johnson charts the progress of two young noblemen's education in politeness, a sorry tale of their gradual degradation. Both young men's mothers insist that their son will not go near a school but must be taught at home by a tutor. Since conversing with books produces awkward scholars who are at once tongue-tied and pedantic, they ensure that their sons' contact with books, learning and even their tutor, are kept to a minimum. From a young age, both young men spend a great deal of time in polite company, especially that of women, so as to become fluent and easy in their conversation. One of these noblemen, admired and petted from a young age by women, becomes so effeminate that when older he is shunned by other men assembled in the masculine company of a coffee house. 'Observations upon sleeves, buttonholes and embroidery' form the substance of the other young nobleman's conversation. Learning French is indispensable, as well as the acquisition of such polite knowledge as the 'rules of visiting', and the 'early intelligence of fashions'. The more delighted the mother is with her son's progress, believing that these skills and accomplishments prepare him for future 'eminence', the more obvious is the inevitability of his degradation. Eventually he brings his whole family to near ruin. 'Women always judge absurdly of the intellect of their boys', Johnson comments dryly.[50] Polite education is about instilling in the young male the ease, vivacity and confidence necessary for social success. But, Johnson argues, such early confidence can be produced only by ignorance and 'fearlessness of wrong'. What boys need is a confidence produced by the 'hardening of long familiarity with reproach', and the struggle of learning to 'suppress their emotions'. The language Johnson uses speaks of the effeminacy of polite education contrasted with a training that would make men out of boys. What an education in politeness ultimately produces, then, is a male who is incapable of self-regulation, a male who is therefore not a man. Emblematic of this lack of regulation is his language:

> He has changed his language with his dress, and, instead of endeavouring at purity or propriety, has no other care than to catch the reigning phrase or current exclamation till, by copying whatever is peculiar in the talk of all whose birth or fortune entitles them to imitation, he has collected every fashionable barbarism of the present winter, and speaks a dialect not to be understood among those who form their style by poring upon authors.[51]

Because he lacks the inner, manly virtue which an education like Euphranor's would have cultivated, he succumbs to the superficial and frivolous attractions of fashionable life, and has no language but what he can ape. Like David Fordyce, Johnson does not derogate politeness as such, only the politeness that women – in this case mothers – produce.[52] Politeness is thus implicated in the problematization of masculinity, because it blurs gender boundaries with its emphasis on softening, pleasing and polite (that is, fashionable) conversation. The construction of the English gentleman is located at the intersection of multiple and contradictory positionings. Can he be both polite and manly?

The best way to acquire manners and *politesse* was to go to France and spend time in the best company; that of the French nobility. But travel had another purpose: it removed the young male from the effeminating influence of his mother. The last we hear of Johnson's young nobleman is that he is being sent abroad with a French governor.

4

THE GRAND TOUR OF THE ENGLISH GENTLEMAN

Travel is 'requisite to ... accomplish a gentleman', declared William Ramsay in 1669, and Obadiah Walker, writing about the gentleman's education, recommended travel abroad to:

> learn the Languages, Laws, Customes, and understand the Government, and interest, of other Nations ... To *produce* confident and comely behaviour, to perfect conversation ... To *satisfy* [the] mind[s] with the actual beholding such rarities, wonders, and curiosities, as are heard or read of. It *brings us* out of the company of our Relations, acquaintances and familiars; making us stand upon our guard, which renders the mind more diligent, vigorous, brisk, and spiritfull. It *shews us*, by consideration of so many various humours, and manners, to look into and form our own; and by tasting perpetually the varieties of Nature, to be able to judge of what is good and better. And it is most useful *for those* who by living at home, and domineering among servants, &c. have got a habit of surliness, pride, insolence, or other resty and slovenly custome. As also *for those*, who are entangled with unfitting companions, friends, loves, servants. *For those* who are seized upon with the vices of their own Countrey, such with Drinking, rusticity, sourness in conversation, laziness, &c. and then, every one must be sent into the place most proper to reforme him.[1]

Though travel had long been considered the final stage, the 'crown' of liberal education, it was in the late seventeenth and early eighteenth centuries that it became the fashion for young men of rank to go on what Lassels in 1670 was the first to call the 'Grand Tour'.[2]

Why did travel suddenly expand at that particular time, for that particular group of people?[3] According to Abbé Le Blanc, whose *Letters on the English and French Nations* were published in 1745, the English travelled more than other people of Europe because they were surrounded by the sea. 'They look upon their isle as a sort of prison; and the first use they make of their liberty is to get out of it'.[4] A more plausible explanation is that it was part of the process that Lawrence Klein has described as the diffusion of the courtly tradition over the English élite, a process which also accounts for the rise of politeness after the Restoration.[5] Thus, Chesterfield's son Philip spent several years travelling on the Continent, David Fordyce's Plan of Education included travel abroad as the final 'finish', and most eighteenth-century texts on the education of the gentleman included a section on travel.[6] My aim in this chapter is to describe the way in which the Grand Tour, embodying an eighteenth-century notion of courtly education, was a major constituent in the fashioning of the English gentleman.

As an educational institution, the Grand Tour can be placed in the courtly tradition.[7] Young men of rank were sent to France to learn gentlemanly accomplishments as well as French with a good accent. Blois was often recommended, as the French spoken there was thought to be particularly 'pure'.[8] They were also expected to learn about men, manners and political institutions, lose national prejudices and acquire a broad perspective. Those with letters of introduction would be received at the French Court or in aristocratic *salons*, where conversation would effect its polish. They were accompanied by a tutor who was usually expected to possess, among his many qualities, a command of foreign languages. The tour lasted between two and five years, after which the young men returned to England, ideally accomplished and finished, complete gentlemen.[9]

Accomplishments featured centrally in courtly education. An accomplishment was what 'perfected'.[10] Humanist education aimed to produce 'the human ideal, the ideal of man in a generic sense' through an education that was 'at once intellectual, moral and physical'. Accomplishments were essential to that project. Locke, whose educational work situates him in the courtly tradition,[11] stressed the interdependency of learning and accomplishments in producing the harmonious man, in whom the outside – civility and breeding – was but a reflection of the inside: virtue. Without polish, Locke asserted, the rough diamond cannot shine. And while polite accomplishments might be the 'ornaments' of a gentleman's education, they were 'Marks of Distinction' which could not be denied to those of rank. Thus, riding and fencing were 'necessary Qualifications in the Breeding of a Gentleman', and dancing not only produced graceful bearing but, most importantly, Locke claimed, it gave 'Manliness, and a becoming Confidence'. Earlier in the century Howell had made similar claims for the learning of French: the French tongue, 'bold and hardy like its Gentry', would 'take away the mothers milk' and 'enharden with confidence'.[12]

Not only had languages, in the humanist tradition, been considered the most appropriate study for young men of rank,[13] but breeding implied cultivation and refinement of the tongue as well as of manners. As a good French accent was considered particularly difficult to acquire, travel to France would ensure a correct pronunciation would be learned. No gentleman could be said to be accomplished if he did not know French.

'A gentleman is a man of conversation', Steele declared in the *Tatler*.[14] Just as conversation produced the *honnête homme* in France, so too did it produce the English gentleman. But whereas in France, the gentleman's tongue was cultivated in the feminine space of the *salon*, a *dépaysement* seems to have first been necessary for the Englishman, a time during which he was expected to break with his mother('s) tongue to speak another.

Paradoxically, attitudes to this foreign tongue were now equivocal: French was said to be not only refined and polished, but *too* refined and *too* polished;[15] and at the same time as young Englishmen were sent to France to study the 'Elements and the Alphabet of Breeding' and 'delicacy and the formulae of polite intercourse' from the French nobility, they were warned not to imitate them: Frenchmen's masculinity was suspect because they spent so much time in gallantries with ladies.[16] These are not the only paradoxes of the Grand Tour.[17] Another concerns the gap between the age at which boys were usually sent abroad and what they were expected to achieve during their stay. Although most youths set out for the continent in their mid- to late teens,[18] there was widespread criticism of early travel. From Steele to Goldsmith, critics complained that 'children' were sent abroad who could only stare and gape at the 'strange things' they saw.[19] As Vicesimus Knox eventually remarked in 1784, 'to expect that boys should make observations on men and manners, should weigh and compare the laws, institutions, customs, and characteristics of various people is to expect an impossibility'.[20] The age at which foreign travel would be most beneficial remained a contentious issue throughout the eighteenth century.[21] One final puzzling question remains, a question posed by Jeremy Black but which, even after consulting numerous archival and manuscript sources he still could not answer: why did young men from noble families travel abroad – a notoriously dangerous undertaking – at a time of crisis for the English aristocracy when there were often not enough male heirs to ensure direct descendence?[22] To answer this question requires telling a different story about the Grand Tour from the one that has usually been told. To begin with, we must first look at the early education of boys in high-ranking families from the late seventeenth century onwards.

Where best to educate the young man of rank – at home or at school – was the subject of intense debate throughout the eighteenth century.[23] In the late seventeenth century, most aristocratic families chose to educate their sons with a tutor at home. They were supported in this by the views of such educators as Gilbert Burnet, Jean Gailhard and John Locke, who claimed that schools encouraged vice and moral corruption and narrowed boys' experience of society. At the same time, however, these same educators warned that home education was not without its dangers.[24]

MOTHERS AND THE EDUCATION OF BOYS

The main danger of a home education for the boy lay in the domestic and emotional comforts it provided. Locke warned that boys 'bred like Fondlings at home' often developed a 'sheepish softness'. This must be avoided 'for Vertue's sake' because it enervated them and made them susceptible to corruption. Though both parents were accused of overfondness, it was the mother's tenderness that was said to be 'the loss of children'.[25] And it was with regard to their sons' education and breeding that mothers' influence was said to be most pernicious. From Jonathan Swift in the early part of the century to James Fordyce towards the end, the same picture was painted of the mother in families of rank. Overly concerned about the ill effects of study on her son's health and/or social skills, afraid that he will learn the manners of a scholar and not those of a gentleman, the mother denigrates study and claims at the same time that her 'darling' is far too clever for the education a mere tutor can provide. As a result, the young man, 'under the Conduct and Tuition of his Mamma, becomes, instead of a fine Scholar . . . a compleat Fop'.[26] By interfering with her son's education, the mother prevents him from attaining, through learning, the virtue emblematic of the gentleman.[27] Worse still, her appropriation of her son prevents him from becoming a man. As long as he remains under her influence and authority he cannot 'improve' and, above all, achieve manliness.

In the *Spectator* no. 364, Steele tells the story of a lady who is convinced that her son has made such 'prodigious Improvements' that he is now beyond 'Book-Learning' and is ready to learn about 'Men and Things'. She decides that he should make the tour of France and Italy. However, because she cannot bear to have him out of her sight, she intends to go with him. Steele's reaction seems extreme: 'I could not but believe that this Humour of carrying a Boy to Travel in his Mother's Lap . . . is a Case of an extraordinary Nature, and carries on it a particular Stamp of Folly'. Why did he find this resolution so 'extravagant', so grotesque? Because travel was expressly about getting the boy away from his mother: it 'take[s] us out of the company of our aunts and grandmothers, and from the track of nursery mistakes'.[28] That is the nub of the issue. The concern that emerges is for the boy to be toughened. Travel involved not just leaving behind the softness of mothers and 'all tenderness and seeking . . . ease too much; all effeminateness and delicateness', but the experience of 'wholesome hardship'. François Misson, who described in lavish detail the difficulties of travel – the roughness of the weather, the 'hard Lodging and worse Diet' – as well as the additional 'many Dangers', also told of surmounting them.[29] The young man travelled abroad not only to become a gentleman, but to become a man. The Grand Tour 'could produce men. It had a way of setting men free to be themselves'.[30]

TRAVEL AND THE CONSTRUCTION OF THE GENTLEMAN

Paradoxically, the fear also loomed that travel to France (and Italy) might effeminate the young man. By going abroad the youth may be 'polished . . . out of his rusticity . . . but may easily wear himself into the contrary defect, an effeminate and unmanly foppery'.[31] That travel abroad could corrupt rather than improve young men had long been a commonplace. In the seventeenth century, Howell was already urging that returned travellers 'abhore' affectations that 'speak them travellers' such as body positions or 'a phantastique kind of ribanding themselves'.[32] But when Costeker, nearly a century later, complained that the young gentleman returned corrupted from his Grand Tour, the emblem of this corruption was his self-display: exhibiting himself, now that he was an accomplished gentleman, 'in all the most fashionable and publick Places'. 'The Mall, the Play, the Ring, the Opera, is dull, insipid all, without the fine Appearance of my Lord'. Everything was ostentation, 'even Virtue, which the gentleman used to screen his Vices'.[33]

As long as the Grand Tour lasted, young men of rank returning from travel abroad were accused of ostentation and display, although the most extreme must have been the Macaronis, who formed the Macaroni Club in the 1770s and claimed to represent the standard of taste in fashion as well as in 'polite learning, the fine arts and the genteel sciences'. Satires of the Macaronis, (and these abounded) all focused on their failing to be men. Said to be concerned solely with display, Macaronis could be only empty shells, enervated parodies of males. 'Of man, they only bear the name; they are perfect nothingness'.[34] The true gentleman, on the other hand, displayed neither his foreign clothes nor his foreign tongue. He was expected not to display even his knowledge of languages, though that knowledge might never be tested or verified. The point is, it did not need to be. Not only must the true gentleman's achievements never be displayed, but the more invisible his powers the more infinite they are assumed to be, as were those of the *honnête homme* in seventeenth-century France. John Barrell has aptly captured this fundamental paradox: in the eighteenth century, a gentleman is one who is 'in, so to speak, a condition of empty potential, one who is imagined as being able to comprehend everything, and yet who may give no evidence of having comprehended anything'.[35]

Since travel could corrupt as well as improve, it could therefore be the test which would distinguish the man of sense from the fool. In James Burgh's words, the contrast is telling:

The first returns from foreign parts improved in easiness of behaviour, in modesty, in freedom of sentiment, and readiness to make allowances to those who differ from him, in a useful knowledge of men and manners. The other brings back with him a laced coat, a spoiled constitution, a gibberish of broken French and Italian, and an awkward imitation of foreign gestures.[36]

For most of the century, accounting for the failures of the Grand Tour served to sustain it and the fiction that its practices could indeed produce 'accomplished' gentlemen. As late as 1784, Vicesimus Knox was asserting that boys whose acquisitions abroad had been 'grimace, affectation and an overbearing insolence' must have been the weak ones, those who had been bound to fail. Travel, he advised, was suitable only for boys 'with parts'.[37] Yet, for a long time too, the accomplishments that the Grand Tour was expected to provide had been criticized. Most returning youths were found wanting. They had been sent abroad to lose narrow home-grown prejudices and returned having acquired new ones, foreign to boot. They had been sent abroad to become polished gentlemen, men of conversation. They returned with broken tongues. They had been sent abroad to learn about men and manners and appreciate their own country knowingly. They returned Frenchified. By the 1760s, however, it was not just French politeness and polite accomplishments that were under attack, but the very notion of travel as a means of fashioning the gentleman; in other words, the Grand Tour as a technology of the self.

The most significant illustration of this shift is Richard Hurd's *Dialogues on the Uses of Foreign Travel*. Written as a conversation between *Locke* and *Shaftesbury*,[38] it is ostensibly about foreign travel but in fact about how best to produce not just gentlemen, but *English* gentlemen. Although some writers on the Grand Tour have treated Hurd's text as if it represents the views of its real interlocutors,[39] it is in fact anachronistic: Hurd speaks with the voice of the 1760s, not that of the 1690s. And it is precisely because of the anachronisms that the *Dialogues* highlight the shifts that have taken place in the conception of the gentleman since the late seventeenth century.

Shaftesbury supports foreign travel, because it is 'the most essential part' of the education of the nobleman, polishing the

'illiberal and ungraceful' effects of English education. *Locke*
opposes it, because it promises only 'shewy and ornamental
accomplishments' and he is concerned to produce not 'fine
gentlemen' but men who will be 'worthy citizens of England'.
The contrast between 'fine gentlemen' – especially meant ironically – and citizens of England was not one that preoccupied
John Locke. The most telling anachronism, however, concerns
Locke's attitude to manners, good breeding and politeness.
Whereas in *Some Thoughts Concerning Education*, John Locke had
set a very high value upon these components indispensable to
the fashioning of the gentleman, for *Locke*, they are accomplishments of little value whose worth has been fixed by the
ladies, for whom appearances, the mere display of good
breeding, is a sufficient indication of merit.[40] And while for
John Locke, gestures and manners were the 'Language whereby
that internal Civility of the Mind is expressed', for *Locke*, the
'excessive sedulity' about manners which civility entails is effeminating.[41] Not only, argues *Locke*, does the concern for politeness
come from women, but politeness itself is born of subjection in
an absolute monarchy. 'Let [it] flourish in France' where insinuation, not merit, brings favour or distinction, but 'let a manlier
character prevail here' he exclaims. Having constructed an
exquisitely polite but effeminated, subjected Other, *Locke* then
produces an English gentleman out of the rejection of all that
John Locke had thought indispensable to his construction: 'Let
our countrymen' *Locke* decrees, 'be indulged in the plainess, nay
the roughness of their manners: But let them atone for this defect
by their useful sense, their superior knowledge, their public
spirit, and, above all, by their unpolished integrity.'[42] It is no
longer politeness, a foreign and effeminating import, but its
opposite, manly sincerity, that is set to produce the English
gentleman.[43]

As important to John Locke as civility and breeding, was a
knowledge of French, which he had 'advocated forcefully'.[44]
Locke, on the other hand, condemns this 'pretense' to fit the
gentleman for conversation 'with foreign acquaintances' as a
waste of time which would be better spent in the study of the
learned languages, 'and perhaps his own.'[45] Between the real John
Locke and Hurd's *Locke*, the techniques for shaping the gentleman had become a means of representing not only the French as
an effeminate other, but politeness and accomplishments as alien

to the English national character. Thus, twenty years later, John Andrews reminded the young gentleman setting out for France that travel abroad was precisely *not* about learning politeness and 'engaging manners'. These are best learned at home, he declared, especially as English manners are not only 'more becoming but more manly than those of the French'.[46] By then, that was what mattered.

Hurd's *Dialogues* are significant because they indicate that the courtly ideal of gentlemanly education was disintegrating by the 1760s. Soon, the cohesion between intellectual, physical and social accomplishments constituting that education would no longer make sense. The very meaning of accomplishments, politeness and speaking French shifted as the discourse in which they had been central was changing, and they became detached from the idea of 'education'. Thus, by the end of the eighteenth century, dancing and fencing were considered merely frivolous accomplishments, and though still thought necessary by some, were unambiguously secondary to the 'solid' improvements of a classical education.[47] Similarly, while a knowledge of French was to remain indispensable for a young man 'who proposes to mix in elegant and respectable companies' until at least the second decade of the nineteenth century,[48] language learning was now said to be an insipid occupation. Fluency in foreign languages ceased to be central to the fashioning of the gentleman, for not only did it not guarantee, John Andrews remarked, that a man would be 'conversant in any knowledge', but, he added, 'the best linguists are found among illiterate people'.[49] Finally, when it could be said that the single best thing that French politeness could produce was obedient servants,[50] the *raison d'être* of the Grand Tour as a means of producing the gentleman was no more.

Historians of the Grand Tour rarely discuss why it ended.[51] Nevertheless, I would want to suggest one reason for its demise. As a means of producing the gentleman, the tour was discontinuous with other practices of liberal education in that its failures were visible (and audible), as James Burgh (cited above) makes clear. The gentleman's powers must specifically not be tested or questioned, yet the Grand Tour was also treated as a test, and its results meant to be displayed. While the end of the gentleman's education was, writes John Barrell, 'simply, to "appear", to "shine"': he 'polish[ed] himself so that he [might] "shine in the world",'[52] display itself was highly problematic.[53] Condemnations of display targeted women as well as men. Women's display was a transgression of modesty and propriety; men's display was a transgression which spoke of effeminacy and of the corruption brought about by consorting with the foreign.[54]

I would argue, then, that display was one condition both for the end of the Grand Tour and for the emergence of a technology for the construction of a gentleman in which his failures could remain invisible, subsumed to the promise of his boundless potential.

5

THE ACCOMPLISHMENT OF THE EIGHTEENTH-CENTURY LADY

'The question', declared John Burton in 1793, 'is whether a woman who is ignorant and uninformed will be more pleasing in her manners, be better qualified to instruct her children, and manage the affairs of a family, than one, who is sensible and intelligent.'[1] Would education imperil women's commitment to their domestic responsibilities, or would it enhance it? Would education 'undomesticate' women or make them better 'companions' to their husbands, and mothers who could be entrusted with the teaching of their children at home?[2] Would it produce pedantic learned women, 'monsters' who are 'feared by their own sex and disliked by ours',[3] or 'fashion the young lady into blushing timidity'?[4] Anxiety about the effects education might have on women's femininity and their relation to the family was unallayed throughout the century, and was far from being assuaged even in the next.[5]

If the question really was, as Burton put it, whether to educate girls or leave them ignorant, why, then, did no one ever say that girls should *not* be educated? Even Thomas Gisborne, who, in 1796 (somewhat nostalgically) represented the measure of 'female perfection' in a 'last age' as mastery of the 'sciences of pickling', the 'mysteries of cross-stitch and embroidery' and the 'family receipt-book', conceded that it was no longer acceptable to restrict 'the intellectual powers of women' to the 'arts of the housekeeper'.[6] What preoccupied moralists and educationists was not, in fact, *whether* to educate girls, but the education girls *were* getting, what they called the 'modern system of education', with its emphasis on 'accomplishments'.

Even though the term 'accomplishment' was on the tip of every moralist and educationist's pen, there was less agreement than one would therefore expect regarding not only what counted as an accomplishment, but whether accomplishments should be censured, tolerated or approved. Attitudes to the learning of French illustrate the ambiguity of the concept. Some considered it an indispensable accomplishment, arguing that it was an intellectual acquirement which graced a polite education. To others, French was merely an 'ornamental' accomplishment, but one that it was 'highly proper' to possess. Others still condemned it as a 'Foreign' and useless accomplishment.[7] The most interesting development, which I will discuss more fully below, was its fracture into two components: *speaking*, a showy accomplishment, and *reading*, which was not only useful but also a 'solid' attainment.

What interests me here is not simply the ambiguity of the concept of accomplishments but the fact that by the second half of the century they had become the object of increasing concern. Since accomplishments – that 'perfected' – had been integral to the courtly ideal of education, the question that needs to be asked is why they became problematized at that particular period.

When James Fordyce railed against the 'fashionable system of female education', it was not just because of its content – dress, dance, a bit of bad French, conceited airs – nor because it was likely to have been acquired at a boarding-school, but because it 'inevitably' led parents to 'show' their daughters, or, as he himself put it, 'let them see company; by which is chiefly meant exhibiting them in public places'. As the varying and contradictory attitudes to French reveal, it was not accomplishments *per se* that provoked the indignation of moralists and educationists. In fact, to be 'accomplished' continued to designate an ideal to which young men and women were encouraged to aspire. What was at issue is more complex. My claim is that accomplishments came to be valued or criticized depending not on what they were, but on whether they could be, or were meant to be, 'displayed'. It was not 'shining' that was the problem, James Fordyce assured the female readers of his *Sermons*, but affecting 'to shine anywhere but in [your] proper sphere'.[8] This 'proper sphere', a place where it was acceptable and even legitimate for a woman to shine and where 'feminine ambition might express itself', was the 'domestic' sphere. A woman could thus be accomplished – and have learning as an accomplishment – as long as these accomplishments were not displayed. As Hannah More would put it, the 'watchful mother must have the talents of her daughter cultivated, not exhibited'.[9]

ACCOMPLISHMENTS AND THE SOCIAL SPACE

While it is reasonable to assume that the 'domestic' space is usually associated with the home, not all areas in a home are necessarily domestic, nor even private.[10] It is important, too, to remember that 'domestic', 'public' and 'private' are also idealized, metaphorical spaces whose boundaries are neither fixed, nor simply corresponding to a physical location, and whose meanings are shifting and historically specific. Thus, although concepts of public and private have long been assumed to be 'highly gendered',[11] ironically, it is precisely the consideration of gender in the eighteenth century that has posed the most serious challenge to the simple sexualization of these spaces into male and female spheres. The 'publicity' of women, and the centrality of their conversation to the construction of men's politeness could not be accommodated within a 'private' sphere synonymous only with domesticity.[12]

However, since coffee houses and clubs, what Habermas calls the 'authentic public sphere,'[13] were primarily masculine spaces, and there was no English equivalent of the French institutionalized space for mixed conversation, the *salon*, what were the discursive spaces for the mixed company of the sexes, this 'Golden State'[14] of social relations?

I want to suggest that eighteenth-century practices of sociability generated 'social' spaces,[15] spaces which accommodated not only the publicity of women but the fashioning of the gentleman in their company and their conversation. These social spaces were both more ambiguous and less stable than the *salon* in France, because they referred to a 'space-between', hovering between inside and outside – comprising the tea-table, assemblies, mixed social gatherings, visiting, the spaces for cultural production, company, as well as the 'society' to whose gaze the mothers censured by James Fordyce and Hannah More exhibited their daughters and their accomplishments.

Acknowledging that the meanings of 'public', 'private' and 'domestic' are historically specific has been crucial to an understanding of sociability and the shaping of identities in the eighteenth century.[16] But identifying these meanings' historical specificity is not sufficient. I want to argue in addition that they were *mutually* constituted and reconstituted. I want to argue in particular that the 'domestic' sphere that emerged in the latter part of the eighteenth century was not just as an idealized space but that it was constructed as the social's moral and virtuous 'other'.

By the 1760s, society and the 'public' were increasingly associated with the threat to female virtue. In 'company', girls become 'intoxicated' and think only of 'how to appear abroad with the greatest advantage', while 'the utmost of a woman's character is contained in domestic life'.[17] By the end of the century, the dangers were more explicit, the warnings more shrill, and the contrast between social and domestic starker: 'Public company' exposed girls to the 'seductions of gaiety and pleasure', their judgements were 'ruled by the caprice of fashion, the folly of pride, and the affectations of vanity'. In domestic retirement, on the other hand, they learned 'wisdom and prudence'.[18] This 'domestic' sphere was not just the moral, but, I will be arguing, the *national* antithesis of what the social and its practices had come to represent – dissipation, effeminacy, and the corrupting influence of the French.

To illustrate how the discourse on 'modern education' and accomplishments was articulated in relation to the social and domestic spaces, I have chosen to discuss two texts concerned with women's education both published in the last decades of the century, John Burton's *Lectures on Female Education and Manners*, and Hannah More's *Strictures on the Modern System of Female Education*.[19]

JOHN BURTON'S LECTURES

Throughout these *Lectures* addressed to girls at a boarding-school,[20] Burton aims to show that education will make the 'domestic' and the 'social' compatible. The success of his enterprise depends on his redeeming both by blurring the boundary between them, which he does by domesticating social accomplishments and glamorizing domestic duties. He declares that education is most important in domestic life not because he believes that women should be educated *for* domestic life but because women should be rational companions for their husbands. Husbands, in turn, should not confine their wives to 'domestic servitude' but treat them as friends. 'The two sexes are designed for mutual happiness; and for enjoying a reciprocation of sentiments and affections'. The very success of the companionate marriage (which, it must be remembered, also regulates husbands) thus depends on women being educated. The domestic arena, he continues, also privileges women as early instructors of their children of both sexes. Because children are the 'future hopes of the Community', from the most private of all spaces, women have direct influence on the most public of all spaces, the polity: 'political Government may be said to derive from the strength of the nursery'. Educated women's commitment to their domestic responsibilities thus ensures the health of the nation.

While celebrating the domestic sphere, Burton also concedes to its ambivalence and acknowledges that girls are 'fond of ornamental accomplishments'. The accomplishments which girls should acquire, he advises 'are those which will contribute to render you serviceable in domestic, and agreeable in social life'. Reading, the main means of attaining knowledge, provides occupation and amusement in domestic retirement and equips you for society as a means of pleasing in conversation. And what is more 'ornamental' than the 'art of pleasing in conversation'? Needlework, the quintessential female accomplishment, can also be shown to be both useful and ornamental. And, if drawing, music and dancing are only ornamental accomplishments, they are justifiable because embellishment, grace and the art of pleasing are the 'province' of the female sex.[21]

HANNAH MORE'S *STRICTURES*

For Hannah More, the social and the domestic – far from being reconcilable – are dislocated. More's goal in the *Strictures* is to demonstrate how an education based on accomplishments fails not just women but men and the whole of society. The meaning of 'accomplishment', she complains, has been perverted. A term which used to mean 'completeness, perfection', is now more 'abused, misunderstood or misapplied' than any other word. Since a 'phrenzy of accomplishments' has infected all ranks of society, the education of 'accomplished' young ladies is a parody of that original definition. 'Accomplishments falsely so called' produce 'talents which have display as their object', and neither 'assist the development of the faculties', nor prepare women's heart and mind 'to love home, to understand its occupations, to enliven its uniformity, to fulfil its duties, to multiply its comforts'.

Originally meant, More claims, to give women the means of enjoying leisure hours and solitude, these false accomplishments 'despise the narrow stage of home: they demand mankind for their spectators and the world for their theatre'.[22]

Conversation best illustrates the failure of an accomplishment-oriented education. It ought to be the social situation where mutual understanding reigns, and where

> the rough angles and asperities of male manners are imperceptibly filed and gradually worn smooth by the polishing of female conversation; while the ideas of women acquire strength and solidity by associating with sensible, intelligent and judicious men.[23]

But, More complains, because young ladies' 'sprightliness has not been disciplined by a correct education', their tongue lacks discipline, and they spoil the conversation. Not accustomed to look into the depth of a subject, they are apt to suddenly divert the direction of talk, and are captivated by what More calls 'the graces of rhetoric' rather than the 'justest deduction of reason'. Worse still, they transform conversation into a stage for display, where all the defects of their education coalesce to form an image of frivolity, superficiality and vanity.[24]

Not content with decrying the effects of a 'showy education' on girls' conversation, More censures even what other writers on education and conduct celebrated as qualities peculiar to females – their fluency, their quickness, perceptiveness and memory.[25] She claims that these only betray women's shallowness, superficiality and lack of higher mental powers. Women, she admits, may be quick to solve a problem, but it is only because[26] they do not see the 'perplexities' of the question. Though she concedes that 'men of deep reflection often sound confused', she takes this very lack of fluency to be evidence of the depth of their mental powers. In contrast to the 'rash dexterity' of women, men's slowness demonstrates their power of penetration. Thus, women's very mental agility is taken to signify a lack of deep understanding, and an ultimate concern with mere appearances.[27]

It is inevitable, More concludes, that men of sense should consider the society of ladies as 'a scene in which they are rather to rest their understandings than to exercise them'; ladies, in turn, believe it a 'welcome flattery to the understanding of men to renounce the exercise of their own' and 'affect to talk below their natural and acquired powers of mind'.[28] Communication has become opaque and the very meaning of conversation falsified. A situation which ought to have brought out the best in both sexes produces precisely the opposite. In an age when, More alleges, 'inversion is the character of the day', the 'showy' education of girls perverts not only their minds and character, but also language and its basis of shared meanings. Even taking into account the 'mutability of language', she asks, could a time have been foreseen when the words '[I] shall be at home' would 'present to the mind an image the most "undomestic" which language can convey?' Even the word 'home', she laments, is now bereft of its former association with the 'joys of the fireside'. For nowadays, she explains, when a lady announces she will be 'at home' on a particular night, far from referring to quiet domestic retirement, this just means that the houses of all her acquaintances will have been emptied. Fashionable couples, more social than domestic, are no longer joined by mutual dependence, affection and obligations. They are companions no longer. Conversation has been corrupted, and mutuality, that 'cement which secure[s] the union of the family as well as of the state', has disintegrated. The very fabric of society is being rent.

More's solution is to argue that woman's best conversation is her silence. 'The silence of sparkling intelligence' is more becoming and advantageous to a woman than an 'abundance of florid talk', as it allows her the simultaneous expression of 'rational curiosity and becoming diffidence'. Eloquent silence and attention have the added advantage of encouraging 'men of sense and politeness' to pursue topics they might not otherwise have chosen to discuss in the presence of women.[29] Thus, despite the importance More attaches to the companionate marriage as the foundation of society, she strikes a heavy blow to the mutual conversation that produces it. It is her inversion that has the last word. Though she deplores the shifts of meaning which she sees as emblematic of the perversion and corruption of her time, she herself radically alters the meaning of mutuality and conversation, disciplining woman's tongue by simply cutting it off.

More's attitude to accomplishments was not wholly shared by such contemporary writers on education as John Burton, John Bennett and Erasmus Darwin. In particular, they had different views on the subject of girls learning French. Burton, Bennett and Darwin may have thought of French as an 'accomplishment', but this did not detract from its value as an intellectual acquirement because, as a language, it was the key to literature.[30] Why did More single out for her most vituperative critique of accomplishments, the 'predominant excellence to which all other excellences must bow down', the attainment of a good French accent? All sorts of 'risks' are taken and 'sacrifices' made, she wrote bombastically, 'to furnish our young ladies with the means of acquiring the French language in the greatest possible purity'.[31] This was neither new, nor limited to girls, for, as we have seen earlier, boys sent on the Grand Tour went to Blois for just that reason. But girls did not go on educational grand tours. The accent had to be imported, as it were, usually in the form of a governess who was likely to be Roman Catholic. More was probably referring to the fact that after the French Revolution, aristocratic refugees might be employed as French governesses.[32] Their class and their French, held to be the most pure since spoken at Court, would have made them highly attractive to English families of rank.[33] The only concession parents are willing to make to religion, More commented indignantly, is to ensure that it is never 'agitated' between teacher and pupil. Girls are thus exposed to this danger for the sake of learning the language of an impious country whose 'contempt for the Sabbath ... and relaxed notions of conjugal fidelity' have already been imported into England by ladies who have resided abroad.[34] It is not surprising, then, that More should have denounced what she saw as the sacrifice of piety to a correct pronunciation. To her, it was emblematic of the corruption of girls' education.

The ability to speak implies by its very nature a performance, French therefore seems a useful tool for examining the problematization of accomplishments, and the relation between accomplishments, display and the emergence of an idealized domestic sphere.

SPEAKING FRENCH AS AN ACCOMPLISHMENT

A number of writers of French language teaching texts published in the second half of the eighteenth century were deploring the fact that learning to speak French had too much to do with display, although this was clearly also a way of advertising their own, more 'thorough' method. Thus in 1772, Chambaud claimed that he had taken a lot of trouble with his grammar because he did not expect his pupils 'just to prattle something, or rather, to shew in an assembly that they can speak some French words and phrases'. He blamed parents who were so keen to have their children show off their French that they wanted them to speak it as soon as they had started to learn it. Worse, many chose to send their boys to schools where, forced to speak 'nothing else but French', they 'acquire[d] the knack of talking a glittering gibberish'.[35] Earlier in the century, two female characters in David Fordyce's *Dialogues Concerning Education* had been praised because, although they knew French, they made no display of that acquirement. No one could have guessed from Cleora's behaviour, commented Eugenio, that she had been 'improved by any extraordinary education', or that she spoke both French and Italian. The well-brought up daughter of a gentleman was commended because she 'reads and talks the French prettily, but neither values herself for it, nor is forward to shew it'.[36] Serious young ladies did not display their knowledge of French. Better still, they chose not to learn to speak it. Fanny Burney tells us that she had learned to read French in order to enjoy its literature, but as for speaking it:

All my time . . . was due to my dearest Suzette with whom I've been reading French: having taught myself that charming language for the sake of its bewitching authors – for I shall never want to speak it.[37]

The difference between serious young ladies and others is illustrated by two characters in Thomas Day's novel *The History of Sandford and Merton*. Martha, whose mother has ensured she has had the best education, talks French better than English. Miss Simmons, on the other hand, does not speak French, though she has *read* the best French as well as English authors. Martha's mother is concerned only with polite society and manners; Miss Simmons, an orphan, was brought up by her uncle, a gentleman who 'waged war with most of the polite and modern accomplishments', and was even reluctant to allow her to learn to read French. Whereas Martha's other accomplishments included drawing and playing 'most divinely upon the piano', Miss Simmons's education comprised the 'established Laws of Nature, and the rudiments of Geometry'. But the major difference between their education has to do with the positionings it produced for them. Miss Simmons was taught to believe that 'domestic economy is a point of the utmost consequence to every woman who intends to be a wife and mother', and understands 'every species of household employment'. Martha's education is meant for display, it positions her in the social space. Miss Simmons's positions her in the domestic. The author leaves us in no doubt as to which is the more virtuous young lady.[38] Hannah More saw the cultivation of a French accent as a 'showy' accomplishment which epitomized all the defects of what she called an education 'for a crowd'. 'To women' she advised, 'moral excellence is the grand object of education; and of moral excellence, domestic life is to women the proper sphere'.[39]

THE DOMESTICATION OF POLITENESS

Hannah More was not alone in feeling that words were losing their meaning or that they were being misunderstood. In the *Lectures* he addressed to young girls at a boarding-school, John Burton had also complained, even though he was concerned not with accomplishments but with politeness: 'there is no word in the English language that is less under-stood' than politeness.[40] Most writers on girls' education and conduct in the latter part of the century included some discussion of politeness and supplied their own definition of the term. For Hester Chapone it was 'a delightful qualification', universally admired but possessed by few 'in any eminent degree'. To be 'perfectly polite', she recommended, a young woman must possess or cultivate two indispensable qualities: 'great presence of mind, with a delicate and quick sense of propriety'. Politeness was not just 'a most amiable quality', wrote John Bennett, it was also an art, 'the art of being easy ourselves, in company, and of making all others easy about us'.[41] The specifically social character of politeness, its emphasis on 'consider[ing] others more than yourself', on self-effacement, 'annihilating, as it were, ourselves', made it easy to accommodate within Christianity, the 'religion which requires us to love one another'. Chapone and Bennett spoke with one voice on the special relation of Christianity to politeness. It is Christianity that gives 'the best lesson of politeness', and its best 'rules'.[42] Exterior manners and graces are 'requisite', conceded Bennett, but only if they 'proceed from inner virtue, gentleness, complacency, affability'. Only then can politeness, the 'sovereign enamel', provide the finishing touch which gives a 'lustre'' to all qualities.[43] A politeness defined as compatible with Christian values not only erases the gap between exterior and interior,[44] but itself becomes the link between the two. True politeness, then, is the 'intercourse of sentiment and civility'.[45]

Just as accomplishments could be false, so too could politeness. Fashion, with its 'insipid routines of ceremony and compliment', its 'affectation and Parade', was the epitome of false politeness. So were, of course, 'dissimulation', 'ceremonious attitudes or fulsome compliments', 'flattery, insincerity'. Even the 'alphabet of breeding' – presenting yourself carefully, knowing how to enter a room, appropriate gestures, which Lassels and Chesterfield had thought so important – could be dismissed as merely a mechanical process, something that could be 'acquired by early education', or simply by associating with good company.[46] But, as Klein has pointed out, politeness was an 'idealized vision of human intercourse . . . situated wherever gentlemanly (or lady-like) society existed'.[47] It was not just behaviour, it was also a locus. False politeness consisted not only in 'the scrupulous observance of fashionable customs' but in 'mixing with the fashionable world, at all Places of genteel resort'.[48] By the end of the eighteenth century, the main problem of politeness was that it was located in the social space, a dangerous space where boundaries of gender and propriety were transgressed in display and ostentation, under the aegis of an ideal which was itself ambiguously gendered.

If, as I have argued earlier, politeness could be rejected as an attribute for men in that it was incompatible with masculinity and the English national character,[49] this was more difficult to do in the case of women. The main characteristics of politeness – desire to please, self effacement, softness, and 'the graces' – were precisely those that delineated and enhanced the feminine ideal. 'Gentleness of manners is perfectly consonant to the delicacy of [the female] form', Burton told his young audience.[50] So too were 'polite' learning and accomplishments. Thus, Hester Chapone advised her niece that

> politeness of behaviour, and the attainment of such branches of knowledge and such arts and accomplishments

as are proper to your sex, capacity, and station, will prove so valuable to yourself throughout life, and will make you so desirable a companion, that the neglect of them may reasonably be deemed a neglect of duty.[51]

It is not surprising, therefore, to find a concern to reclaim politeness for females. If the social space distorts and corrupts politeness reducing it to empty gestures, artifice and display, then true politeness is to be found within. Where can this be but in the domestic space? 'Your behaviour at home, when withdrawn as it were, from the public eye ... will be the real criterion of courtesy', Burton informed his young listeners. It is towards members of one's own family that politeness is most necessary, insisted Bennett, Burton and More. This is why 'politeness is compatible with sincerity', concluded Burton.[52]

One problem remains: the relation of politeness to France. The most vitiating form of false politeness, declared Burton, is that performance of 'unmeaning ceremonies and ridiculous distinctions ... whence all the social and benevolent feelings of the heart are excluded', that 'grimace' of 'ceremony and ostentation' which, he tells us, was called the *Ton*. This 'air' followed by all fashionable society is a 'vortex' that saps their 'spirits' and 'corrupts their Principles'.[53] The language Burton uses suggests at the same time as it highlights the foreignness and Frenchness expressed by the word *Ton*. Associated with the foreign name are the disparaging terms usually deployed to describe not only the French, but also the English who imitated the French: the grimace, as of a monkey,[54] and the performance of meaningless ceremonies associated with a society enslaved by an arbitrary government. The warning is that the French corrupt not just English manners, but their very spirit.

However, politeness could be redeemed if it could be shifted from the social to the domestic space and mostly appropriated by that space. Domesticating politeness freed it from two of the elements that constituted its problematics: gender ambiguity and insincerity. Thus, though politeness had always been situated – problematically – where women were, by shifting its locus it ceased to be a means of producing a social, public, male élite, and became instead the site for the production of virtuous domesticity.

Domesticating politeness transformed it into a virtue, severed it from its roots in the courtly tradition, and cleansed it once and for all of its parentage with the French. Above all, a domesticated politeness could finally and unproblematically incorporate women. It became women. 'What woman is most really admired in the world? The domestic. What women has all the suffrages of the sensible and the good? The domestic', rhapsodizes Bennett.[55] And it is the domestic woman, the woman who has refused to be enslaved by the social with its connotations of Frenchness and artificiality, who wins the prince charming. I will let Maria Edgeworth, whose novel *Patronage* is a fictional version of some of the themes discussed in this section, have the last words. Count Altenberg, a German noble, has recently met Caroline Percy, a paragon of true politeness and real accomplishments.

> It was reserved for Count Altenberg, to meet in England a woman, who to the noble simplicity of character, that was once the charm of Swisserland (sic), joined the polish, the elegance that was once the pride of France; a woman possessing an enlarged, cultivated, embellished under-standing, capable of comprehending all his views as a politician, and a statesman; yet, without the slightest wish for power, or any desire to interfere in public business, or political intrigue. – Graced with knowledge and taste for literature, capable of being extended to the highest point of excellence, yet free from all pedantry, or pretension – with it, conversation talents, and love of good society, without that desire of exhibition, that devouring, diseased appetite for admiration, which preys upon the mind insa-tiably to it's torture, to it's destruction; without that undefineable, untranslateable French love of *succès de société*, which substitutes a precarious, factitious, intoxicated existence in public, for the safe self-approbation, the sober, the permanent happiness of domestic life.[56]

That woman can only be English, and is of course Caroline Percy. Although the Count's path to domestic happiness is strewn with difficulties arising from his courtly duties, he vanquishes them all because he too has refused the hypocrisy of politeness. For him, this is achieved not through its domes-tication, but through the quintessential manly attribute of the late eighteenth century, sincerity.[57]

DOMESTICITY AND NATIONAL VIRTUE

The emergence of the domestic space through the derogation of the social space is not without ambiguity. Caroline Percy does not shun good society and conversation. Her virtuous domesticity implies not a blunt rejection of the social, but a distillation of its best features. In her, More, Burton and Bennett's 'true' accomplishments and politeness are realized. What makes this possible is not simply that she is English, but that she is not French. If, as Davidoff and Hall have suggested, the 'idealized position of women was a central theme in nationalistic claims to English superiority',[58] then the construction of French women as other can be said to have served the same purpose and have been as much of a fiction as French politeness and effeminated French men: it forged and emphasized national difference. Whereas for men, the site where this difference was produced was the tongue, for women, it was the domestic space.

Whereas French ladies are said to be willing to sacrifice 'the quiet and comforts of the home' for *Succès de Société*, writes John Andrews in 1783, English ladies are usually 'exemplary' in the 'assiduity and diligence' they bring to the domestic responsibilities with which they are 'principally taken up'.[59] He does not portray French women as wicked; on the contrary. Like many other Englishmen and women, he admires their intelligence, their authority in matters of literary taste and, above all, their conversation. But French women's conversation rules the social space. It makes them omnipotent and they cannot be contained. For fashionable French women are also consumed by a 'national disease', the 'appetite for admiration'. This is part of their seductiveness, but it is also what makes them dangerous. For Andrews, the 'native sprightliness', the 'natural . . . eloquence' of French women is also a flaunting of their tongue akin to a flaunting of their sexuality. It is indeed saturated with sexuality, it is 'irresistible' and thus renders men submissive. French men's masculinity is thus doubly threatened, by the absolute rule of their women and that of their monarch, a connection that Andrews does not fail to make: 'subjection of some kind or other seems necessary for a Frenchman'.[60]

Hannah More, John Burton, Thomas Day and Maria Edgeworth operated in different discursive domains, but their critique of accomplishments, politeness and speaking French was underpinned by one common feature: the critique of French morality and the political system in general, and French women in particular. The French represented the moral ills that ensued when women were positioned only in the social space. It is because Caroline Percy's conversation is grounded in the domestic space that it is not destructive of manliness, but constructive of the companionate marriage. The integrity of the English nation rests on virtuous domestic womanhood.

6

THE SEXED MIND

Women, wrote Hannah More in the introduction to her *Essays* (1785),

> have generally quicker perceptions; men have juster senti-
> ments. – Women consider how things may be prettily laid –
> Men how they may be properly laid. – ... Women speak to
> shine or to please, men to convince or confute. – Women
> admire what is brilliant, men, what is solid ... Women are
> fond of incident, men of argument. – Women admire passion-
> ately, men approve cautiously ... Men refuse to give way to
> the emotions they actually feel, while women sometimes
> affect to be transported beyond what the occasion will justify.[1]

Hannah More was not the first to assign different traits to
each sex. But when James Fordyce, for instance, had addressed
young women on the subject in his *Sermons*, twenty years earlier,
what he put to them was that 'Nature' had 'formed' their 'faculties' with 'less vigour' than those of men. This did not mean
that women were incapable of 'the judicious and solid', but,
Fordyce reminded them, women's primary concern must remain
their 'destination in life'. Your 'chief business', he told them, was
to 'read men, in order to make yourselves agreeable and useful'.
It was the 'sentimental' talents, not the 'argumentative', that
women must cultivate.[2]

As Fordyce saw it, the difference between men and women was
relative, a matter of degree. Hannah More was more radical. The
'mind of each sex', she argued, has 'some kind of natural bias'. It
was this difference in *mind* that constituted the 'distinction of
character' that 'marked' the sexes and determined the 'respective,
appropriate qualifications' she catalogued so definitively.[3]

Whether the greater weakness of women's minds was merely a 'natural' extension of their 'more delicate frame',[4] as Fordyce claimed, or whether men and women's minds were radically different, as Hannah More suggested, the discourse on the sexed mind implied a major shift in the meaning of education. While it served, in the first place, to justify an education that positioned women firmly in the domestic space, it had far-reaching consequences for the education of boys and for the way males and females have been positioned by the discourse on achievement.

To examine how the discourse on the sexed mind was constituted, I have chosen to discuss three texts concerned with female education published between the end of the eighteenth and the beginning of the nineteenth centuries: Hannah More's *Essays on Various Subjects*, John Bennett's *Strictures on Female Education*, and J.L. Chirol's *Enquiry into the best System of Female Education*.[5] More, Bennett and Chirol were unanimous about the quickness, vivacity and versatility of woman's mind, and unanimous as well that these constituted the visible manifestation of her mental inferiority. Vivacity, wrote Bennett, is unfavourable to 'profound thinking and accurate investigation', while More counterposed women's 'quicker perceptions' to men's 'juster sentiments'. Chirol was more blunt: woman has scarcely a thought she can call her own, except 'what is fugitive and transient as lightning'. 'The very structure of woman's mind renders her incapable of the profound thought and careful reasoning that carry knowledge to its zenith of perfection', Bennett concluded.[6] What is striking about these comments is that the very presence of certain mental qualities in the female constructs her as lacking, whereas their absence in the male is held to construct *his* mental powers: the more invisible, the greater their strength. Nowhere is this more evident than in Bennett's discussion of the differences between little girls and boys, which he used to mark the precise 'bounties of nature' to each sex to demonstrate the natural truth of difference. Though he reckoned that little girls are quicker and generally more advanced than boys the same age,[7] this was not a proof of their general superiority. Quite the opposite. It is the boy's thoughtfulness that prevents more brilliant and showy exertions. The deep and true worth of the boy's mental apparatus and the shallow and worthless brilliance of the girl's were summarized in one sentence: 'gold sparkles less than tinsel'.[8] By a rhetorical *tour de force*, the sexed mind was constructed so that the female's would generate not only the physical space for the domestic comfort and felicity of man,[9] but the mental space which guaranteed the superior intellectual powers of the male.

The discourse on the sexed mind constituted the male intellect as higher, deeper and stronger than the female's. Strength was the essence of manliness and access to knowledge – to science – was predicated on that strength. Women were excluded by virtue of their constitutional weakness. Women lacked the 'intellectual strength' necessary to 'penetrate into the abstruser walks of literature', declared Hannah More. 'Woman's outward frame seems not to be calculated for such efforts of thinking as the more abstracted sciences require', asserted Bennett. Chirol, writing in the first decade of the nineteenth century, went further. Contrasting men's strength and robustness with the delicacy and feeble constitution which made women liable to 'almost incessant infirmities,' he concluded that woman was therefore incapable of 'intense application' and had 'no aptitude for the study of sciences'. It was 'morality' that should be woman's 'principal study', not just because it was 'within her mental capacity', but because it was by morality alone that she could 'influence the virtues of men', make 'her situation more comfortable' and 'find her happiness and glory even in the sacrifice of her inclinations'.[10]

The principal object of Bennett and Chirol's texts had been a fierce denunciation of boarding-schools for girls, while vaunting their advantages for boys. As I have already shown, see note 2 in Chapter 5, Chirol focused on the dangers of these schools to girls' virtue. Bennett's chief anxieties were of a different nature: the very reasons why boarding-schools were beneficial for boys made them 'abhorrent' for girls. Boarding-schools, for one, established in boys the 'confidence so necessary for any publick character or employment'; confidence in women, however, was a 'horrid bore'.[11] Both Chirol and Bennett favoured instead a home-based education,[12] which positioned females firmly in the domestic space and as men's inferiors. Chirol's prescriptions are almost brutal. Women were 'created for the domestic comfort and felicity of man'. Mothers must 'train their daughters to consider a Husband as a Master; and Matrimony as the grave of Liberty . . . a state of Pain'. Bennett, who made the same point more mildly, resorted to nature to demonstrate that gender roles were natural and superiority providentially lodged in the male: do not male birds display greater strength, and females more brilliant plumage?[13]

The shift in the meaning of education implied by the discourse on the sexed mind had different consequences for the education of males. Educating the gentleman now meant exercising and disciplining his mental faculties. This is why, explains the historian of education Sheldon Rothblatt, the nineteenth century was the age of the teacher: only he could determine which faculties needed strengthening, and consequently, which programme of study was best suited to the student. He alone could discipline male minds. It also accounts, argues Rothblatt, for the dominance of faculty psychology in that period: 'cultivating the faculties was the single most important educational learning theory of the nineteenth century' and was a direct result of the rise of the teacher.[14] It seems to me, however, that the process unfolded the other way around. I shall argue that the rise of the teacher was a product of the new discourse on the sexed mind and that the rise in importance of faculty psychology was one component of that discourse. It was the shift from cultivating the tongue and manners of the gentleman (best achieved by women), to exercising and training his masculine faculties that created the space and conditions for the emergence of a male expert. Most importantly, this involved a shift from the teacher as a means of producing the authoritative voice of his pupil to that of the teacher himself being the authoritative voice.

The discourse on the sexed mind implied not that males had minds and females not,[15] but that the faculties of each sex must be cultivated to follow 'nature'. Both sexes must be educated for their 'destination in society': men for the 'more public exhibitions on the grand theater of human life', and women 'to constitute the happiness of the other half'.[16] This did not mean that women had to remain ignorant. On the contrary. Since the sexed mind constituted difference it was more imperative than ever that what women learned enhance their femininity. Education was meant to emphasize gender difference, not to 'obliterate the natural difference' between the sexes. Thus, Frances Power Cobbe remarked ironically in 1862, Latin kept a man masculine by exercising and strengthening his mental faculties. Learning French, on the other hand, kept a woman 'feminine in mind'.[17]

It may now be a commonplace that French was the language without which no young lady would be considered accomplished in the nineteenth century. What is not so well remembered, however, is that in the eighteenth century it was the language without which no *gentleman* had been considered accomplished. French thus shifted from contributing to the fashioning of males in the eighteenth century to being central to the construction of femininity in the nineteenth. This shift, ignored in histories of language teaching as well as general histories of education, transformed the study of French in England.

French has a unique position in the history of education in England because it was the only 'serious' subject learned by both sexes until the late eighteenth–early nineteenth century, when it came to be associated predominantly with females. The fact that this gendering took place at the time the discourse on mental differences was emerging is not accidental. Tracing the history of the learning of French *by both sexes* in the eighteenth and the nineteenth centuries can, as I will show in this and the next chapter, provide an insight into the practical consequences of the discourse on the sexed mind on education and on the techniques for constructing the gentleman.

LEARNING FRENCH IN THE EIGHTEENTH CENTURY

Major histories of language teaching all focus on boys, and girls are virtually absent, except in Kathleen Lambley's *The Teaching and Cultivation of the French Language*.[18] The justification for not discussing girls – when a justification is made at all – is that most girls learned French at home, and as such were not part of organized instruction.[19] This suggests that home education is of no concern to the history of education, though it has never caused aristocratic boys' private education to be ignored.

If girls outnumber boys by perhaps a third in today's French classrooms, the situation was very different then. 'French', the author of *An Essay in Defense of the Female Sex* (1697) had remarked, 'has become a very fashionable language. There are now almost as many Ladies as Gentlemen speaking it'.[20] Though we know that boys either learned or perfected their French while on the Grand Tour, girls' French instruction has to be established more indirectly. From Locke's observations on the conversational method we find out that girls learned French at home with governesses.[21] We can also infer from their biographies that girls born in families of rank might acquire French as their sole first language, as did Sarah Lennox, daughter of the Duke and Duchess of Richmond, born in 1744. She had a French governess and 'spoke nothing but French' at five years of age.[22] Later in the century, Mrs Delany advised her niece to 'read the Psalms for the morning in French, and some French lesson before breakfast, if there was time.'[23] From the French language textbooks themselves we can infer that girls also learned the rudiments of French at home from visiting tutors as did their brothers.

Visiting tutors with foreign language skills were probably common in the many boarding-schools which thrived throughout the eighteenth century.[24] Contemporary advertisements targeting both boys and girls all boast inhouse or visiting tutors who will teach French. Thus, the boarding-school for young gentlemen newly established in 1745 at Theobald's House near Cheshunt, claims that 'for the Ready Attainment of French, a Native of the Country attends Youths from Morning till Night, both in School and at their Diversions'. The language is taught 'both by Rote and Grammar'. In November 1785, Mr Praval, 'hopes his Lessons, united to a Constant Opportunity of conversing in French' will soon make the pupils attending Mrs Praval's boarding-school 'speak that Language with Fluency and Elegance'.[25]

The difference between learning French at home with a governess, mainly by conversational methods, and learning it with a tutor, at home or at school, is not without implications. For if the governess spoke French all the time with her pupil, the language would be acquired as a first or second language, whereas if a tutor came for French instruction, it would be learned as a foreign language.[26] French acquired through conversation at home could eventually be spoken fluently. Fluency would be more difficult to attain if it was learned as a foreign language, as was likely at boarding-school, because of the conditions generally prevailing in a school. Even when claims were made that there would be 'constant opportunity' to speak French, the practice was undoubtedly very different. One might even suspect that the prominence given to such claims in the advertisements to be evidence of how little success was generally achieved in that area.

CONVERSATION OR GRAMMAR

A comparison of French language teaching texts published in the first and second half of the eighteenth century reveals that a major shift had taken place. Comparing what two writers said was the best way to learn to speak French highlights the nature of this shift: for Cheneau (1723), it was by constant practice. For Chambaud (1772), it was by understanding the rules of the language. Although the original impetus to learn French grammatically lay in the concern to achieve and maintain a standard of correctness,[27] late seventeenth-century texts, Lambley tells us, 'reduced rules to "as small a compass as possible" because what mattered was not the grammar but the ability to speak.'[28] The number of pages allocated to the sections on 'grammar' and 'language' between the 1729 (tenth) edition of a typical and popular text, Abel Boyer's *The Compleat French Master for Ladies and Gentlemen*, and the last posthumous edition, the twenty-first, in 1767, is most indicative of this change of emphasis. In the earlier edition, the grammar section contains 157 pages and the language section 215. In the last, the section on grammar had increased by 31 pages, the rest of the text remaining virtually unchanged.[29]

Why the shift to grammar? One reason was given by Cheneau: '[La méthode] d'apprendre par coeur est fort difficile, on ne peut pas mettre les règles en pratique . . . on est fort long à apprendre' [The method of learning by heart is very difficult, one cannot apply rules . . . it takes a very long time].[30] Learning by rote, without organizing principles, the large amount of vocabulary and dialogues constituting the texts published in the earlier part of the century was very time-consuming. Grammar represented an attractive short cut – at least for boys. For not only was grammar education taught in Latin, which girls did not customarily learn, but French syntax had been stretched to fit the framework of Latin, and French grammar texts used the terminology of Latin grammar.[31] Yet, as the initial dialogue in Claude Mauger's *French Grammar* illustrates, this was not seen as an insurmountable obstacle for females.

'Entre une Dame et le Maître de Langues' shows how the problem might have been met.

> 'Monsieur, je n'ai pas appris la langue Latine, je ne sais pas ce que c'est que Grammaire, qu'un Nom, qu'un Verbe . . . et je voudrais pourtant bien apprendre par Règles, et non par Routine. Je vous prie de m'en informer.'
> 'Il est très raisonnable . . . La Grammaire est l'Art de bien Parler.'
>
> ['Sir, I have not learned Latin, and do not know what is meant by grammar, noun, verb . . . and I would prefer to learn by rule

rather than rote. Please let me know what they are.'
'It is very reasonable . . . Grammar is the art of speaking.']

The lady then asks what is a syllable, then a phrase, then the parts of language and so on. Far from being a tedious list of rules, the dialogue is charmingly lively and the lady's ignorance never used to make her appear lacking or stupid; on the contrary, as the exchange about grammatical gender should demonstrate.

'Mais je vous demande une chose, pourquoi les autres noms des choses inanimées sont-ils Masculins ou Féminins?'
'Madame, vous objectez fort bien, je vous le dirai: ils le sont par accident. Si un e que nous appelons Féminin, c'est à dire faible, qui n'est point prononcé, finit un mot, généralement il est Féminin à cause de cet e.'[32]

['But tell me, why are the names of inanimate objects masculine or feminine?'
'Madam, this is a good question. I will tell you why: by accident.[33] If an e that we call feminine, that is weak and not pronounced, ends a word, generally it is feminine because of this e.']

Not only was grammar perceived not to present particular problems to females, but they might, like Fauchon's pupil Isabella Carr, make more progress 'without any previous knowledge of Grammatical Rules' than someone trained 'Scholastically'.[34] In addition, by learning French grammar, a girl entered hallowed ground and became one of the initiates: the Art of Grammar was 'the Golden Key to unlock all other liberal Arts and Sciences', and 'the Gate' that would give an 'easy entrance' into all foreign languages.[35]

By the end of the eighteenth century, even though it was conceded that learning grammar was often 'disagreeable' and made the study of language 'dry, tedious and disgustful to young people', it was held to be 'the only effectual means of acquiring a perfect knowledge of any language'.[36] Method was associated both with rationality and virtue, and was believed to 'form the mind'.[37] Though being able to hold a conversation in French was still held to be of the utmost difficulty, the communicative function of language had come to take second place. In the 1770s, Chambaud was already expressing contempt for the 'common compliments', and the 'trifling topics of familiar discourse' which constituted the knowledge of those taught French conversationally without a thorough grounding in principles of the language.[38] Chambaud was probably referring to the textbooks and methods published in the earlier part of the century.[39] These consisted in the main of shorter and longer dialogues. The shorter ones, called 'Familiar Phrases', usually involved what we would today call 'functional' notions, such as how to inquire about the health of one's interlocutor, how to thank, agree, consent and deny, get angry, what to say when playing cards or billiards. The longer ones often painted vignettes of the life of the time, such as a dialogue between two friends concerning marriage, between two young ladies, between a man and his mistress and so on. These dialogues were not graded for difficulty, nor were they designed to illustrate grammatical points. They were meant to be memorized. In Bernard Calbris' *A French Plaidoyer Between Five Young Ladies* (1797), five young noblewomen are engaged in a contest, organized and arbitrated by their learned aunt, the Marquise de. . ., which consists of explaining clearly and elegantly the rules of French syntax. There is no other conversation between them.[40] The difference between this text and the dialogues between young ladies in Mauger, Boyer and even Peyton could not be more dramatic. Even meaning was becoming a by-product of grammar teaching. Henri Gratte, for instance, claimed that

> On ne peut pas douter que quand un enfant aura appris et récité attentivement toutes les Règles contenues dans cette grammaire avec leurs exemples, il ne sache la signification des mots qui y sont enfermés.[41]

> [There is no doubt that when a child will have learned and recited attentively all the rules and their examples contained in this grammar, he will know the significance of all the words it contains.]

LEARNING FRENCH IN THE NINETEENTH CENTURY

A convenient vantage point for considering the way in which French was studied in the nineteenth century is provided by the evidence of the two major Royal Commissions on education in the 1860s, the Clarendon and the Taunton Commissions.[42] Not only do they afford a detailed picture of the overall state of boys' education in public schools and grammar schools, but the

Taunton Commission had also agreed to investigate girls' schools. Because these had been regarded till then as dispensing not education but mere accomplishments, it marked, as Josephine Kamm put it, 'the opening of a new epoch'.[43]

The Clarendon Commission

Given how important speaking French had been for upper-class males in the eighteenth century, one might have thought that in the nineteenth century, as the public school which trained the men who occupied most of the highest government and diplomatic posts,[44] Eton would sustain something of that tradition. But no. Of the nine public schools investigated by the Clarendon Commission, Eton was the only one in which French was not part of the curriculum. 'It is a complete impossibility to teach French at Eton in class', Mr Vaughan, a classics master, said to Lord Clarendon.[45] It was available only as an extra, and had to be paid for. As Mr Tarver, the sole French master at Eton at the time of the inquiry put it, he was 'a mere *objet de luxe*'.[46] French was offered at the other public schools and was even obligatory at Westminster and Harrow, but it tended to be despised and treated as an inferior subject.

Public schools in general, and Eton in particular, saw disciplining and strengthening the mind as their principal educational aim. It was necessary to teach 'strong subjects', subjects which 'require a strain upon the mind'.[47] The complex structure of Latin – rated as difficult because of its inflections – was thought to fulfil this function. Because it lacked declensions and its grammar was considered simple, French could not discipline the mind. The proof of its simplicity was that it could be learned 'empirically', as a 'vernacular or half-native tongue at home'.[48] Not only was a knowledge of French seen as no indication of a boy's mental abilities, but John Walter, an old boy, even declared that 'people may be first rate scholars in a language and not be able to hold a conversation'.[49] When French was taught, it was usually for two hours a week. To allow it more time, said Revd H.M. Butler, Headmaster at Harrow, might 'damage . . . the intellectual tone of the place'.[50]

French in public schools

Mr Tarver provides the most detailed account. His pupils were expected to attend twice a week for one hour – though many did not. During the lesson, they were to 'read and construe, write by ... dictation, translate into French or into English according to their capacity'. They also had to have prepared 'a piece of composition' and if they were not able to do as much as that, 'a grammatical exercise'.[51] At Winchester, where French was held to be taught 'effectively', the work of the class consisted of 'translating French into English, translating English into French, and answering grammatical questions'. At Harrow, where French was compulsory, knowledge of French was defined as reading and translating. This was expected to enable boys to 'acquire afterwards in a *short time* what cannot be taught in a public school, the power of speaking fluently'.[52] French was taught grammatically, ostensibly because Englishmen could not be expected to teach pronunciation, and Englishmen were preferred teachers of French because Frenchmen were said to be unable to maintain discipline.[53]

What was really at issue, however, was the low esteem in which oral fluency was held. At Rugby for instance, French conversation classes, timetabled at the same time as games, were attended 'reluctantly'. Max Müller, the Taylorian Professor of Modern Languages at Oxford, declared that servants and couriers spoke French very well, and he did not see the attainment of 'fluency in conversation', or of a 'perfect accent', to be within the purview of public schools.[54] Nor can the meaning of the term conversation be taken for granted: at Rugby, it meant reading French aloud.

The Taunton Commission

French in boys' schools

French was taught in most of the higher grade grammar and private schools investigated by the Taunton Commission,[55] but, just as in the public schools, it held a subordinate position, and was considered an inferior subject.[56] Throughout the country it was assumed that boys attending such schools would go on to university, and a classical curriculum was therefore required. The assistant commissioners judged that, although there were some notable exceptions,[57] French was badly taught. Translations from English into French, 'the true test of a knowledge of the language', were full of the most elementary errors; even if the boys could manage to turn French into English tolerably well, this did not represent 'a sound grammatical knowledge'. The teaching of French was 'unintelligent', commented another assistant commissioner, with too much stress on 'minute rules with long lists of exceptions' and on pronunciation and idioms, and too little on the 'main outlines of etymology and syntax'; there was, in other words, insufficient explanation of the 'universal principles of language'.[58]

Like John Walter, assistant commissioner Bryce believed that one reason for these defects was that French was a living language, and teachers 'apt to hesitate between two modes of treatment, the grammatical and the colloquial'. The latter often slipped into superficiality and grammatical slovenliness.[59] Another major cause of concern was the status of French masters. Frenchmen were not respected as professionals either by their colleagues or by their pupils and were considered a 'serious source of weakness' in the teaching of French. Not only were they generally considered incapable of maintaining discipline and commanding authority over boys, but their very availability made them suspect: 'a good Frenchman unwillingly expatriates himself'. To inspire respect, a teacher ought to be a 'scholar and a gentleman'. The implication was that French masters were neither. Worse still, they could not be, when their French accent in English, and the 'peculiarities of a foreigner', made them figures of fun to schoolboys.[60] In other words, French masters were ridiculed for their Frenchness. Girls apparently did not have that response, something assistant commissioner Fearon found difficult to explain. Nor was any such ridicule directed at French women teachers. If they were suspect, it was because their 'standard of propriety' did not measure up to that of English women, and worse, they might introduce their female pupils to 'too much freedom of thought and discussion, especially about theological matters'.[61] The danger that French women might have an immoral influence was nothing new. The crucial shift was in the image of the male French teacher who seems to have been collapsed with that of the eighteenth-century stock figure of caricature, the effeminate French dancing master.[62]

French in girls' schools

French was so commonly taught in girls' schools that it was taken by the Commission as 'the means of testing their general linguistic cultivation', that is, their educational standard. In other words, the attitude to French in girls' schools was the exact opposite of those just described in boys' schools, where French was not important enough to be 'a subject by which the efficiency of the teaching may be fairly judged'.[63] The best test of this linguistic cultivation was believed to be translation with critical (i.e., grammatical) questions. The assistant commissioners were severe: even in the best private schools the results were poor. The most serious criticism of girls' French instruction, however, was directed at the use of the spoken language. The assistant commissioners complained that the French lesson was too often conducted entirely in French and opportunities for explaining grammar (in English) were lost.[64] Seventy years earlier, Lévizac and Gratte, for instance, had insisted on the use of French, especially in the teaching of grammar, so as not to waste any opportunities of using the language.[65] Now, the practice, common in the best schools, of enforcing constant use of French for a fixed number of hours outside class was considered 'mischievous', and even 'injurious to morals'. The assistant commissioners also believed it would encourage 'triviality and poverty of thought' because conversations would be limited to the subjects within the reach of the available vocabulary, and the resulting language would be slovenly and inaccurate.[66]

Overall, the assistant commissioners were critical of what they saw as false priorities in girls' French language classes. Assistant commissioner Fitch's disapproval is representative of their sentiments: 'a pure Parisian accent is regarded as of more consequence than grammatical knowledge, familiarity with literature or the power of explaining principles'.[67] Assistant commissioner Bompas' complaint that 'the advantage of gaining fluency was greater than the evil of incorrectness' is intriguing: it speaks of the moral disapproval of the tongue and its display, in contrast to the rectitude of its containment through the regulation of grammar.

The aim of language instruction was mental discipline, and accuracy in translation its main manifestation. Girls' performance did not meet this criterion, so the assistant commissioners concluded that no girls were found whose mind had been trained or strengthened by learning French. At the same time, they noted not only that girls 'knew French better than the boys', but that girls performed better than the boys in a number of other subjects.[68] Each time, however, that achievement was explained

away. Girls were said to have 'a correct ear', 'quicker perception', 'greater aptitude'; they had spent more time learning the
subject, and they were more mature than the boys.[69] Should we
be surprised that the discovery that girls outperformed boys did
not have the force of a revelation for the assistant commissioners?
Because no attempt had been found to teach grammar 'as a
science' in girls' schools, knowing French was no indication of
mental ability and discipline. The way girls' performance was
conceived did not locate it in their intellect, it was not based
'on the same intellectual foundations as the performance of
boys'.[70] At the same time as girls' achievement was noticed, it
was rendered insignificant and immaterial.

Thus, when the Direct Method, inspired by the German Reform
School[71] was hailed at the turn of the twentieth century as a revolution in language teaching methods, as early as 1905 one of its
foremost proponents could write: 'In pre-reform days ... the
learner never handled the language himself for the purpose of
expressing his own experiences and ideas'.[72] This was precisely
what the assistant commissioners had criticized so severely in
girls' language classrooms. In fact, the main 'innovative' tenets of
the Direct Method comprised precisely those features of girls'
French instruction condemned by the Taunton Commission: it
advocated the use of French at all times in the classroom and
opposed parsing, analysis and translation.[73] Because girls' French
instruction had been judged 'unsystematic' and wanting in
'soundness and accuracy' – as had their education in general – it
had not qualified as a method. What history has recorded is the
'slipshod chatter' of French conversation lessons in nineteenth-
century girls' schools.[74]

The assistant commissioners cannot be charged with having
failed to see the 'truth' deriving from the 'evidence'. Nor can they
be accused of deception: they reported girls' superior achievement.
Indeed, it was their conclusion that girls were able to learn 'the
various subjects of education' which made it possible for girls to
have access to the same education as boys. What the assistant commissioners' final assessment demonstrates is the power of the
dominant discourse on mental differences, a power which their
Report served to reinforce. Ultimately, it sanctioned the differential
positionings of boys and girls in the discourse on achievement,
positionings that have shaped educational practices ever since.[75] It
is these gendered positionings that I want to address now.

THE DISCOURSE ON ACHIEVEMENT

The assistant commissioners' main criticism of French instruction was that for both sexes, there was insufficient explanation of the 'universal principles of language'.[76] Discussing boys' schools, assistant commissioner Fearon suggested that one reason for this state of affairs was the textbooks. Most of the grammars used were not only 'exceedingly bad', they were also 'defective in the scientific treatment of the language'. The editions of French authors for English pupils were, if anything, worse. The notes lacked any 'scholarship'; there was, Fearon specified,

> no attempt to grapple with the real syntactical or idiomatic difficulties in a true spirit of philology ... I did not see one note in which any attempt was made to illustrate French usages or constructions by the light of parallel or analogous expressions in Latin, German or English authors; not one in which the origin and derivation of words and phrases was discussed, or they were traced through their various changes of signification; in short, not one in which any use or application was made of the stores of knowledge which modern studies in comparative grammar and philology have accumulated.[77]

Similar deficiencies were noted in girls' schools. Even in the best private schools, girls could not

> discuss the origin and derivation of words and phrases; trace them through their various phases of signification; reconcile their employment, or point out their disagreement, with the general laws of grammar, illustrate the growth of such usages by other examples from the French or other languages.[78]

Ostensibly the criticisms are similar, except for one crucial detail. Boys' failure was attributed to their textbooks, girls' failure to something in them. Yet, boys *were* taught mostly 'grammatically' but girls were not. It should have come as no surprise that they could not 'answer such questions upon their French authors, as boys in the upper sixth form of our public schools are expected to answer upon their Latin authors'. But it did. Fearon was surprised that girls who were having 'conversational lessons in literature with Parisian teachers' were unable to construe, translate or conjugate verbs accurately. This confirmed the 'want of early and systematic mental discipline' and 'want of cultivation of the logical and reasoning faculties' of their education.[79] Thus, girls may well have 'known' French better than the boys, but that very success was taken as evidence of their failure, since it was also believed at the time that 'modern languages inherently weakened the mind and made it more superficial'.[80]

My argument is that the very terms of the discourse on education are organized so that practices, then as now, have the achievement of boys as their main concern. It is neither a conspiracy, nor a deliberate attempt to discriminate against girls, but is just how the discourse is structured. This is particularly true in French, where the present 'crisis' in modern languages has been constituted by the gender imbalance in take-up and achievement favouring girls.[81] The discourse presupposes that boys' failure and girls' success are due to something exterior to them – a pedagogical practice, a method. That girls' success and boys' failure might be due to something in them is not envisaged, for the possibility that boys might be deficient – at least in comparison to girls – is ruled out. One consequence is that boys tend to be perceived as potentially, if not actually, able, but not so girls.[82] Not only have these gendered positionings had a long history, but the assumption of boys' potential has been integral to the construction of males since at least the late seventeenth century, when the ability to comprehend everything was, as John Barrel has suggested, just 'empty potential'. The gentleman was never required to 'give any evidence of having comprehended anything'.

Thus when Locke observed how quickly and successfully little girls learned French just by 'pratling' with their governess, it was not because he wanted to discuss how clever little girls were. By attributing girls' success to a mere *method*, he was able to correct gentlemen's 'misapprehension' that their sons might be 'more dull or incapable than their Daughters'.[83] For Locke, as one concerned with the education of gentlemen, it was inconceivable that boys might be less able than girls. Yet, Locke was not ignoring how well little girls were doing. Indeed, the visibility of girls' achievement was necessary because it held the promise of boys' achievement.

The 'empty potential' of boys and men was woven into the fabric of gender difference at the turn of the eighteenth century when, as I have already argued, the superior male intellect was constituted *as* potential in contrast to girls' evident superiority. A dialogue in Porny's *Practical French Grammar* illustrates this very clearly. I have already reviewed how in the eighteenth century, both males and females of rank were expected to learn French and to speak it fluently. However, if the learning of French was not gendered,[84] achievement in it seems to have been. In this story, (meant to be learned by heart) a girl who has been learning French for six months 'understands it better ... construes it, writes it, and even speaks it better' than her brother who has been learning it for six years at school.[85] Two features of the dialogue are of interest. The first involves the boy. Though his reluctance to learn is obvious – he finds French 'too hard' and does not see 'what use it is' – his failure is located in an aspect of the educational process, the method. ' 'Tis none my fault' says the boy, and his interlocutor concurs; the blame rests with the master. Bad methods were commonly held responsible for boys' 'aversion' to French and 'sometimes even their books and master', they were the 'bad Tools' Englishmen had to work with.[86] The complaint was frequent, even though there was no consensus as to what constituted a bad method.[87] If, on the other hand, it was girls who were said to be 'discouraged' by French, the problem was not lack of motivation or interest because of the method, but was in their 'nature': their 'more nice and tender constitutions' are not 'able to endure those rugged and thorny Difficulties in the Methods hitherto practiced'.[88] The second feature involves the girl. Though her achievement is meant to discipline the boy,[89] we should not lose sight of that achievement nor of how is it constructed. The girl does not conceal the fact that she takes 'much pains' to learn: on the contrary, she believes that 'Science and Languages are only acquired by diligence and labour', and that without effort, knowledge would not be of much value. She succeeds not because she is able, but because she is diligent and has a good teacher. 'Good girls' are those who rely on hard work because they lack 'that elusive gift, "brilliance".'[90] Positioned as hard working rather than able, the girl in the story does not undermine or threaten the boy's potential. Indeed, once he is convinced of the 'benefits' of learning French, he endeavours to 'take so much pains' that he is sure to speak it in a short time.[91]

There is one corollary to my story. Histories of education tell us that change comes from 'struggles for reform', or from the ideas of the great men (and occasionally women) who have inspired them; of progress and innovation.[92] In this perspective, improvement in girls' education is measured by its approximation to boys', the 'powerless' follow the 'powerful'. But what if the suspicion were raised that 'the direction of change is not necessarily one way'?[93] Girls tend to be positioned as passive in educational discourse, yet, could their *achievement* be a condition of possibility for the emergence of educational practices? Since girls' failure is believed to result from something in them, interventions promoting girls' achievement in the past twenty years have been organized as compensations for a deficit: their 'nature', their conditioning had to be altered, their subjectivity changed.[94] Although boys underachieve in French, there is no question of deficiency or conditioning. Their failure is ascribed to external conditions.[95] Motivating boys to take up and do well at French is a matter of changing not the boys, but the methods. Since girls' success is attributed to a method, change in practices would then emerge on the assumption either that a method must be good, since it causes girls to do well (Locke's observation), or that a method must be bad, since it causes boys to do badly.[96] In this perspective, girls' achievement would be implicated in shifts in educational practice, but because their achievement is treated ambiguously, the mechanism of the shift is not clear. One example of this is Eric Hawkins' comment that teachers have developed ways of helping boys to compensate for the 'unfairness of having to compete in verbal learning tasks with girls'.[97]

Thus, when Bob Powell attributes girls' superior achievement in French to their accepting to do the 'repetitive and meaningless tasks' required in present (1985) language teaching methods, but boys' failure to an appropriate rebellion against these inadequate methods, he is merely endorsing a long tradition. Girls, both conditioned and compliant, are doubly passive. Boys, neither 'conditioned' nor docile, are doubly active. It is ostensibly in response to their rebellion that Powell suggests changes in method, such as making language learning more 'mathematical' by introducing more computer-based teaching and problem-solving exercises.[98]

Raising the suspicion that the direction of change is not necessarily one-way means re-examining the taken-for-granted assumption that girls are excluded from what boys have access to, it may be that boys are removed from what girls do. The consequence is that while there is no space for the achieving girl, girls' achievement itself continues to create the space for the fiction of boys' potential to be sustained.

7

TONGUES, MASCULINITY AND NATIONAL CHARACTER

Why did the attitude to French undergo such a dramatic change? The standard reply to this question is that the fashion for learning and speaking French must necessarily have been one of the casualties of the French Revolution and the Napoleonic Wars. Yet it is difficult to draw such a straightforward conclusion about English attitudes to France over that period. These were varied, extremely complex – contradictory even – and altered as events unfolded.[1] There is also a lack of consensus among historians even about the effects of the French Revolution on England not least because it influenced historiography itself.[2]

None the less, while it is expected that the period 1789–1815 would have repercussions on English attitudes to France, it is also important to consider what did not change. Gerald Newman, who cites as an instance of anti-French nationalism Hannah More's objection, in 1799, to the 'sacrifices' made to ensure that young English ladies learn the purest French, omitted to mention that More conceded at the same time that a young lady might 'excel in speaking French', because such skill was 'elegant' and becoming.[3] It's not that Hannah More ignored the events following the French Revolution. On the contrary, having already condemned French ladies' immoral practices and lack of religion, she reminded her readers of the 'malignity' and 'turpitude' of the 'practices and principles' of modern France, and called for a patriotic resistance to the foreign 'contagion'. Why then would she accept that French was a language English ladies might still wish to learn? Could it be attributed to her 'religious faith in the distinction between social classes'?[4] If so, her attitude suggests that French had remained a powerful social marker after the French Revolution. In fact, far from declining, the fashion for learning French actually increased after the French Revolution and the Napoleonic Wars.[5] While it has been argued that this increase affected mainly girls, Linda Colley provides evidence that French was still 'a prerequisite for entry into high society or high office' – therefore for men – at the end of the second decade of the nineteenth century.[6] No argument about a direct link between the political upheavals of the period 1789 to 1815 and the change in attitude towards French can thus be sustained.

Yet by the 1860s it had become a virtual commonplace that the English gentleman did not speak French, as Frances Power Cobbe tells us,[7] and the Clarendon (1864) and the Taunton (1868) Commissions alike revealed the contempt in which the study of French was now held by males. Why, and how, did a language which, throughout the eighteenth century, had been central to the accomplishment of young males of rank and for which – to misquote Hannah More – enormous financial sacrifices had been made to ensure that it would be learned with the purest accent, become the object of such scorn barely a century later?

It is indisputable that by the 1860s, learning French had acquired entirely different meanings. Not only did boys, according to their masters, despise the study of French because they said it was 'girls' business' whereas Latin was boys',[8] but, learning French, held throughout the eighteenth century to be difficult, was now thought so easy that schools treated it as a subject for the less able. As one master put it, boys who could never 'make anything of Latin could at least do French.'[9] At the same time, it had become the language without which no young lady would be considered accomplished.[10]

Ostensibly, speaking French appears on the one hand to have lost the prestige it had maintained for centuries and, on the other, to have become gendered. In the last section of this book, I will attempt to identify the conditions for the emergence of what was a rather dramatic shift which, though ignored by historians of language teaching,[11] still governs attitudes to the study of French today.

THE GRAND TOUR AND THE PUBLIC SCHOOL

One of the most important educational institutions of the eighteenth-century élite was the Grand Tour. From Obadiah

Walker in the late seventeenth century to Oliver Goldsmith in the mid-eighteenth, the Grand Tour was expected to 'enrich and broaden the mind, give insight into things and men' and give the young man of rank an opportunity to learn the languages, laws and customs of other nations, as well as understand their governments. He would thus gain the experience that would render him 'serviceable to his Country and an Honour to his Family'. Above all, it was expected to improve him and polish his manners: 'Home-bred Gentlemen are only rough cast'. It was travel that would bring the young man 'to the Standard of a fine Gentleman.'[12]

This is why Richard Hurd's *Dialogues on the Uses of Foreign Travel Considered as a Part of an English Gentleman's Education*, (1764) signals a turning point. Although the discussions between *Locke* and *Shaftesbury*[13] are ostensibly about the role of travel, the text is in fact about two divergent conceptions of the gentleman, the old and the new. Whereas *Shaftesbury* wants to fashion a 'citizen of the world', a man who can converse not only in English but in the universal language of the time, French, for *Locke*, the education of the young man of rank must produce not polite gentlemanliness, but citizenship, public spirit and integrity.[14] The sentiments Hurd's *Locke* expressed against polite education were not new. Less than twenty years earlier, David Fordyce had highlighted the limitations and failings of polite education and recommended instead an education that would produce men of civic virtue.[15] Significantly, David Fordyce's Plan of Education included foreign travel as final polish. What was new in Hurd's *Dialogues* was the outright rejection of both foreign travel, of the Grand Tour as part of the English gentleman's education, and of the polish it was supposed to effect. For *Locke*, the accomplishments acquired during foreign travel were not only potentially effeminating but alien to the national English character. Although the 'manly' national character might be distinguished by his 'rough manners', these would be amply compensated by his 'unpolished integrity'. In the curriculum *Locke* prescribed for the construction of the English gentleman, foreign travel was irrelevant and learning French a waste of time.

This is why I want to suggest that the Grand Tour ended not by being transported into Britain as 'internal' tourism, as Linda Colley argues,[16] but by being transformed into another institution for the shaping of the gentleman, the public school.

It was the public school that took over and recast a number of the educational aims of the tour and produced new ones, the two most important being patriotism and masculinity.[17]

Thus, while the *Shaftesbury* of Hurd's *Dialogues* maintained that foreign travel was indispensable to correct the 'mischiefs' of a public school education, which left boys 'timid at the same time as rude; illiberal, and ungraceful ... clownish, coarse, ungainly',[18] for George Chapman, writing in 1773, 'get[ting] the better of [boys'] rawness, and ... awkward bashfulness' was precisely what public education[19] achieved. Public schools, he claimed, provided not only the beneficial company of other boys but more importantly, the training to be 'a good [English] citizen'. Writing in 1797, John Moore was categorical. The most effective means of educating a 'young man of rank of our country' is a public school in England. Not only will it 'make him an Englishman', but it will develop his 'manliness of character'.[20]

By 1800, Colley points out, '80 per cent of all English peers received their education at just four public schools, Eton, Westminster, Winchester and Harrow'. This provided not only a 'more uniform patrician education' and a new 'source of cultural identity', but, she argues, it must also have shaped attitudes to the British nation.[21] However, the Grand Tour had also been a form of patrician education and a source of cultural identity. One major difference between the two educational institutions was the way in which they shaped attitudes to the British nation. A principal aim of the Grand Tour had been to root out

> *National* ... Prejudices ... a certain Partiality to our own Country, and Attachment to our own Manners and Customs, in Opposition to those of other Countries, an Attachment which savours something of ancient Barbarity, that had need to be worn off, to bring him to the true Standard of a Fine Gentleman.[22]

By contrast, it was patriotism, 'patrician patriotism *in the British present*',[23] that the public schools aimed to develop.

GRAMMAR AND THE TONGUE

The three major features that Colley highlighted as characterizing public schools – the study of the classics, patriotism and manliness – were underpinned and legitimated by the discourse on the sexed

101

mind and the educational practices that derived from it. This explains why cultivating the faculties was so important in the nineteenth century.[24] In their evidence to the two Royal Commissions on education, public and grammar school Heads and masters were unanimous in their belief that Latin (i.e., grammar), was the best means of achieving this aim. Yet, in the late seventeenth century, Locke had condemned the arduous learning of Latin through grammar, recommending instead that it be taught by conversation. The only grammar that could usefully be learned by a gentleman, he argued, was that of his own language, to avoid making errors unbecoming to his rank. Grammar was necessary to train the tongue of the gentleman, to distinguish his English from the vernacular.[25] In the early eighteenth century, Latin was considered imperative for a gentleman in so far as the primary aim of education was to '[form] the mind to virtue'.[26] By the 1780s, however, Vicesimus Knox was declaring that learning Latin grammar had the 'most valuable effect of exercising and strengthening the mind', a conviction shared by Lewis Chambaud, who claimed that learning grammar was the only way to learn the French language methodically and rationally.[27] The belief that grammar trained the faculties was held up as a 'scientific' truth by the witnesses of the Clarendon and the Taunton Commissions less than one hundred years later. However, as Michael Stubbs has argued, grammar is at best an elusive notion. For Locke, it meant mostly rules. In the nineteenth century, it had acquired quasi mystical properties.[28] In the words of J.S. Mill, in his Inaugural Address at St Andrews,

> Consider for a moment what grammar is. It is the most elementary part of logic. It is the beginning of the analysis of the thinking process. The principles and rules of grammar are the means by which the forms of language are made to correspond with the universal forms of thought . . . The structure of every sentence is a lesson in logic. The various rules of syntax oblige us to distinguish between the subject and predicate of a proposition, between the agent, the action, and the thing acted upon; to mark when an idea is intended to modify or qualify, or merely unite with, some other idea; what assertions are categorical, what only conditional; whether the intention is to express similarity or contrast, to make a plurality of assertions conjunctively or disjunctively; what portions of a sentence, though grammatically complete

within themselves, are mere members or subordinate parts
of the assertion made by the entire sentence. Such things
form the subject matter of universal grammar, and the languages which teach it best are those which . . . provide dis-
tinct forms for the greatest number of distinctions in thought
. . . In these qualities, the classical languages have an incom-
parable superiority over every modern language.[29]

Grammar also served as a discourse of exclusion. For Locke,
knowledge of grammar served to mark the gentleman's class.
In the nineteenth century, it served to mark gender. The logical
analysis defined by Mill as grammar was attempted in boys'
schools,[30] especially the élite grammar and public schools. The
grammar which boys learned was 'the science of language'. The
grammar that girls learned was a catechism of rules.[31]

'Even as mere languages, no modern European language is so
valuable a discipline to the intellect as those of Greece and Rome,
on account of their complicated structure', Mill also declared in his
Inaugural Address.[32] Witnesses to the two Royal Commissions
held the same view: even when it was taught grammatically,
French was not thought to be adequate as a means of mental training. Its 'simple and uniform' sentence structure and its lack of
inflections meant that it could not illustrate many grammatical
principles and 'demand[ed] less thought and ingenuity than
Latin'. The fact that French could be learned 'empirically', by
imitation, proved the point. Imitation was believed to involve no
rational thought since this was how infants were thought to
acquire their mother tongue. Latin grammar, on the other hand,
aimed to train not the tongue but the faculties of the mind. This
was the critical difference: the purpose of classical studies was
expressly *not* to learn to speak in Latin. The education of the
English gentleman is at odds with the learning of French, declared
old Etonian John Walter, for 'a gentleman requires a classical
education and the object of learning modern languages is merely
to speak them'.[33]

THE PROBLEMATIZATION OF THE TONGUE

Why was speaking problematized in the nineteenth century? In
the eighteenth century, the gentleman was produced in conversation, and the cultivation of the gentleman's tongue had been

central to his self-fashioning. At the same time, the tongue had been the focus of a number of problematizations and anxieties, due in part to the slippages between its various meanings – as organ of speech and national language, not to mention 'women's' tongues. One anxiety was that 'too much' conversation with women would effeminate men, another that English would be debilitated and 'enervated' by French. The fop, who embodied both these fears, was characterized by his tongue: a voluble tongue that charmed women, a tongue which aped the French and their language.

On the other hand, taciturnity had also been considered a problem. But, though it was one associated with the English national character, it was English *men*, not women, that were said to be taciturn. The tongue of English women was as 'flexible'[34] as any women's tongue; from Swift to James Fordyce and even Hannah More, English women's verbal talents had been celebrated. Hannah More put it most forcefully:

> In the faculty of speaking well, ladies have such a happy promptitude of turning their slender advantages to account, that there are many who, though they have never been taught a rule of syntax, yet by a quick facility in profiting from the best books and the best company, hardly ever violate one; and who often exhibit an elegant and perspicuous arrangement of style without having studied the laws of composition.[35]

In contrast to women, men were said to lack both ease and elegance of expression. James Fordyce's explanation for this failure had been men's education in the classics. It gave them 'habits of accuracy' which 'often [hamper] the faculties'. This produced – and excused – their awkward and graceless conversation.[36] Thirty years later, in 1799, Hannah More counterposed fluency of tongue to depth and penetration of mind. She claimed that men's very inarticulateness was the testimony of the strength of their mind. Women's voluble tongue and easy conversation, on the other hand, were the evidence *par excellence* of the weakness of theirs. In young women, More asserted, 'speaking accompanies and sometimes precedes reflection; in men, reflection is the antecedent'.[37] It was the strength of men's minds that provided the self-regulation and restraint on their tongues that women lacked constitutionally. Taciturnity, once held to result from the 'Clog upon [the] tongue' of the Englishman,[38] had become the emblem of his self-discipline, and his strength – in other words, of his manliness.

By the middle of the nineteenth century, taciturnity would be transformed into a virtue. It was the 'talent of Silence' that Carlyle celebrated, a silence that characterized his strong and manly heroes.[39] In the nineteenth century, cultivating the tongue did not just fail to strengthen the male mind, it could actually emasculate it.[40] Nothing conveys this so clearly as the belief current at that time that modern languages – languages learned to be spoken – inherently weakened the mind.[41] Only languages which were learned neither *by* nor *for* conversation were appropriate for males.

THE TONGUE AND THE SOCIAL

Cultivating the tongue of the gentleman, a cultural practice of the social, could not be achieved without women, but training boys' mental faculties was a man's job. It required the expertise and authority of schoolmasters. Thus, Eton 'professe[d] to train the mind and to ground boys in that which is the best training of the mind, the classics.' Yet, some masters pointed out disapprovingly, parents, who were 'no judges at all' of 'the best means of training the mind and strengthening the faculties', still thought that French ought to be taught in school because 'a gentleman is scarcely educated' unless he knows French.[42] Criticism of parents was not something new; throughout the eighteenth century, parents, particularly mothers, had been blamed for interfering with their children's education – especially their sons'. What was new was that masters and headmasters were indignant not just because parents apparently underestimated and undervalued the magnitude and significance of the teachers' task but because they confused educational – serious – and social – frivolous – goals. Some parents even sent their sons to Eton mostly for the 'manners and connexions' they might form there, one master complained.[43] In the eighteenth century, the social aptitudes of the gentleman had prevailed over his scholarly attainments. In the nineteenth century, the social was not just at odds with the educational; it was believed to subvert it.

This is even more clear in the criticisms directed at parents of schoolgirls. Parents are 'indifferent' to the 'mental cultivation'

105

of their daughters, reported assistant commissioner Fitch. Governesses had complained to him that parents could not '"see the use of" any subject of instruction except plain rudiments and accomplishments'. Those governesses who strove to improve the quality of their instructions, Fitch concluded, had to do so 'under the great difficulties of parental apathy or discouragement'. Assistant commissioner Bryce commented: 'As to thorough mental training, the formation of intellectual habits and taste, it was not the wish of parents to foster these'.[44] The disparagement of the social also comes across particularly clearly in school mistresses' own testimonies to the Taunton Commission. Asked whether the girls at the North London Collegiate School for Girls learned French 'in an empirical manner, merely to enable them to talk and read in French', Frances Mary Buss declared that no, 'they study the syntax carefully and closely'. This was meant to demonstrate not just the seriousness of her educational purpose and the thoroughness of her instruction, but her contempt, shared by every assistant commissioner, for what had become a merely social accomplishment, French conversation.[45] What was it about conversation that prompted such unanimous condemnation?

CONVERSATION AND NATIONAL CHARACTER REVISITED

Conversation had been celebrated throughout most of the eighteenth century; mixed conversation had epitomized a 'Golden State' of society,[46] and most education and conduct books for both males and females included a chapter or section on its importance and practice. While this might seem to be putting a value on the voice and the tongue, the image of the English gentleman remained one of taciturnity.[47] In my earlier discussion of the taciturnity of Englishmen, I suggested that, although it was seen as a national trait, attitudes to it were at least equivocal. The English 'delight in Silence', had written Addison, but Thomas Wilson had complained about national laziness, and worried that English negligence about their tongue adversely affected the reputation of England as a nation.[48] Indeed, throughout the eighteenth century foreign visitors commented on Englishmen's taciturnity. The English are 'little versed in conversation of mere amusement, being naturally silent', noted the anglophile Abbé Trublet. Taciturnity, and what Abbé Le Blanc called 'that disagreeable bluntness of character', had long been been attributed to Englishmen neglecting the company of ladies. It was not just Frenchmen who maintained that ladies were 'the best school for politeness'.[49] In 1753, a contributor to the *Monthly Review* had declared that 'Commerce with the ladies is the best nursery for those qualities which constitute a man of the world'.[50] But while women's conversation was indispensable to the refinement of the gentleman, it was also dangerous because it was held to be effeminating. This anxiety was inscribed on the tongue.

Because language and national character were thought to be interrelated, taciturnity was held to be a product not just of the English character but of the English language as well. Monosyllabic, it was eminently suited to an 'enemy of Loquacity', observed Addison. At the time, few had agreed with him, arguing, like Swift, that a monosyllabic language was one that had not been polished.[51] By the end of the eighteenth century, however, the monosyllabic English tongue and the taciturnity of its native speakers were fused into a common national trait, manliness. English, a 'plain, rational and monosyllabic tongue' was suited to its 'manly and laconic' speakers. By contrast, French was a language suited only for 'graceful trifling'.[52]

The derogation of the tongue entailed the derogation of tongues. By the end of the eighteenth century, the learning of languages, for so long a central feature of the gentleman's education and the hallmark of his accomplishment, was now rated as an 'insipid occupation to a solid, thinking mind'. Learning to speak a language, asserted John Andrews in 1785, was, after all, only a matter of learning 'combinations of sounds and letters'. In particular, the 'attention to the nicety of diction' necessary for speaking French, 'frequently destroys manliness of thinking.' Though Andrews conceded that this focus on the tongue had 'purified' French, it was something 'judicious Frenchmen' themselves deplored.[53] To be concerned with one's articulation and pronunciation – one's tongue – resonated with connotations of effeminacy. Alexander Jardine even condemned the 'false delicacy' which led

> those who formed the French ... to prefer such combinations of sounds and articulations, as are contrary to the

real principles and mechanical means of full fine expression, and as tend to form such positions and habits of the organs as contract and debilitate them, instead of assisting and fortifying their exertions.[54]

Conversation and fluency of the tongue had been accomplishments valued mainly in the social space, the space where the cultural practices of sociability were to produce the gentleman. Speaking French on the other hand had always been ambiguous, simultaneously valued as an accomplishment and derogated if displayed. In the nineteenth century, French conversation – because it was believed to have no educational value – was not only associated with the social and its display, but fused with it, itself becoming a 'superficial' and 'showy' female accomplishment. Thus, Miss Porson, the virtuous English governess in Catherine Sinclair's moral tale *Female Accomplishments* (1836), holds that reading French is a means of training the female mind but is contemptuous of mere training in tongues, which tells of an education meant only for display in the drawing room.[55] This accounts for the ambiguity of the transformation in the study of French in the nineteenth century. It is not simply the case either that French became gendered or that it lost its prestige and was dismissed as a school subject because, as has been suggested, the educational establishment was 'obsessed' with classical methods and values.[56] It was, I want to argue, as a consequence of the derogation of the tongue that French was split apart and its tongue was severed from its grammar. French was in effect divorced from its 'Frenchness', and to that extent, from its effeminacy. In this divorce, French also became gendered: the split between grammar and tongue was also a split mapped onto gender difference.

In their final report, both the Clarendon and the Taunton Commissions nevertheless recommended that French be taught in schools. But there was one condition: oral work was to be excluded. As Max Müller, Taylorian Professor of Modern Languages and Literature at Oxford, put it, the aim should be to secure 'an accurate knowledge of grammar' and not to attempt 'fluency and the attainment of a perfect accent'. Similar sentiments were expressed by Charles Cassal, Professor of Language and Literature at University College London. In his report to Lord Taunton, he argued that although French lacked 'flexional declensions it had at least a verb which is as complicated almost as the Latin Verb'. It could discipline the mind and ought to be taught 'in a systematic, scientific or philosophical way', just like Latin.[57]

The derogation of the tongue generated not just gender but national difference. If the taciturnity of Englishmen differentiated them from the voluble and shallow sprightliness of English females, it also served to distinguish them from Frenchmen. From an English perspective, there was, in France, no difference between men and women's tongue. Frenchmen's many 'pretty ways of insinuating what they mean[t]' positioned them precisely as opposite to Englishmen's 'forcible and manly ways'.[58] Frenchmen's 'esprit' and brilliance, essential features of their success in the conversation of the *salon* were construed by the English as mere flexibility of the tongue.[59] Their conversational skills, their 'wit and vivacity' suggested that they 'must perhaps be proportionately deficient in judgement'.[60] A caustic comment of Mary Wollstonecraft's sums it up: because, she argues, the French language is 'more adapted to rhetorical flourishes' than other languages,

> The French therefore are all rhetoricians and they have a singular fund of superficial knowledge, caught in the tumult of pleasure from the shallow stream of conversation; so that if they have not the depth of thought which is obtained only by contemplation, they have all the shrewdness of sharpened wit; their acquirements are so near their tongue's end that they never miss an opportunity of saying a pertinent thing, or tripping up, by a smart retort, the argument with which they have not strength fairly to wrestle.[61]

Taciturnity and the restraint of the tongue, on the other hand, were emblematic of the manliness of the English male.

MASCULINITY AND THE SILENCING OF WOMEN'S CONVERSATION

'Of all the various causes which tend to influence our conduct and form our manners, none operate so powerfully as the society of the other sex', wrote William Alexander in 1779. But, he continued,

If perpetually confined to their company, they infallibly stamp upon us the effeminacy, and some other of the signatures of their nature; if constantly excluded from it, we contract a roughness of behaviour, and slovenliness of person, sufficient to point out the loss we have sustained. If we spend a reasonable portion of our time in the company of women, and another in the company of our own sex, it is then only that we imbibe a proper share of the softness of the female, and at the same time retain the firmness and constancy of the male.[62]

If women's conversation could polish the gentleman out of rude nature it could also fashion him into an effeminate 'other'. To 'retain' manliness, as Alexander puts it, men had to remove themselves from women's company and from their conversation and create or maintain a private space in which to preserve their manliness. The 'public' school was one of those private spaces.

In the last decade of the eighteenth century, woman's best 'conversation' was said to be a responsive silence not just because, as Hannah More claimed, it enabled men better to express themselves, but also because, as Thomas Gisborne feared, women's witty tongue might emasculate them.[63] By the nineteenth century, when the education of the male had shifted from the cultivation of his tongue and conversation to the training and disciplining of his mental faculties, women's conversation became superfluous. One critical consequence of the end of conversation as a technology of the self for the gentleman was the silencing of women's conversation.

At the same time as women's verbal conversation was silenced, so too was their active participation in sexual conversation and generation. While the discipline, restraint, absence even, of tongue produced the strength of the male mind, passionlessness produced the strength of the female's.[64] In the early nineteenth century woman's verbal and sexual conversation was disempowered and woman made passive to promote the male by effacing herself. This, in essence, was the Victorian ideal of femininity.

NOTES

PREFACE AND INTRODUCTION

1 The *Guardian*, 6 May 1994, p. 1.
2 The *Guardian*, 6 May 1994, p. 10, my emphasis.
3 This seems to be the assumption of the four-week language course, starting with a 'free audio-tape' offered by *The Observer* newspaper in the week of the inauguration of the Channel Tunnel. The blurb read: 'Many people learn French at school but never use it regularly enough in conversation to achieve fluency. Starting next week, *The Observer* is giving away four pull-out booklets to help people who know a little of the language but need to unlock their conversational skills'.
4 See, for example, H.H. Stern, *Fundamental Concepts of Language Teaching*, Oxford, Oxford University Press, 1984; William T. Littlewood, *Foreign and Second Language Learning: Language Acquisition Research and its Implications for the Classroom*, Cambridge, Cambridge University Press, 1984; Bernard Spolsky, *Conditions for Second Language Learning*, Oxford, Oxford University Press, 1989; E. Halsall, 'Linguistic Aptitude', *Modern Languages*, vol. 50, no. 1, March 1969, pp. 18–23.
5 In 1945, however, one writer noted that in England, 'it isn't "done" to be good at languages' E. Allison Peers, *'New' Tongues*, London, Pitman, 1945, p. 13.
6 Titles of some recent articles convey the tenor of the concern: J. Batters, 'Do Boys Really Think Languages are Just Girl-Talk?', *Modern Languages*, vol. LXVII, 1986, pp. 75–79; R. Loulidi, 'Is Language Learning Really a Female Business?', *Language Learning Journal*, no. 1, March 1990, pp. 40–43. See also Department of Education and Science, *Boys and Modern Languages*, H.M.I Inspection Report, London, 1985.
7 Stephen Greenblatt, *Renaissance Self-Fashioning: from More to Shakespeare*, London, University of Chicago Press, 1980, p. 9.
8 Joan W. Scott, 'Deconstructing Equality-Versus Difference: Or, the Uses of Poststructuralist Theory for Feminism', *Feminist Studies*, 14, no. 1, Spring 1988, p. 35. S.J. Hekman, *Gender and Knowledge: Elements*

111

of a Postmodern Feminism, Oxford, Polity Press, 1990.

9 This book is concerned with conversation, not oratory. The one was a social and the other a political discourse. However, because both required eloquence, there are interesting tensions and overlaps between the two. See, for example, Adam Potkay, 'Classical Eloquence and Polite Style in the Age of Hume', *Eighteenth-Century Studies*, vol. 25, Part 1, 1991, pp. 31–56.

10 As Olivia Smith puts it, 'the belief that the self and language co-existed in a simple and direct relation', *The Politics of Language 1791–1819*, Oxford, Clarendon Press, 1984, p. 21, and John Barrell, *English Literature in History 1730–1780: An Equal, Wide Survey*, London, Hutchinson, 1983.

11 Jim Secord, private communication. Peter Burke makes not a single reference to the tongue in the chapter on conversation in *The Art of Conversation*, Oxford, Polity Press, 1993.

12 Except in particular expressions like 'mother tongue' and 'speaking in tongues', that is in language teaching and religious discourses.

13 Samuel Johnson, *A Dictionary of the English Language*, London, 1755, preface, p. 10.

14 [Richard Allestree], *The Government of the Tongue*, Oxford, 1674; Daniel Defoe, 'An Academy for Women', in *An Essay Upon Projects*, (1697), facsimile reprint, Menston, The Scolar Press, 1969; Thomas Sheridan, *A Rhetorical Grammar of the English Language*, (1781), facsimile reprint, Menston, The Scolar Press, 1969. p. 163; Henry Hooton, *A Bridle for the Tongue*, London, 1709.

15 Lisa Jardine, *Still Harping on Daughters: Women and Drama in the Age of Shakespeare*, Sussex, The Harvester Press, 1983; Marina Warner, *From The Beast to the Blonde: On Fairy Tales and Their Tellers*, London, Chatto & Windus, 1994. The exception is Patricia Parker, 'On the Tongue: Cross Gendering, Effeminacy and the Art of Words', *Style*, vol. 23, no. 3, Fall 1989, pp. 445–465.

16 Barrell, *English Literature in History*; Pat Rogers (ed.), *The Context of English Literature: The Eighteenth Century*, London, Methuen, 1978; Smith, *Politics of Language*; Sterling A. Leonard, *The Doctrine of Correctness in English Usage*, New York, Russell & Russell, 1962.

17 Johnson, preface to the *Dictionary*, p. 14; Thomas Wilson, *The Many Advantages of a Good Language to Any Nation*, London, 1729, p. 36; Thomas Sheridan, *A Dissertation on the Causes of the Difficulties which Occur in Learning the English Tongue*, London, 1762, pp. 212–213. See also Defoe, *Essay Upon Projects* and Jonathan Swift, 'A Proposal for Correcting, Improving and Ascertaining the English Tongue', in T. Roscoe (ed.), *The Works of Jonathan D.D. Swift*, 2 vols, London, Geo. Bell & Sons, 1880.

18 Leonard, *The Doctrine of Correctness*.

19 See L.E. Klein, 'The Rise of "Politeness" in England, 1660–1715', Ph.D. thesis, Baltimore, Johns Hopkins University, 1984. See also Burke, *Art of Conversation*.

20 The tongue was the source of many offences against the conduct of polite conversation – talkativeness, raillery, swearing, licentiousness.

See Allestree, *The Government of the Tongue*; Laurent Bordelon, *La Langue*, Rotterdam, 1705, published in London one year later as *The Management of the Tongue*.

21 John Andrews, *A Comparative View of the French and English Nations in their Manners, Politics, and Literature*, London, 1785, p. 185.

22 Addison, *Spectator*, no. 135; John Andrews, *A Comparative View of the French and English Nations*, pp. 144, 317.

23 This was said throughout the century. See for example Addison, *Spectator* no. 135; Wilson, *Advantages of a Good Language*; *The Connoisseur*, Thursday 16 September 1756; B.N. de Muralt, *Lettres sur les Anglois et les François*, Cologne, 1727; *The Art of Speaking and Holding one's Tongue*, 1761. Rousseau too had noticed, writing 'Nous avons passé une matinée à l'anglaise, réunis dans le silence' [We spent the morning in the English manner, united in silence], Jean-Jacques Rousseau, 'Julie ou La Nouvelle Héloise', in *Oeuvres Complètes*, Paris, Gallimard, 1964, vol. II, 5ième partie, Lettre III, pp. 557–558.

24 Harold E. Palmer, *The Scientific Study and Teaching of Languages*, 1917, reprinted Oxford, Oxford University Press, 1968, p. 166.

25 *Spectator* no. 433.

26 John Millar, *The Origin of the Distinction of Ranks*, London, 1779, pp. 122–123. See also William Alexander, *The History of Women*, 2 vols, London, 1779.

27 Shaftesbury, quoted in George Barker-Benfield, *The Culture of Sensibility: Sex and Society in Eighteenth-Century Britain*, London, University of Chicago Press, 1992, p.117; Joseph Spence, *Letters from the GRAND TOUR 1730–1741*, S. Klima (ed.), London, McGill–Queen's University Press, 1975, pp. 9–10.

28 John Barrell, '"The Dangerous Goddess": Masculinity, Prestige, and the Aesthetic in Early Eighteenth-Century Britain', *The Birth of Pandora and the Division of Knowledge*, London, Macmillan, 1992, p. 75.

29 'The Dangerous Goddess', p. 64. See also L.E. Klein, 'Liberty, manners and politeness in early 18th century England', *The Historical Journal*, 32, no. 3, 1989, pp. 583–605.

30 However, though self-control was always manly, as a virtue, it was available to women as well. See Carolyn D. Williams, *Pope, Homer, and Manliness: Some Aspects of Eighteenth-Century Classical Learning*, London & New York, Routledge, 1993.

31 Marcia Pointon, 'The Case of the Dirty Beau', in K. Adler and M. Pointon (eds), *The Body Imaged: The Human Form of Visual Culture Since the Renaissance*, Cambridge, Cambridge University Press, 1993, pp. 175–189.

32 See David Kuchta, 'The Semiotics of Masculinity in Renaissance England', in James Grantham Turner (ed.), *Sexuality and Gender in Early Modern Europe: Institutions, Texts, Images*, Cambridge, Cambridge University Press, 1993. One historian has been puzzled by the contradiction, noting that 'Frenchmen, *despite* their heightened sexuality, were effeminate, not quite men'. Sheila Cottrell, 'The Devil on Two Sticks: Franco-phobia in 1803', in Raphael Samuel (ed.),

Patriotism: the Making and Unmaking of British National Identity, London & New York, Routledge, 1989, p. 268. (My emphasis).

33 John Sekora, *Luxury: The Concept in Western Thought, from Eden to Smollett*, London, The Johns Hopkins University Press, 1977, p. 75.

34 This relationship is highlighted by John Barrell in 'The Dangerous Goddess'.

35 Sekora, *Luxury*, pp. 48–49. See also Kathleen Wilson, *The Sense of the People: Politics, Culture and Imperialism in England, 1715–1785*, Cambridge, Cambridge University Press, 1995.

36 Barker-Benfield, *The Culture of Sensibility*.

37 Sekora, *Luxury*, p. 75.

38 G.S. Rousseau, 'Sodomy – that utterly confused category' – in R.P. Maccubin, *'Tis Nature's Fault: Unauthorized Sexuality during the Enlightenment*, Cambridge, Cambridge University Press, 1987; Randolph Trumbach, 'The Birth of the Queen: Sodomy and the Emergence of Gender Equality in Modern Culture, 1660–1750', in Martin Duberman, Martha Vicinus and George Chauncey, Jr (eds), *Hidden from History: Reclaiming the Gay and Lesbian Past*, Harmondsworth, Penguin, 1989, p. 493. See also Kristina Straub 'The Guilty Pleasures of Female Theatrical Cross-Dressing and the Autobiography of Charlotte Charke', in Julia Epstein, and Kristina Straub, (eds), *Body Guards: The Cultural Politics of Gender Ambiguity*, London & New York, Routledge, 1991, p. 162.

39 Harriet Guest, 'A Double Lustre: Femininity and Sociable Commerce, 1730–60', *Eighteenth-Century Studies*, vol. 23, no. 4, Summer 1990, p. 482.

40 Wilson, *The Sense of the People*, pp. 72, 185–205.

41 Michel Foucault, *The Archaeology of Knowledge*, London, Tavistock, 1974, p. 151.

42 John Brown, *An Estimate of the Manners and Principles of the Times*, London, 1757, pp. 67, 141; and London, 1758, vol. 2, p. 40.

43 Linda Colley, *Britons: Forging the Nation*, London, Yale University Press, 1992, p. 88. Colley is referring to George Newman, *The Rise of English Nationalism: A Cultural History 1740–1830*, London, Weidenfeld & Nicolson, 1987.

44 James Burgh, *Britain's Remembrancer: or, the Danger is not over*, London 1746, pp. 20, 46. (My emphasis.)

45 Thomas Sheridan defined 'to Frenchify' as 'to infect with the manners of France, to make a coxcomb', *Dictionary*, London, 1780.

46 Colley, *Britons*, p. 90.

47 John Butley, cited in Colley, *Britons*, p. 90; *Spectator*, no. 45.

48 Johnson, *Dictionary*, Sheridan, *Dictionary*; *OED*. See also, Carolyn Williams, *Pope, Homer, and Manliness*, p. 37. Alhough Trumbach has claimed that the first meaning had disappeared by the early eighteenth century, there is evidence this usage was still current at least in the 1740s: see James Burgh, *Britain's Remembrancer: or, the Danger is not over*, London 1846. For a critique of Trumbach's periodization, see Alan Bray, *Homosexuality in Renaissance England*, London, Gay Men's Press, 1982.

49 Epstein and Straub (eds), *Body Guards*, p. 11.
50 Vern L. Bullough and Bonnie Bullough, *Cross-Dressing, Sex, and Gender*, Philadelphia, University of Pennsylvania Press, 1993, p. 124.
51 See Lynne Friedli, '"Passing Women": A Study of Gender Boundaries in the Eighteenth Century' and Terry Castle, 'The Culture of Travesty: Sexuality and Masquerade in Eighteenth Century England', in G.S. Rousseau and R. Porter (eds), *Sexual Underworlds of the Enlightenment*, Manchester, Manchester University Press, 1987.
52 Williams, *Pope, Homer and Manliness*, p. 9.
53 Friedli, ' "Passing Women"', p. 250; R.W. Connell, 'The Big Picture: Masculinities in Recent World History', *Theory and Society*, vol. 22/5, October 1993, p. 608; Michael S. Kimmel, 'The Contemporary "Crisis" of Masculinity in Historical Perspective', in Harry Brod (ed.), *The Making of Masculinities*, London, Allen & Unwin, 1987.
54 What Suzanne Moore calls 'freedom from the binary prison', 'Getting a Bit of the Other – the Pimps of Postmodernism', in R. Chapman and J. Rutherford (eds), *Male Order: Unwrapping Masculinity*, Lawrence and Wishart, 1988, p. 167.
55 As intimated, for example, in Terry Castle's analysis of the *potential* for gender subversion of the masquerade in 'The Culture of Travesty'.
56 Williams, *Pope, Homer and Manliness*, p. 3.
57 Kimmel, 'The Contemporary "Crisis" of Masculinity', p. 127. Arthur Brittan, *Masculinity and Power*, Oxford, Blackwell, 1989. Michael Roper and John Tosh, 'Historians and the Politics of Masculinity', in M. Roper and J. Tosh (eds), *Manful Assertions: Masculinities in Britain since 1800*, London, Routledge, 1991, p. 18.
58 Williams, *Pope, Homer and Manliness*, p. 10. Anthropologist David Gilmore has noted the 'recurrent notion that manhood is problematic' in a variety of cultures and 'at all levels of sociocultural development', *Manhood in the Making: Cultural Concepts of Masculinity*, London, Yale University Press, 1990, p. 11.
59 Roper and Tosh, *Manful Assertions*, p. 18. See also Peter Brown, cited by Ann Rosaling Jones and Peter Stallybrass, 'Fetishizing Gender: Constructing the Hermaphrodite in Renaissance Europe', in Epstein and Straub (eds), *Body Guards*, p. 86. and Fletcher, *Gender, Sex and Subordination*, London, Yale University Press, 1995.
60 Anthony Fletcher, *Gender, Sex and Subordination*, p. 95. See also Michael McKeon, 'Historicizing Patriarchy: The Emergence of Gender Difference in England, 1660–1760', *Eighteenth Century Studies*, vol. 28, no. 3, Spring 1995, pp. 295–322.
61 Barrell, 'The Dangerous Goddess'; Klein, 'Liberty, Manners and Politeness'.
62 *Spectator*, no. 92.
63 See also Parker's discussion of 'national types' in relation to 'excesses of the tongue', 'On the Tongue', p. 448.
64 Andrews, *A Comparative View of the French and English Nations*, p. 72.
65 There has also been some debate about the exact relation between archaeology and genealogy. See J. D. Marshall, 'Foucault and educational research', in S.J. Ball (ed.), *Foucault and Education: Disciplines*

and Knowledges, London, Routledge, 1990.

66 Phil Bevis, Michèle Cohen and Gavin Kendall, 'Archaeologizing genealogy: Michel Foucault and the economy of austerity', in Mike Gane and Terry Johnson (eds), *Foucault's New Domains*, London, Routledge, 1993, p. 194; Julian Henriques, *et al.*, *Changing the Subject: Psychology, Social Regulation and Subjectivity*, London, Methuen, 1984, p. 104; Michel Foucault, 'Nietzsche, genealogy, history', in D.F. Bouchard (ed.), *Language, Counter-Memory, Practice*, Ithaca, Cornell University Press, 1977. Alan Sheridan, *Foucault: The Will to Truth*, London, Tavistock Publications, 1980, p. 104.

67 Peter De Bolla, *Discourses of the Sublime: Readings in History, Aesthetics and the Subject*, Oxford, Basil Blackwell, 1989, pp. 9, 15.

68 See for example J. Black, *The British and the Grand Tour 1713–1793*, London, Croom Helm, 1985; G. Avery, *The Best Type of Girl: A History of Girls' Independent Schools*, London, Deutsch, 1991.

69 Klein, 'The rise of "politeness"'; Peter France, *Politeness and its Discontents: Problems in French Classical Culture*, Cambridge, Cambridge University Press, 1992; David Jarrett, *England in the Age of Hogarth*, London, Yale University Press, 1986.

1 CONVERSATION AND THE CONSTRUCTION OF THE HONNÊTE HOMME IN SEVENTEENTH-CENTURY FRANCE

1 See Alain Montandon, 'De L'Urbanité: Entre Etiquette et Politesse', in Alain Montandon (ed.), *Etiquette et Politesse*, Association des Publications de La Faculté des Lettres et Sciences Humaines de Clermont Ferrand, 1992.

2 Though it was not until the nineteenth century that the term *salon* denoted a space for social gatherings, it has become the practice to use it in early modern studies to refer to the social space in which the seventeenth-century *ruelle* was located. See Dena Goodman, 'Enlightenment salons: the convergence of female and philosophic ambitions,' *Eighteenth-Century Studies*, 22, Spring 1989 pp. 329–350; Erica Harth, *Cartesian Women: Versions and Subversions of Rational Discourse in the Old Régime*, London, Cornell University Press, 1992.

3 A *ruelle* was an alcove-like space in a room where the day bed was placed. See *La Vie Quotidienne des Femmes au Grand Siècle*, Claude Dulongi (ed.), Paris, Hachette, 1984, p. 132. For illustrations of *ruelles* see J. Fowler and J. Cornforth, *English Decoration in the Eighteenth Century*, London, Barrie and Jenkins, 1978; Peter Thornton, *Seventeenth-Century Interior Decoration in England, France and Holland*, London, Yale University Press, 1978.

4 For a discussion of the class composition of the women as well as the men who frequented the *salons*, see Carolyn Lougée, *Le Paradis des Femmes: Women, Salons and Social Stratification in Seventeenth-Century France*, Princeton, Princeton University Press, 1979. See also Michael Moriarty, *Taste and Ideology in Seventeenth-Century France*,

Cambridge, Cambridge University Press, 1988, and Marc Fumaroli, *Le Genre des genres littéraires Français: la conversation*, The Zaharoff Lecture for 1990–91, Oxford, Clarendon Press, 1992.

5 It is crucial to the arguments I develop in this book to distinguish *politesse* from what the English were to call 'French politeness'.

6 Chalesme, cited in Domna C. Stanton, *The Aristocrat as Art: A Study of the Honnête Homme and the Dandy in Seventeenth- and Nineteenth-Century Literature*, New York, Columbia University Press, 1980, p. 139. Claude Favre de Vaugelas, *Remarques sur la Langue Française*, (1647), R. Lagane (ed.), Paris, Larousse, 1975. It was said that women's language was pure because they had not been 'contaminated' by the study of Latin or Greek. See also Dominique Bouhours, 'La Langue Française', in *Entretiens d'Ariste et d'Eugène*, Paris, Brossard, 1920; Wendy Ayres-Bennett, *Vaugelas and the Development of the French Language*, London, The Modern Humanities Research Association, 1987, pp. 14, 198–199.

7 J-P. Dens, *L'Honnête Homme et la Critique du Goût: esthétique et société au XVIIe Siècle*, Lexington, KY, French Forum, 1981, p. 46; Jean-Baptiste Morvan de Bellegarde, *Modèles de conversation pour les personnes polies*, (1697), La Haye, 1719, p. 23.

8 The word *honnête* has no English equivalent, and cannot be translated as 'honest'. It suggests civility and gentlemanliness. Eighteenth-century French language teaching grammars such as Chambaud's *The Art of Speaking French*, Dublin, 1772, noted the idiomatic uses of the term. See also L.E. Klein, 'The rise of "politeness" in England 1660–1715', Ph.D. thesis, Baltimore, Johns Hopkins University, 1984, pp. 75–76.

9 Antoine Gombauld, Chevalier de Méré, *Oeuvres Complètes*, (1668–1677); Charles H. Boudhors (ed.), 3 vols, Paris, Fernand Roches, 1930, vol. III, p. 75. All further references to Méré are from this edition.

10 *Bienséance* refers broadly to social propriety and appropriateness. 'It governs all forms of social practice, including linguistic ones', Moriarty, *Taste and Ideology*, p. 67.

11 See for example Harth, *Cartesian Women*.

12 Thomas Crow, *Painters and Public Life in Eighteenth-Century Paris*, London, Yale University Press, 1985, p. 67; see also Anne Goldgar, *Impolite Learning in Conduct and Community in the Republic of Letters 1680–1750*, Yale University Press, 1995, Moriarty, *Taste and Ideology*, and Stanton, *Aristocrat as Art*.

13 Méré, *Oeuvres*, III, p. 70.

14 'L'Urbanité . . . est un assemblage de plusieurs manières aisées et délicates . . . et qui est directement opposé à la rusticité'. [Urbanity . . . is a collection of easy and delicate manners . . . and is the exact opposite of rusticity], Antoine Renaud, *Manière de Parler*, Paris, 1697, p. 144. According to Jean-Louis Guez de Balzac, it was 'the science of conversation and the ability to please in good company', cited in Daniel Gordon, *Citizens Without Sovereignty: Equality and Sociability in French Thought, 1670–1789*, Princeton, Princeton University Press, 1994.

15 Jean Baptiste Morvan de Bellegarde, *Réflexions sur ce qui peut plaire ou déplaire dans le commerce du monde*, Paris, 1690, p. 281.
16 Méré, *Oeuvres*, III, p. 88.
17 Méré, *Oeuvres*, III, pp. 70, 78. See also Moriarty, *Taste and Ideology*.
18 Méré, *Oeuvres*, I, p. 21; III, p. 72. See also L.K. Horowitz, *Love and Language: A Study of the Classical French Moralist Writers*, Columbus, OH, Ohio State University Press, 1977.
19 Bouhours' 'entretien' on the meaning of the *je ne sais quoi* illustrates what Moriarty terms 'the deliberate vagueness of the dominant cultural discourse'. Le *'Je ne sais quoi'*, argues Bouhours 'ne serait plus un je ne sais quoi si l'on savait ce que c'est' [the *je ne sais quoi* would not be an 'I don't know what' if we knew what it was], Bouhours, *Entretiens d'Ariste et d'Eugène*, p. 247; Moriarty, *Taste and Ideology*, p. 163.
20 Maurice Magendie, *La politesse mondaine et les théories de l'honnêteté en France de 1600 à 1660*, Paris, Presses Universitaires de France, 1925.
21 Paris, 1630.
22 Stanton, *Aristocrat as Art*, p. 11.
23 Stanton, *Aristocrat as Art*; Moriarty, *Taste and Ideology*.
24 Michel Foucault, 'The concern for truth', in L.D. Kritzman (ed.), *Michel Foucault: Politics, Philosophy, Culture: Interviews & other writings of Michel Foucault 1977–1984*, London, Routledge, 1988, p. 259. For a different perspective on the same question, see S. Greenblatt, *Renaissance Self-Fashioning: From More to Shakespeare*, Chicago, University of Chicago Press, 1980.
25 Méré, *Oeuvres*, III, p. 121.
26 Gérard Genette notes that for half of the seventeenth century, *l'Astrée* was, both at Court and in Town, 'le bréviaire des sentiments et des bonnes manières' (the Bible of sentiments and good manners), 'Le Serpent dans la Bergerie', *Figures I*, Paris, Seuil, 1966, p. 109. See also Magendie, *Politesse mondaine*.
27 Madeleine de Scudéry, *Clélie, Histoire Romaine*, Paris, 1658–66, Book II, part 3, pp. 1381–1382.
28 Méré, *Oeuvres*, II, p. 81.
29 In French, to be tongue-tied is *perdre sa langue*, literally to 'lose one's tongue'.
30 Méré, *Oeuvres*, III, pp. 74–75.
31 Moriarty, *Taste and Ideology*, p. 101.
32 Horowitz, *Love and Language*, p. 26.
33 See Act III Scene 1 in Molière's 'Les Femmes Savantes', where the expectation of Trissotin's poem sends Philaminte, Bélise and Armande, the three *femmes savantes*, into an erotic paroxysm resulting in symbolic consummation, fecundation and the 'birth' of his poem. It is because they have misunderstood the relation between love and language that they are ridiculous.
34 Kritzman, *Michel Foucault*, p. 259.
35 Moriarty, *Taste and Ideology*, pp. 99–100. Moriarty himself does not elaborate on this topic.
36 Nicolas Faret, *L'Art de plaire à la cour*, Paris, 1630; François de La

Rochefoucauld, *Maximes et Réflexions*, (1662), Paris, 1965; Jacques Du Bosc, *L'Honneste Femme*, Lyon, 1665; René Bary, *Journal de conversation*, Paris, 1674; Madeleine de Scudéry, *Les Conversations sur divers sujets*, Amsterdam, 1686; Jean de La Bruyère, *Les Caractères ou les moeurs de ce siècle*, (1688), Paris, Garnier Frères 1962; Pierre Ortigue de Vaumorière, *L'Art de la conversation*, Paris, 1690; Morvan de Bellegarde, *Modèles de conversation*.

37 As in Antoine Baudeau de Somaize's *Dictionnaire des Précieuses*, (1661), Charles-L. Livet (ed.), Paris, H. Welter, 1856. On verbal portraits in the seventeenth century, see Erica Harth, *Ideology and Culture in Seventeenth-Century France*, London, Cornell University Press, 1983. See also Stanton, *Aristocrat as Art*.

38 Baldessare Castiglione, *The Book of the Courtier*, Eng. trans., Harmondsworth, Penguin, 1967, pp. 76–81, 213–214; Faret, *L'Art de Plaire*, pp. 88–89.

39 Morvan de Bellegarde, *Modèles de conversation*, p. 3.

40 Scudéry, 'De la Conversation' in *Les Conversations*, p. 1; Vaumorière, *L'Art de plaire*; see also Jean Pierre Dens, 'L'Art de la Conversation au Dix-Septième Siècle', *Les Lettres Romanes*, vol. 27, 1973.

41 Méré wrote 'Il ... faut ... bien dire et bien faire pour être *honnête homme*' [To be an *honnête homme* one must speak well and act properly], *Oeuvres*, I, p. 46; see also Dens *L'Honnête Homme*.

42 'Il n'y a rien de plus juste, de plus propre et de plus naturel que le langage de la plupart des Françaises'. [There is nothing so right, proper and natural as the language of French women], Bouhours, *Entretiens*, p. 57.

43 Morvan de Bellegarde, *Modèles de conversation*, p. 225.

44 Bouhours, *Entretiens*; Stanton, *Aristocrat as Art*.

45 All of the *auteurs mondains* agreed that women were central to the process, notes Dens, 'L'Art de la Conversation', p. 142; See also Stanton, *Aristocrat as Art*; Peter France, *Politeness and its Discontents: Problems in French Classical Culture*, Cambridge, Cambridge University Press, 1992.

46 Antoine Furetière, quoted by R. Duchêne, 'Honnêteté et Sexualité', in Y-M. Bercé (ed.), *Destins et Enjeux du XVIIième Siècle*, Paris, Presses Universitaires de France, 1985, p. 120. I am deliberately avoiding the use of the terms 'public' and 'private' to describe this gender difference.

47 François de Grenaille, quoted in Ian Maclean, *Woman Triumphant: Feminism in French Literature 1610–1652*, Oxford, Clarendon Press, 1977, p. 125.

48 Du Bosc, *L'Honneste Femme*, part 3, p. 376.

49 Robert A. Nye, *Masculinity and Male Codes of Honour in Modern France*, Oxford, Oxford University Press, 1993; see also Dens, *L'Honnête Homme*.

50 'De parler trop ou trop peu et comment il faut parler', *Choix de Conversations de Mademoiselle de Scudéry*, P.J. Wolfe (ed.), Ravenna, Longo, 1977, p. 36.

51 Morvan de Bellegarde, *Modèles de conversation*.

52 Du Bosc, *L'Honneste Femme*, p. 35. This, from a man who has been taken to represent the 'feminist' tendency in the seventeenth century, principally because of his support for women's education. See Carolyn Lougée, *Paradis des Femmes*, and Maclean, *Woman Triumphant*.

53 Scudéry, *Conversations sur divers sujets*, p. 6.

54 Wolfe (ed.), *Choix de Conversations*, p. 28.

55 Morvan de Bellegarde, *Modèles de conversation*, p. 230.

56 The notion of *bagatelles* illustrates the paradox of women's talk: the ability to talk agreeably about the most trifling topics as well as the most serious ones was the essence of good conversation, a testimony to the achievement of the *honnête homme*. However, women on their own talking about *bagatelles* served to confirm their shallowness and triviality.

57 Bellegarde, *Réflexions*, p. 280. See also pp. 348 and 362.

58 Scudéry, *Conversations sur divers sujets*, 1686; Bellegarde, *Réflexions*; Faret, *Art de plaire*; Du Bosc, *L'Honneste Femme*.

59 Scudéry, *Conversations sur divers sujets*, 1686, p. 7.

60 For Méré, for example, 'Esprit consiste à comprendre les choses ... à juger nettement ce qu'elles sont, et de leur juste valeur, à discerner ce que l'une a de commun avec l'autre, et ce qui l'en distingue ...' [Esprit consists in understanding what things are, judging clearly what they are, and their value, in discerning what things have in common and how they differ ...] 'De L'Esprit', in *Oeuvres*, vol. II, p. 64.

61 Du Bosc, *L'Honneste Femme*, p. 42.

62 Stanton, *Aristocrat as Art*, p. 139. Christopher Strosetzki has argued that the *honnête homme* is 'grafted' onto women: his desire to please women copies the desire usually attributed to women to want to please men. *Rhétorique de la Conversation: sa dimension littéraire et linguistique dans la société française du XVIIe siècle*, Paris, Biblio 17, 1984, p. 144. The concern that commerce with women might soften men's courage was raised only to be dismissed by Bellegarde, who argued that the desire to please eliminated only the brutal and ferocious aspects of that courage. See Morvan de Bellegarde, *Modèles de conversation*, p. 236.

63 The gap betwen *être* and *paraître* concerned Méré and most other seventeenth-century authors, and was, according to Stanton, 'the central and most obsessive problem in *honnêteté*'. Stanton, *Aristocrat as Art*, pp. 8, 187. See also Dens, *L'Honnête Homme*.

64 Stanton, *Aristocrat as Art*, p. 96; One of the qualities indispensable to *honnêteté* was 'ce génie qui pénètre ce qui se passe de plus secret' [the genius which penetrates the innermost secrets], Méré, *Oeuvres*, III, p. 72 and *passim*. For a discussion of the gender of 'genius' in the early modern period, see Christine Battersby, *Gender and Genius: Towards a Feminist Aesthetics*, London, The Women's Press, 1994. The terms 'genius' and 'penetration', used again and again by Méré, illustrate Joan Scott's concept of gendered coding, which she discusses in 'Gender: a useful category for historical analysis', *American Historical Review*, 91, November 1986, pp. 1053–1075.

65 Antoine Baudeau de Somaize, in the introduction to his *Dictionnaire des Précieuses*, presented them as beings from a foreign land, a sort of Amazon country where women reigned. He claimed his book would disclose their history, give a summary of their origins and customs, and a description of their Estates, Empire, cities etc. *Le Dictionnaire des Précieuses* (1661), Charles-L. Livet (ed.), Paris 1856. Michel de Pure introduced *'la prétieuse'* as 'un animal d'une espèce autant bizzare qu'inconnue' [an animal of a weird and unknown species], *La Prétieuse ou le mystère des ruelles*, 2 vols, (1656–58), Emile Magne (ed.), Droz, Paris, 1938, Première Partie, p. 62. See also Mlle de Montpensier, 'Portraits des Précieuses', in Edouard de Barthelémy (ed.), *La Galerie des Portraits de Melle de Montpensier*, Paris, Didier, 1860.

66 Barthelémy, *Galerie des Portraits*. Méré, *Oeuvres*, III, p. 79.

67 Somaize, *Dictionnaire des Précieuses*, p. 23; Somaize also defines 'une *précieuse* véritable' (a true *précieuse*) as 'Une vieille fille qui a de l'esprit', (a witty old maid) and 'une *précieuse* ridicule' as 'une fille coquette et qui veut passer pour un bel esprit' (a coquette who wishes to be thought witty). *Le Grand Dictionnaire des PRECIEUSES ou la clef de la langue des Ruelles*, Paris, 1661, p. 29. The association of *précieuses* with age has echoes in the early satires of the modern women's movement: only old women, women whom men no longer want, could possibly wish to be identified with female groups.

68 As Pelous puts it, no woman could declare that she was a *précieuse* and be proud of it. J.-M. Pelous, *Amour précieux, amour galant 1654–1675*, Paris, Klincksieck, 1980, p. 373. See also Domna Stanton, 'The fiction of *préciosité* and the fear of women', *Yale French Studies*, vol. 62, 1981, pp. 107–134.

69 See Molière's 'Les Précieuses Ridicules', 1662 and 'Les Femmes Savantes', 1672. Discernment is a mental trait that particularly distinguishes the *honnête homme*. The *précieuses* in Molière's plays and in Somaize's 'Les Véritables Précieuses' have no discernment: they cannot tell the mask from the essence, the *paraître* from the *être*, and they judge a man's mind by the state of the clothes he wears. Somaize, 'Les Véritables Précieuses', in G. Mongrédien (ed.), *Comédies et Pamphlets sur Molière*, Paris, Nizet, 1986.

70 Although St Evremont suggested that they might enjoy the pleasures of love in each other's arms, cited in Pelous, *Amour précieux*, p. 337. La Carte de Tendre is an allegorical map of the itinerary of the affections invented by Madeleine de Scudéry. See N. Aronson, *Mademoiselle de Scudéry ou le voyage au Pays de Tendre*, Paris, Fayard, 1986.

71 They are referred to as 'des vieilles pucelles' – literally old virgins – in 'La Déroute des Précieuses', in V. Fournel (ed.), *Les Contemporains de Molière: recueil de comédies rares ou peu connues jouées de 1650 à 1680*, Paris, Firmin Didot Frères, 1863, vol. 1, p. 505.

72 Pelous, *Amour précieux*, p. 311.

73 Charles Sorel, *La Connaissance des bons livres*, (1671), quoted in Stanton, 'Fiction of *Préciosité*', p. 112.

74 Pelous and Stanton also list the large number of texts about *précieuses*

that appeared at the time.

75 Maclean, for one, was convinced, and claims that the utterances of the *précieuses* were 'faithfully recorded' by de Pure. See Maclean, *Woman Triumphant* p. 118. According to Harth, however, de Pure was a 'notoriously unreliable commentator on the *salons*'. *Cartesian Women*, p. 35. Somaize's *Grand Dictionnaire* too was 'taken as gospel' by literary historians. (Stanton, 'Fiction of *Préciosité*', p. 127).

76 'La Prétieuse de soi n'a point de définition', de Pure, *La Pretieuse*, Première Partie, p. 67.

77 This is particularly important given the concern to distinguish the 'true' from the 'false' or 'ridiculous' *précieuse*, both in the seventeenth century and in the subsequent historiography. See Stanton, 'Fiction of *Préciosité*'.

78 Charles-L. Livet, *Précieux et Précieuses: caractères et moeurs littéraires du XVIIième siècle*, Paris, H. Welter, 1856; Aronson, *Mademoiselle de Scudéry*; R. Lathuillère, *La préciosité: Etude historique et linguistique*, Geneva, Droz, 1966; E. Avigdor, *Coquettes et précieuses*, Paris, Nizet, 1982. See also Harth, *Cartesian Women*.

79 Y. Fukui, *Raffinement précieux dans la poésie Française du XVIIe Siècle*, Paris, Nizet, 1964; R. Bray, *La préciosité et les Précieux*, Paris, Nizet, 1968; Stanton notes that in literary history the *précieux* becomes 'masculinized and progressively valorized as a poetic tendency effacing the "female specificity" of la *précieuse*'. See 'Fiction of *Préciosité*', p. 110.

80 Lougée, *Paradis des Femmes*, Maclean, *Woman Triumphant*; Dulong, *La Vie quotidienne*. This is possible only if the *précieuses* are conflated with one of their representations, the *femme savante*, as Pelous also notes in *Amour précieux*, p. 353.

81 Harth, *Cartesian Women*, p. 43. In her analysis of the *précieuses*' dissent, Harth too has reduced them to a unitary, homogeneous figure, that of 'learned women'.

82 Mongrédien, *Comédies et Pamphlets*, p. 22. Thus, even if one ignored the derisory association of *précieuse* and 'vieille fille', Somaize's entry concerning the ampersand – or rather its absence, abolished by the *précieuses* because they refuse any 'conjunction', an allusion to their sexual prudery – should be sufficient to make one wonder how the *Grand Dictionnaire des Précieuses* could possibly have been treated as a serious record. At the same time, there is an ambiguity: most of the portraits Somaize drew of '*précieuses*' in his *Dictionnaire Historique* are not satires, on the contrary. These portraits laud women (and some men) for their learning and their conversation.

83 Stanton, 'Fiction of *Préciosité*', p. 113.

84 Pelous, *Amour précieux*, p. 366; Stanton, 'Fiction of *Préciosité*,' p. 113.

85 Du Bosc, *L'Honneste Femme*, p. 30. Their opposite are vices, especially *babil*, i.e. chatter.

86 Pelous, *Amour précieux*, p. 355.

87 De Pure, *La Prétieuse*, p. xxxvii.

88 Stanton, 'The Fiction of *Préciosité*', pp. 127, 129.

89 See Stanton, 'The Fiction of *Préciosité*'. In the eighteenth century

Molière's 'Les Femmes Savantes' and 'Les Précieuses Ridicules' were said to have administered the fatal blow by ridicule to the 'sect', as the *précieuses* were also known. In England, John Andrews claimed that Molière 'drew so faithful and striking a portrait of that species of foible, that a general correction was almost instantaneously effected by them'. *Remarks on the French and English Ladies*, London, 1783, p. 26.

90 What Lougée characterized as their wanting 'the traditional prerogatives of the aristocratic male', *Paradis des Femmes*, p. 25.

91 See, for example, the story of Isotta Nogarola, in Anthony Grafton and Lisa Jardine, *From Humanism to the Humanities*, London, Duckworth, 1986, and Lisa Tickner's discussion of hysteria in relation to women's struggle for the vote in *The Spectacle of Women: Imagery of the Suffrage Campaign 1907–14*, London, Chatto and Windus, 1987.

92 The *honnête homme* must always be desirable and desired: he must be 'souhaité partout' (desired everywhere). Méré, *Oeuvres*, III, p. 74. However, Ninon de Lenclos, the seventeenth-century courtesan, earned the honour of being called an *honnête homme*. See Duchêne, 'Honnêteté et Sexualité', in Bercé (ed.), *Destins and Enjeux*, pp. 129–130.

93 Stanton, 'The Fiction of *Préciosité*' p. 126.

94 Méré, *Oeuvres*, II, 75; Morvan de Bellegarde, *Modèles de conversation* and *Réflexions*.

95 The analogy between woman's tongue and her sexuality has been noted by L. Jardine in *Still Harping on Daughters: Women and Drama in the Age of Shakespeare*, Sussex, The Harvester Press, 1983. P.-G. Boucé points out that the unbridled tongue evokes women's rapacious and unbridled sexuality, one of the 'major sexual myths traceable in many medical handbooks'; 'Some sexual beliefs and myths in eighteenth-century Britain', in P.-G Boucé (ed.), *Sexuality in Eighteenth-Century Britain*, Manchester, Manchester University Press, 1982, pp. 41–42. Ann Rosalind Jones discusses the tensions around women's conversation in the courtly ideal of conduct, 'Nets and bridles: early modern conduct books and sixteenth-century women's lyrics', in Nancy Armstrong and Leonard Tennenhouse (eds), *The Ideology of Conduct: Essays on Literature and the History of Sexuality*, London, Methuen, 1987.

96 See Scudéry's portrait of Mme de Rambouillet as Arténice in *Célinte, Nouvelle Première*, (1661), A. Niderst (ed.), Paris, 1979, p. 53. Madame de Rambouillet is held up as the ideal, the best model of a pure, true *précieuse*, in comparison with whom all emulations are but degenerate imitations. 'Mme de Rambouillet est le type le plus pur et le plus élevé de la vraie précieuse dans le meilleur sens du mot', Livet, *Précieux et Précieuses*, p. xxxiv; Stanton argues, however, that the 'binary model' of the *précieuses* has the 'rhetorical function of underscoring the rarity of the pure and the overwhelming predominance of the ridiculous *précieuse*'. See Stanton, 'The Fiction of *Préciosité*', p. 111.

97 See Peter France, *Politeness*, chapter 4.

98 A vicious example is provided in Somaize's *Les Véritables Précieuses*. In the play-within-the-play 'La mort de Lusse-tu-cru lapidé par les femmes' (the death of Lusse-tu-cru stoned by women), Lusse-tu-cru complains that he is being persecuted by 'La femme acariâtre' (the shrewish woman) and 'sa langue maudite et empestée' (her cursed and foul tongue). An extra dimension to the story is provided by a gruesome illustration: Lusse-tu-cru is the *opérateur céphalique*: husbands bring him their wives' heads which they want reformed because they talk too much. He operates on them with a hammer, on an anvil. The workshop is full of decapitated women's heads. 'Tableau de lustrucru', in E. Fournier *Variétés Historiques et Littéraires* vol. 9, pp. 79–89. See also Marina Warner, *From the Beast to the Blonde: On Fairy Tales and Their Tellers*, London, Chatto and Windus, 1994, pp. 27–29.

2 THE ENGLISH GENTLEMAN AND HIS TONGUE

1 In this book I use the term 'gentleman' to refer primarily to the man of rank after the manner of Swift and Chesterfield. See Jonathan Swift, 'An Essay on Modern Education', in T. Roscoe (ed.), *The Works of Jonathan D.D. Swift*, London, George Bell & Sons, 1880, vol. 2, p. 291; Stanhope Philip Dormer, Earl of Chesterfield, *Letters to his Son*, 1737–1768, (1774), London, W. W. Gibbings, 1890, Letter CCXIV. At the same time, as scholars writing about the early modern period have noted, the term remains imprecise: see J.A. Sharpe, *Early Modern England: A Social History 1550–1760*, London, Edward Arnold, 1987; John Barrell, *English Literature in History 1730–1780: An Equal, Wide Survey*, London, Hutchinson, 1983. See also Peter Borsay, *The English Urban Renaissance: Culture and Society in the Provincial Town, 1660–1770*, Oxford, Clarendon Press, 1991.

2 John Locke, *Some Thoughts Concerning Education*, (1693), J.W. and J.S. Yolton (eds), Oxford, Clarendon Press, 1989, pp. 240–241. All further references to Locke will be from this edition.

3 Locke, *Some Thoughts*, pp. 226, 244.

4 Locke, *Some Thoughts*, pp. 216, 217, 244. R.C. Stephens, The Courtly Tradition in English Education from Sir Thomas Elyot to John Locke, , Ph.D. thesis, University of Belfast, 1955.

5 W.A.L. Vincent, *The Grammar Schools: Their Continuing Tradition, 1660–1714*, London, Murray, 1969; Nicholas Hans, *New Trends in Education in the Eighteenth Century*, London, Routledge & Kegan Paul, 1966; Richard S. Tompson, *Classics or Charity? The Dilemma of the 18th-Century Grammar School*, Manchester, Manchester University Press, 1971.

6 Locke, *Some Thoughts*, p. 207; *Spectator*, no. 168. For a different perspective on this question, see 'Latin language study as a Renaissance puberty rite', in W.J. Ong (ed.) *Rhetoric, Romance and Technology: Studies in the Interaction of Expression and Culture*, Ithaca, Cornell University Press, 1971.

NOTES

7 John Clarke, *An Essay Upon the Education of Youth in Grammar Schools*, London, 1720, pp. 9–10. *Spectator* no. 230. Locke opposed all language teaching by rule, and recommended the conversational method for teaching even Latin.

8 This charge recurred throughout the eighteenth century. Daniel Defoe, for example, complained that it was the 'Scandal of our Nation' that young gentlemen can 'neither express themselves fluently upon any subject or write elegantly in their mother tongue'. He attributed this to their being expected to declaim in Latin or Greek. *The Compleat English Gentleman*, (c. 1728), Karl D. Bühlbring (ed.), London, 1890, pp. 198, 218, 222. In 1770, James Fordyce attributed men's awkward and graceless conversation to their classical education; *Sermons to Young Women*, London, 1770, p. 153; see also chapter 7 below.

9 Michel Foucault, 'The concern for truth', in L.D. Kritzman (ed.), *Michel Foucault, Politics, Philosophy, Culture: Interviews and Other Writings of Michel Foucault 1977–1984*, London, Routledge, 1988, p. 257. See also Robert Castel, '"Problematization" as a mode of reading history', in Jan Goldstein (ed.), *Foucault and the Writing of History*, Oxford, Basil Blackwell, 1994.

10 L.E. Klein, 'The Rise of "Politeness" in England, 1660–1715'. Ph.D. thesis, Baltimore, Johns Hopkins University, 1984 and 'Liberty, manners and politeness in early 18th-century England', *The Historical Journal*, 32, no. 3, 1989, pp. 583–605.

11 See for example, Peter Burke, *The Fabrication of Louis XIV*, London, Yale University Press, 1992.

12 See also Barrell, *English Literature in History*.

13 Locke, *Some Thoughts*, pp. 225, 244. S.A. Leonard has argued that throughout the eighteenth century grammarians were writing to 'warn' gentlemen against 'inadvertent contamination with the language of the vulgar', and cites Philip Withers who declared in 1788 that 'Purity and Politeness of expression. . .is the only external Distinction which remains between a Gentleman and a Valet; a Lady and a Mantua maker.' Sterling Andrus Leonard, *The Doctrine of Correctness in English Usage*, New York, Russell and Russell, 1962, p. 169. A. Lane, *A Key to the Art of Letters or English as a Learned Language*, London, 1706, introduction, p. x.

14 See for example Locke, *Some Thoughts*; Daniel Defoe, 'Of Academies', in *An Essay Upon Projects*, (1697), Facsimile Reprint, Menston, The Scolar Press, 1969; Thomas Sheridan, *A Rhetorical Grammar of the English Language*, (1781), Facsimile Reprint, Menston, The Scolar Press, 1969.

15 See Klein, 'The Rise of "Politeness"'.

16 Defoe, 'Of Academies', pp. 233, 250; Thomas Sprat, in Thomas Stackhouse, *Reflections on the Nature and Property of Languages*, London, 1731, and Jonathan Swift, 'A Proposal for Correcting, Improving and Ascertaining the English Tongue', in *Works*. For a discussion of earlier proposals for academies, see Joel Reed, 'Academically speaking, language and nationalism in seventeenth-

and eighteenth-century England', Ph.D thesis, University of California, Irvine, 1991. See also Barrell, *English Literature in History*, especially chapter 2, and John Cannon, *Samuel Johnson and the Politics of Hanoverian England*, Oxford, Clarendon Press, 1994.

17 A. Baugh, *A History of the English Language*, London, 1959; reprinted (revised) by Routledge in 1993.

18 Michel Foucault, *Archaeology of Knowledge*, (1969), London, Tavistock, 1972.

19 The Accademia della Crusca was founded in Florence in 1532, and its dictionary, the *Vocabolario degli Accademici della Crusca* was first published in 1612. The Académie Française was set up by Cardinal Richelieu in 1635. In 1673, it adopted a standard spelling, and its dictionary, the *Dictionnaire de l'Académie* was first published in 1694.

20 Baugh, *History*, pp. 306, 308, 316, 344.

21 Locke, *Some Thoughts*, p. 241.

22 Swift, 'Hints Towards an Essay on Conversation', in *Works*, vol. 2, p. 294. See also Klein's remarks on Swift and politeness, L.E. Klein, *Shaftesbury and the Culture of Politeness: Moral Discourse and Cultural Politics in Early Eighteenth-Century England*, Cambridge, Cambridge University Press, 1994.

23 *An Essay in Defense of the Female Sex*, London, 1697. The authorship of the *Essay* is still disputed: according to Ruth Perry, Mary Astell's biographer, when the *Essay* was first published, it was attributed to Mary Astell, but Perry has no doubt that its author is Judith Drake; see R. Perry, *The Celebrated Mary Astell: An Early English Feminist*, London, University of Chicago Press, 1986. Hannah More, *Strictures on The Modern System of Female Education, with a View of the Principles and Conduct Prevalent among Women of Rank*, 2 vols, (1799), London, 1811.

24 See for instance Dominique Bouhours, 'La Langue Française' in *Entretiens d'Ariste et d'Eugène*, (1671), Paris, Brossard, 1920, and Marc Fumaroli, 'Animus et Anima : L'instance féminine dans l'apologétique de la langue Française au XVIIe Siècle', *XVIIième Siècle*, no. 144, July-September 1984, pp. 233–240.

25 Because they did not usually learn Latin. Locke, *Some Thoughts*, pp. 224–225; More, *Strictures*, vol. II, p. 59.

26 James Greenwood, *An Essay Towards a Practical English Grammar*, London, 1711, introduction.

27 [Mary Wray], *The Ladies Library*, published by Sir Richard Steele, London, 1722, pp. 12, 16.

28 'How can [ladies] without blushing be in Company guilty of Errors . . .' Wray, *Ladies Library*, p. 11.

29 Greenwood, *Practical English Grammar*.

30 Charles Gildon and John Brightland, *A Grammar of the English Tongue*, (1711), Facsimile reprint, Menston, The Scolar Press, 1967, Preface. It is interesting to note Locke's remark that a boy's mother 'ignorant of Rhetoric and Logic' usually 'out does' a 'Country School-Master' in teaching her son to express himself 'handsomely' in English, *Some Thoughts*, p. 243.

31 Thomas Wilson, *The Many Advantages of a Good Language to Any Nation*, London, 1729, p. 38. Thomas Wilson was the Bishop of Sodor and Man; [Mary Wray] *Ladies Library*, p. 12.

32 For France, see the discussion of Du Bosc's metaphor of the architect, chapter 1 above, and Morvan de Bellegarde, *Modèles de conversation pour les personnes polies*, 1697; for England, see also Carolyn D. Williams, *Pope, Homer, and Manliness: Some Aspects of Eighteenth-Century Classical Learning*, London, Routledge, 1993.

33 Swift, Introduction to 'A Compleat Collection of Genteel and Ingenious Conversation', *Works*, vol. 2, p. 328.

34 *Essay in Defense of the Female Sex*, p. 144.

35 [Mary Wray], *Ladies Library*, pp. 36–37, 117.

36 [Richard Allestree], *The Government of the Tongue*, Oxford, 1674, p. 10.

37 [Mary Wray], *Ladies Library*, pp. 121–122.

38 Defoe, 'An Academy for Women', in *Essays*, pp. 294–295.

39 [Mary Wray], *Ladies Library*, pp. 117, 118–119; Defoe, 'An Academy for Women', p. 73.

40 Bathsua Makin, *Essay to Revive the Antient Education of Gentlewomen, in Religion, Manners, Arts and Tongues, with an Answer to the Objections against this Way of Education*, London, 1673, p. 11. Defoe also exploited that ambiguity when, having recommended that women be taught French and Italian, he explained that in this case, he 'would venture the Injury of giving a Woman more Tongues than one'. 'An Academy for Women', p. 292. 'The Anatomy of a Woman's Tongue', divided women's tongue into five parts: A Medicine, a Poison, a Serpent, Fire and Thunder, (1638), *The Harleian Miscellany*, vol. 1, London, 1744, p. 167; see also Lisa Jardine, *Still Harping on Daughters: Women and Drama in the Age of Shakespeare*, Brighton, Harvester Press, 1983, chap. 4.

41 John Essex, *The Young Ladies Conduct, or Rules for Education*, London, 1722, pp. 12–14.

42 David Jarrett, *England in the Age of Hogarth*, London, Yale University Press, 1986, p. 107; see also William Alexander, *The History of Women from the Earliest Antiquity to the Present Time*, 2 vols, London, 1779.

43 *Spectator*, no. 135; see also [John Constable], *The Conversation of Gentlemen*, London, 1738; B.N. de Muralt, *Lettres sur les Anglois et les François*, Cologne, 1727; Abbé Trublet, *Essays Upon Several Subjects of Literature and Morality*, 3 vols, London, 1744; *The Connoisseur*, September 16, 1756, to cite a few. A satirical tract, *The Art of Speaking and Holding one's Tongue in and out of Doors*, London, 1761, claimed that foreigners commonly associated taciturnity with the Englishman, whom they saw as 'a pensive Animal, so deeply immerged (sic) in Thought and Spleen that Nothing but repeated Draughts of strong Liquor can raise his Spirits, or render him sufficiently vivacious to express his Ideas for any Length of Time', p. 1.

44 Chauncey Brewster Tinker, *The Salon and English Letters*, New York, Macmillan and Co., 1915, p. 134. Sir N. William Wraxall, *Historical Memoirs of My Own Time*, 2 vols, London, 1815, Part the First, from

1772 to 1780, pp. 155–160. See also Feuillet de Conches, *Les salons de conversation au dix-huitième siècle*, Paris, Charavay Frères, 1882; L.E. Klein, 'Gender, conversation and the public sphere', in J. Stills and M. Worton (eds), *Textuality and Sexuality: Reading Theories and Practices*, Manchester, Manchester University Press, 1992.

45 Pierre Jean Grosley, *A Tour to London*, London, 1772, pp. 251–252; C.H. Lockitt, *The Relations of French and English Society*, London, Longmans, Green and Co., 1920, p. 33.

46 M. Girouard, *Life in the English Country House*, London, Yale University Press, 1978, pp. 204–205. See also J. Fowler and J. Cornforth, *English Decoration in the 18th Century*, London, Barrie and Jenkins, 1978; C. Saumarez-Smith, *Eighteenth-Century Decoration: Design and the Domestic Interior in England*, London, Weidenfeld & Nicolson, 1993; Benedetta Craveri, *Madame Du Deffand and her World*, London, Peter Halban, 1994; Annik Pardailhé-Galabrun, *La naissance de l'intime: 3000 foyers parisiens XVIIe-XVIIIe siècles*, Paris, Presses Universitaires de France, 1988.

47 *Spectator*, no. 135.

48 *The Many Advantages of a Good Language*, p. 36. For a discussion of the meaning of 'spleen', see William B. Ober, 'Eighteenth Century Spleen', in C. Fox (ed.), *Psychology and Literature in the Eighteenth Century*, New York, 1987.

49 Samuel Parker, *Sylva, Letters Upon Occasional Subjects*, London, 1701, p. 76.

50 *Essay in Defense of the Female Sex*, London, 1697, pp. 145–146.

51 [Mary Wray], *Ladies Library*, p. 123. This is likely to be a reference to the *ruelle*, see chapter 2, note 3.

52 [Mary Wray], *Ladies Library*, p. 122. Sexual licence was seen as slavery to the passions.

53 Joseph Spence, *Letters from the GRAND TOUR 1730–1741*, in S. Klima (ed.), London, McGill-Queen's University Press, 1975, pp. 9–10.

54 Politeness was an art of sociability, and taciturnity was 'the extreme of unsociability'. Klein, 'The Rise of "Politeness"', p. 83.

55 See, for example, David Hume's discussion of gallantry in 'Of the Rise and Progress of the Arts and Sciences', in J.W. Lenz (ed.), *Of the Standard of Taste and Other Essays by David Hume*, New York, 1965, pp. 89–94.

56 *Spectator*, no. 435.

57 *Spectator*, no. 128.

58 Also called Beaus, coxcombs, Men of Mode and at times in the *Spectator*, 'Women's Men'.

59 Sir John Vanbrugh, 'The Relapse', (1697), in Michael Cordner (ed.), *Sir John Vanbrugh: Four Comedies*, Harmondsworth, Penguin, 1989, Act II, Scene i.

60 *Spectator*, no. 57.

61 John Ashton, *Social Life in the Reign of Queen Anne*, London, 1883, p. 105.

62 Melantha, in Dryden's *Marriage à la Mode*, distinguished by a 'passion' for 'everything French', especially French words, is the

'female fop'. A. Beaurline and F. Bowers in K. Muir, *The Comedy of Manners*, London, Hutchinson, 1970, p. 51 n. 2.

63 Sir George Etheredge, 'The Man of Mode', (1676), in E. Gosse (ed.), *Restoration Plays*, London, J.M. Dent and Sons, 1968. Vanbrugh, 'The Relapse', Samuel Foote, 'The ENGLISHMAN return'd from Paris' (1756), in P.R. Backscheider and D. Howard (eds), *The Plays of SAMUEL FOOTE*, New York, Garland, 1983.

64 *Spectator*, no. 45.

65 As such, it was particularly important for the future diplomat, as Chesterfield told his son.

66 *Spectator*, nos 165, 405.

67 Linda Colley, *Britons: Forging the Nation*, London, Yale University Press, 1992, p. 90; Henry Felton, *A Dissertation on Reading the Classics and Forming a Just Style*, London, 1723, p. 147; *Spectator*, nos. 165, 405. See also the *Annual Register*, 1758, p. 373. It must be pointed out, however, that towards the end of the century, there were many who considered that borrowing from French improved English and contributed to making it a superior tongue: Lindsay Murray, *English Grammar Adapted to the Different Classes of Learners*, London, 1795, p. 111; John Corbet, *A Concise System of English Grammar*, Shrewsbury, 1784, p. 46. See also G.S. Rousseau, 'Towards a semiotic of the nerve' in P. Burke and R. Porter (eds), *Language, Self and Society: A Social History of Language*, Oxford, Polity Press, 1991, for a discussion of the gender of 'nerves.'

68 Felton, *Dissertation*, p. 89; Stackhouse, *Reflections*, p. 181. For a discussion of the gendered meanings of music in the eighteenth century, see Richard Leppert, *Music and Image: Domesticity, Ideology and Socio-cultural Formation in Eighteenth-Century England*, Cambridge, Cambridge University Press, 1988.

69 Gildon and Brightland, *Grammar*; Stackhouse, *Reflections*; Corbet, *English Grammar*.

70 The copiousness of the English language was a recurrent theme. See for example Stackhouse, *Reflections*; Thomas Sheridan, *A Rhetorical Grammar of the English Language*, (1781), facsimile reprint, Menston, The Scolar Press, 1969.

71 Gildon and Brightland, *Grammar*, Preface. The sense of the moral pollution brought on by French is also conveyed by Johnson in his preface to the *Dictionary*. He specifies that he collected words from writers when English had been 'undefiled', before it had deviated 'towards a Gallick structure and phraseology'. Samuel Johnson, *A Dictionary of the English Language*, London, 1755, Preface, p. 9.

72 Stackhouse, *Reflections*, p. 172. This image echoed the contemporary discourse on generation, according to which venery led to degeneration and weakness. Tobias Smollett for instance, who trained as a physician, wrote: 'the exercise of common venery . . . by ruining the constitutions of our young men, has produced a puny progeny, that degenerates from generation to generation'. 'The Adventures of Roderick Random,' (1748), George Saintsbury (ed.), *The Works of Tobias Smollett*, 12 vols, London, The Navarre Society, n.d., vol. 3, chap. 51, p. 44.

73 See John Barrell, '"The Dangerous Goddess": masculinity, prestige, and the aesthetic in early eighteenth-century Britain', *The Birth of Pandora and the Division of Knowledge*, London, Macmillan, 1992.

74 N. Holland, quoted in Susan Staves, 'A Few Kind Words for the Fop', *Studies in English Literature*, vol. 22, no. 3, 1982, p. 413. Collocations of the term fop in the *Spectator* include: empty, insipid, affectation, falsehood, and, citing Dryden, 'outward form, empty noise', nos. 92, 128, 156, 280.

75 *Spectator*, no. 92.

76 *Spectator*, no. 128; see also no. 92.

77 Staves, for example, is concerned to show that 'foppery was a real social phenomenon, not merely a theatrical convenience', 'A Few Kind Words', p. 419.

78 John Dennis, 'A Defense of Sir Fopling Flutter', (1722), reprinted in E.A. Bloom and L.D. Bloom (eds), *Addison and Steele: The Critical Heritage*, London, Routledge & Kegan Paul, 1980, p. 167.

79 Ashton, *Social Life*, p. 105.

3 POLITENESS

1 L.E. Klein, 'The rise of "politeness" in England, 1660–1715', Ph.D. thesis, Baltimore, Johns Hopkins, 1984. In his recent book, *Shaftesbury and the Culture of Politeness: Moral Discourse and Cultural Politics in Early Eighteenth-Century England*, Cambridge, Cambridge University Press, 1994, Klein has taken up and reworked many of the themes explored in this wide-ranging early work, though the discussion of politeness is now incorporated into and subsumed to the study of Shaftesbury, 'the philosopher of politeness'. The introduction, however, contains a succinct and lucid exposition and summary of the main tenets of politeness. The introduction to my discussion of politeness is indebted to both texts.

2 Klein, 'The rise of "politeness"', pp. 203, 49; see also John Barrell, *English Literature in History: An Equal Wide Survey*, London, Hutchinson, 1983, for a discussion of the role of the polite as authority in language.

3 Klein,'The rise of "politeness"', pp. 30, 80–93, 185–189; *Shaftesbury*, pp. 3, 7.

4 Klein,'The rise of "politeness"', pp. 50, 74–75, 77.

5 L.E. Klein, 'Liberty, manners and politeness in early 18th-century England', *The Historical Journal*, 32, no. 3, 1989, pp. 583–605; 'The rise of "politeness"'. See also John Barrell, '"The Dangerous Goddess": masculinity, prestige, and the aesthetic in early eighteenth-century Britain', in *The Birth of Pandora and the Division of Knowledge*, London, Macmillan, 1992.

6 The ideal classical citizen was 'independent, public minded, martial, frugal and simple', whereas his opposite was 'self-indulgent and private ... soft and sensuous ... expensive ... excessive'. Klein, 'Liberty, manners and politeness', pp. 593, 594. In the eighteenth

century, these terms were used particularly to contrast manliness with effeminacy.

7 Philip Dormer Stanhope, Earl of Chesterfield, *Letters to his Son 1737–1768*, (1774), London, W. W. Gibbings, 1890. All references to the Letters are from this edition. Although Chesterfield's *Letters* range over a period of thirty years starting in 1738, I have selected mainly the ones he wrote to his adolescent son. David Fordyce's *Dialogues Concerning Education* were published in London in 1745–48.

8 For other Scottish views on politeness, see John Dwyer and Richard B. Sher (eds), *Sociability and Society in Eighteenth-Century Scotland*, Edinburgh, The Mercat Press, 1993; and John Dwyer, *VIRTUOUS DISCOURSE; Sensibility and Community in Late Eighteenth-Century Scotland*, Edinburgh, John Donald, 1987.

9 He is also the author of *The English Grammar*, London, 1712.

10 Letter CXLI.

11 Letter CLVII.

12 Letters CLV, LXXIV; Locke uses the same metaphor in *Some Thoughts on Education*, 1693. Chesterfield had read Locke, admired him and sent his son a copy of the text. See Letter CLXVIII.

13 Letter LXIX.

14 Letter CXXXIX. See also Letter CLXI.

15 Letter LXIX.

16 Letter XCV.

17 Letters CI and CLIV.

18 Letters XCVI, CXCV and LXXIV, CLI, CLVII, CCXXIX. See also Locke, *Some Thoughts*, p. 244, and chapter 2 above.

19 Letters XCV, CXCV, CLXVI, CCXLIII. Pierre Ortigue de Vaumorière, *L'Art de plaire dans la conversation*, Paris, 1690; Antoine Gombauld, Chevalier de Méré, *Oeuvres Complètes*, (1668–1677), C. Bouhors (ed.), 3 vols, Paris, Fernand Roches, 1930.

20 Letters XLIV, LXXIII, CCXXXVIII.

21 Business – here refers to official or public engagements. *OED.*

22 Letters CLII, CLXIII: 'An ungraceful manner of speaking, awkward motions, and a disagreeable address are great clogs to the ablest man of business'.

23 Letter CLXIV.

24 Letter CLXI.

25 Letters CXI, CXVIII.

26 James Boswell, *The Life of Samuel Johnson*, (1791), A. Glover (ed.), London, J.M. Dent & Sons, 1925, vol. 1, p. 170.

27 Klein, 'The rise of "politeness" ', p. 44.

28 Charles Whibley (ed.), 'The Characters of Lord Chesterfield', reviewed in the *Times Literary Supplement*, 8 March 1928.

29 Euphranor is the 'Head and Genius' of the academy, and its Master; Cleora is a young woman whom Simplicius meets in the carriage on the way to the Academy. He is struck by her unaffected manner and conversation and by the lack of display she makes of the excellent education she has received from Phylax, a member of the

Academy and her uncle and guardian. She does not live at the academy, just nearby. Philander is Euphranor's assistant.

30 Concerned to educate his niece in polite and virtuous ways, Phylax elaborated a 'Plan for the Education of Women', which Cleora outlines in vol. 2 of the *Dialogues*.

31 *Dialogues*, vol. 1 pp. 46, 48.

32 *Dialogues*, vol. 1, p. 98, vol. 2, p. 327.

33 *Dialogues*, vol. 1, p. 45.

34 *Dialogues*, vol. 1, p. 347.

35 *Dialogues*, vol. 1, pp. 97–98.

36 *Dialogues*, vol. 2, p. 336. It is interesting to compare this perspective with the sentiments of a French contemporary. In his essay on politeness Abbé Trublet argues, like Cleora, that sincerity and politeness are incompatible, but his position is diametrically opposed to hers. Sincerity, he declares, is a natural, universal disposition of mankind. Man 'loves to speak what he thinks, and to give vent to his own sentiments'. To be polite and hold back what might offend is the difficult achievement. It implies a great deal of self-control. Indeed, 'constant dissimulation is a violent state'. Without politeness, he concludes, there is no society. Abbé Nicolas Charles Joseph Trublet, *Essays Upon Several Subjects of Literature and Morality*, London, 1744, vol. 3, pp. 292, 293, 299.

37 *Dialogues*, vol. 2, pp. 62, 297–302, 304–305.

38 For a discussion of the relation between politeness and liberty, see Klein, 'Liberty, manners and politeness'.

39 *Dialogues*, vol. 2, p. 309. The original meaning of virtue was manliness. *OED*.

40 *Dialogues*, vol. 2. p. 327.

41 See Klein, 'Liberty, manners and politeness'.

42 John Andrews, *A Comparative View of the French and English Nations*, London, 1785, pp. 69, 73, 74–75, 84.

43 *Dialogues*, vol. 1, pp. 46–47.

44 *Dialogues*, vol. 1, pp. 45, 46, 48.

45 *Dialogues*, vol. 2, p. 151.

46 *The Rambler*, a Periodical Paper, (1750–1752), London, 1824, Letter no. 98. Johnson distinguished what he called 'genuine' politeness, and the practice of the 'exterior and unessential parts of civility'. The former aimed at putting others before the self and curbing one's vanity; the latter consisted of the minutiae of visiting, and talking 'frippery and slight silks' with the ladies.

47 Abbé Jean Bernard Le Blanc, *Letters on the English and the French Nations*, Dublin, 1747, vol. 2, pp. 237, 238, 239. Battista Angeloni, an Italian Jesuit noted that ' in England, it is considered unmanly and effeminate to dangle after women, to prevail by sighs, tender speeches, long sufferings and perseverance', *Letters on the English Nation*, London, 1756, p. 162.

48 *Dialogues*, vol. 2, p. 151.

49 *Letters*, nos. 109, 132, 194, 195.

50 Johnson, *The Rambler*, Letter no. 194.

51 Johnson, *The Rambler*, Letter no. 195.
52 See Johnson, *The Rambler*, Letter no. 98; see also James Fordyce, *Addresses to Young Men*, 2 vols, London, 1777, the chapter entitled: 'On a manly Spirit, as opposed to Effeminacy'.

4 THE GRAND TOUR OF THE ENGLISH GENTLEMAN

1 William Ramsay, *The Gentleman's Companion*, London, 1669, p. 55; Obadiah Walker, *Of Education*, (1673), facsimile reprint, Menston, The Scolar Press, 1970, Part I, chap. XIV, p. 192.
2 Richard Lassels, *The Voyage of Italy*, Paris, 1670, Preface to the Reader. I am concerned with the Grand Tour, that is, with travel to France, and not with *Il Giro*, to Italy.
3 Young men in other nations travelled as well, but there is no study I know of which analyses the practice as anything other than 'educational'. It is my argument that although education was the ostensible motive for sending English young men of rank abroad for so long and at such expense, there were other important reasons, as this chapter will attempt to demonstrate.
4 Jean Bernard, Abbé Le Blanc, *Letters on the English and the French Nations*, Dublin, 1747, vol. 1, p. 37.
5 L.E. Klein, 'The rise of "politeness" in England, 1660–1715. Ph.D. thesis, Baltimore, Johns Hopkins University, 1984, pp. 194, 203. Klein does not discuss the Grand Tour, but his insights concerning the rise of politeness are congruent with its expansion at that particular time. Other explanations have been suggested: see J. Burke, 'The Grand Tour and the rule of taste', in R.F. Brissenden (ed.), *Studies in the Eighteenth Century*, Canberra, 1968; C. Maxwell, *The English Traveller in France 1698–1815*, London, George Routledge & Sons, 1932; W.E. Mead, *The Grand Tour in the Eighteenth Century*, New York, Benjamin Bloom, 1914.
6 David Fordyce, *Dialogues Concerning Education*, 2 vols, London, 1745–48. From Jean Gailhard, *The Compleat Gentleman or Directions for the Education of Youth as to their Breeding at Home, and Travelling Abroad*, 2 vols, London, 1678, and John Locke, *Some Thoughts Concerning Education*, (1693), J.W. and J.S. Yolton (eds), Oxford, Clarendon Press, 1989, to William Darrell, *A Gentleman Instructed in the Conduct of a Virtuous and Happy Life*, (1704), London, 1720; James Burgh, *The Dignity of Human Nature*, London, 1754 and Vicesimus Knox, *Liberal Education or, a Practical Treatise on the Methods of Acquiring Useful and Polite Learning*, London, 1784, to cite a few. See also George C. Brauer, *The Education of a Gentleman: Theories of Gentlemanly Education in England, 1660–1775*, New York, Bookman Associates, 1959.
7 R.C. Stephens, 'The courtly tradition in English education from Sir Thomas Elyot to John Locke', Ph.D. thesis, University of Belfast, 1955.

8 See, for example, the letter Joseph Spence wrote his mother from Blois, August 9, 1737, *Letters from the GRAND TOUR 1730–1741*, S. Klima (ed.), London, 1975, p. 191. Addison spent one year there learning French, noted Kathleen Lambley, *The Teaching and Cultivation of the French Language in England during Tudor and Stuart Times*, Manchester, Manchester University Press, 1920, p. 218.

9 For a critique of this view, see Michèle Cohen, 'The Grand Tour: constructing the English gentleman in eighteenth-century France', *History of Education*, vol. 21, no. 3, 1992, pp. 241–257.

10 *OED*.

11 Ruth Kelso, *Doctrine for the Lady of the Renaissance*, Urbana, University of Illinois Press, 1956, p. 2; Stephens, 'The courtly tradition', pp. 46, 310.

12 Edward Hyde, Earl of Clarendon, 'A dialogue concerning education', *A Collection of Several Tracts*, London, 1728, p. 322; Locke, *Some Thoughts*, pp. 254, 252; James Howell, *Instructions for Forreine Travel*, (1640), E. Arber (ed.), London, English Reprints, no. 6, 1869, pp. 19, 68–69.

13 Stephens, 'The courtly tradition'.

14 The *Tatler*, no. 21.

15 See, for example, Henry Felton, *A Dissertation on Reading the Classics and Forming a Just Style*, London, 1723, pp. 87–89; Thomas Stackhouse, *Reflections on the Nature and Property of Languages*, London, 1731; [John Constable], *The Conversation of Gentlemen*, London, 1738.

16 Lassels, *Voyage of Italy*, introduction; Gilbert Burnet, *Thoughts on Education*, (1668), J. Clarke (ed.), London, 1761; John Andrews, *A Comparative View of the French and English Nations*, London, 1785; Anthony Burgess and Francis Haskell, *The Age of the Grand Tour*, London, Paul Elek, 1967, p. 14.

17 See Cohen, 'The Grand Tour'.

18 Anthony Ashley Cooper, Third Earl of Shaftesbury was sixteen; Thomas Coke, First Earl of Leicester was fifteen, and Edward, his younger brother, was fourteen, as was Chesterfield's son. R. Voitle, *The Third Earl of Shaftesbury*, London, Louisiana State University Press, 1984; James Lees-Milne, *Earls of Creation*, London, Hamish Hamilton, 1962; Chesterfield, *Letters*, CXI. J.W. Stoye commented 'many of the young men abroad were hardly more than boys, and often they were boys', *English Travellers Abroad 1604–1667*, London, Jonathan Cape, 1952, p. 62.

19 *Spectator*, no. 364; Oliver Goldsmith, 'An Enquiry into the Present State of Polite Learning in Europe', (1756), A. Friedman (ed.), *Collected Works of Oliver Goldsmith*, Oxford, Clarendon Press, 1966, vol. 1, p. 331.

20 Vicesimus Knox, *Liberal Education or, a Practical Treatise on the Methods of Acquiring Useful and Polite Learning*, London, 1784, p. 382.

21 See Cohen, 'Grand Tour'; see also Stephens, 'The courtly tradition'.

22 Jeremy Black, *The British and the Grand Tour 1713–1793*, London, Croom Helm, 1985.

23 For reviews of the debate, see Brauer, *Education of a Gentleman*, Stephens, 'The courtly tradition'. See also *Spectator* no. 313.

24 Gilbert Burnet, *Thoughts on Education*, (1668), J. Clarke (ed.), London, 1761; Gailhard, *The Compleat Gentleman*; Locke, *Some Thoughts*.

25 Burnet, *Thoughts on Education*, pp. 19, 20; Locke, *Some Thoughts*, p. 129. The *OED* defines 'Fondling' as one who is much caressed and petted.

26 J.L. Costeker, *The Fine Gentleman or the Complete Education of a Young Nobleman*, London, 1732, p. 10; There are many other references to the ill effects of mothers' fondness on their sons' education and character. See [Constable], *The Conversation of Gentlemen*; Fordyce, *Dialogues Concerning Education*; Johnson, *The Rambler*, no. 195; James Burgh, *The Dignity of Human Nature*, London, 1754; James Fordyce, *Addresses to Young Men*. This fear is not confined to the eighteenth century, as Christine Heward has shown in *Making a Man of Him: Parents and their sons' education at an English public school 1929–1950*, London, Routledge, 1988.

27 Learning was essential to nobility. See Peacham, *The Complete Gentleman*, (1634; Gailhard, *The Compleat Gentleman*; Locke, *Some Thoughts*. Stephens discusses in detail the relation between learning and virtue in 'The courtly tradition'.

28 Laurence Sterne, 'Sermon on the prodigal son', in *The Works of Laurence Sterne*, London, 1857, Sermon XX, pp. 596–601.

29 Lassels, *Voyage of Italy*, introduction; François Maximilien Misson, *A New Voyage to Italy*, London, 1695, vol. 1, p. 144, vol. 2, p. 305.

30 R.J. White, 'The Grand Tour', in A. Natan (ed.), *The Silver Renaissance: Essays in Eighteenth-Century English History*, London, Macmillan, 1961.

31 Richard Hurd, *Dialogues on the Uses of Foreign Travel Considered as a Part of an English Gentleman's Education: Between Lord Shaftesbury and Mr Locke*, London, 1764, p. 105.

32 Howell, *Instructions*, p. 65; see also Francis Osborne, *Advice to a Son*, Oxford, 1656.

33 However, display of the body as a social symbol was an important aspect of the 'courtly ethic of graceful behaviour' developed by French nobles. M.E. Motley, *Becoming an Aristocrat: The Education of the Court Nobility 1580–1715*, Princeton, NJ, Princeton University Press, 1990, pp. 116–117. See also Christopher Breward, *The Culture of Fashion: A New History of Fashionable Dress*, Manchester, Manchester University Press, 1995. Costeker, *The Fine Gentleman*, p. 14.

34 *The Macaroni Jester and Pantheon of Wit*, London, 1773; Thomas Wright, *Caricature History of the Georges or Annals of the House of Hanover*, London, John Camden Holten, 1868. See also Cohen, 'Grand Tour'.

35 Domna Stanton, *The Aristocrat as Art: A Study of the Honnête Homme and the Dandy in Seventeenth- and Nineteenth-Century Literature*, New York, Columbia University Press, 1980; Barrell, *English Literature in History*, p. 203.

36 Burgh, *Dignity of Human Nature*, Book II, Section VI, p. 148.

37 Knox, *Liberal Education*, p. 382. 'Parts' meant 'abilities, talents', *OED*.

38 To avoid confusion, I will refer to Hurd's apocryphal characters as *Locke* and *Shaftesbury*, and to John Locke, author of *Some Thoughts* as John Locke.

39 See for example R.S. Lambert (ed.), *The Grand Tour – A Journey in the Tracts of the Age of Aristocracy*, London, Faber and Faber, 1935, p. 11; Brauer, *Education of a Gentleman*; White, 'The Grand Tour'; K.S. Dent takes Hurd's text to represent Locke's 'updated' views about the merits or disadvantages of travel in 'The informal education of the landed classes in the eighteenth century, with particular reference to reading', Ph.D. thesis, University of Birmingham, 1974.

40 Hurd, *Dialogues*, pp. 44, 71, 74, 91, 117–118.

41 Locke, *Some Thoughts*, p. 200; Hurd, *Dialogues*, p. 115.

42 Hurd, *Dialogues*, pp. 117–119, 159, 160.

43 Sincerity became 'the philosophical essence of the English nation, its identity, its National Character', George Newman, *The Rise of English Nationalism: A Cultural History 1740–1830*, London, Weidenfeld & Nicolson, 1987, p. 155. See also pp. 127–139.

44 Stephens, 'The courtly tradition', p. 316.

45 Hurd, *Dialogues*, p. 87.

46 John Andrews, *Letters to a Young Gentleman on his Setting out for France*, London, 1784, p. 4.

47 [John Bennett], *Strictures on Female Education*, London, 1787, pp. 134–135. Knox, *Liberal Education*.

48 Linda Colley, *Britons: Forging the Nation*, London, Yale University Press, 1992.

49 Andrews, *Letters to a Young Gentleman*, pp. 32, 40. James Fordyce, who also criticized foreign travel, counterposed 'language learning' to 'the exercise of reason and the attainment of wisdom'. *Addresses to Young Men*, London, 1777; see also, Knox, *Liberal Education*.

50 Hannah Cowley, *The Belle's Stratagem*, Dublin, 1781.

51 Suggestions vary considerably, including the French Revolution and the Age of the Railway – a few believe it never ended. See, for example, R.S. Lambert, *The Grand Tour*; J.A.R. Pimlott, *The Englishman's Holiday: A Social History*, London, Faber and Faber, 1947; Linda Colley, on the other hand, argues it was replaced by internal tourism, *Britons*.

52 *English Literature in History*, p. 38.

53 And had long been. See for example D. Kuchta, 'The semiotics of masculinity in Renaissance England', in J.G. Turner (ed.), *Sexuality and Gender in Early Modern Europe: Institutions, Texts, Images*, Cambridge, Cambridge University Press, 1993.

54 See also Carolyn Williams, *Pope, Homer and Manliness: Some Aspects of Eighteenth-Century Classical Learning*, London, Routledge, 1993.

5 THE ACCOMPLISHMENT OF THE EIGHTEENTH-CENTURY LADY

1 John Burton, *Lectures on Female Education and Manners*, London, 1793, vol. I, p. 109.

2 This was important throughout the period under discussion in this study. Mothers were expected to teach their sons until they were old

enough to be handed over to a tutor, but the main emphasis was on mothers continuing to educate their daughters rather than abdicating this responsibility and sending them to boarding-schools. The charges against boarding-schools included not just the alleged frivolity of their curricula but the dangers to girls' virtue most explicitly alluded to by Chirol, who claims that the 'secret vice' is rife in these unsupervised surroundings. J.L Chirol, *An Enquiry into the Best System of Female Education*, London, 1809. James Fordyce, in *Sermons to Young Women*, (1766), 2 vols, London, 1770, Henry Home, in *Loose Hints upon Education*, Edinburgh, 1781, Vicesimus Knox, in *Liberal Education*, London, 1784, Mary Wollstonecraft, in *Thoughts on the Education of Daughters*, London, 1787, [John Bennett], in *Strictures on Female Education*, 1787 and *Letters to a Young Lady*, 2 vols, 1789, all criticized a boarding-school education for girls. Erasmus Darwin was the outstanding exception, drawing up instead *A Plan for the Conduct of Female Education in Boarding Schools*, London, 1797. At the same time, the figure of the mother as instructor was equivocal, since she was also potentially a corrupting influence on both her sons (as I argued in Chapter 5) and her daughters. Indeed, the virtuous women I discuss in this study have all been educated by men – Cleora, in David Fordyce's *Dialogues Concerning Education*, 2 vols, London 1745–48, Miss Simmons in Thomas Day's *The History of Sandford and Merton*, (1783–1789), London, Ward & Lock, 1860.

3 [John Moir], *Female Tuition, or an address to mothers*, London, 1784, p. 26; Bennett, *Letters*, p. 96.

4 The aim of female education according to Erasmus Darwin, *A Plan*, p. 10

5 In 1862, Frances Power Cobbe was still invoking Sydney Smith's remark that 'A woman's love for her offspring hardly depends on her ignorance of Greek, nor need we apprehend that she will forsake an infant for a quadratic equation'. 'Female education', Paper read at the Social Science Congress, London, 1862, p. 6. The twentieth-century 'solution' to the debate was to subsume femininity and domesticity to the 'special needs' of girls' education, thereby occulting the problem altogether. See Board of Education, *Report of the Consultative Committee on the Differentiation of the Curriculum for Boys and Girls Respectively in Secondary Schools*, London, 1923.

6 Thomas Gisborne, *An Enquiry into the Duties of the Female Sex*, London, 1796, p. 10.

7 Hannah More, *Essays on Various Subjects*, London, 1785, p. 132; David Fordyce, *Dialogues*, Burton, *Lectures*, Knox, *Liberal Education*, Darwin, *A Plan*.

8 James Fordyce, *Sermons*, vol. 1, p. 89.

9 Suellen Diaconoff, 'Ambition, politics, and professionalism: two women painters', in Frederick M. Keener and Susan E. Lorsch (eds), *Eighteenth-Century Women and the Arts*, Contributions to Women's Studies, no. 98, London, Greenwood Press, 1988, p. 201. More, *Essays*, p. 130.

10 See L.E. Klein, 'Gender and the public/private distinction in the eighteenth century: some questions about evidence and analytic procedure', *Eighteenth-Century Studies*, vol. 29, no. 1, 1995, pp. 97–109; John Barrell, 'The private comedy of Thomas Rowlandson', in *The Birth of Pandora and the Division of Knowledge*, London, Macmillan, 1992.

11 Ludmilla Jordanova, *Sexual Visions: Images of Gender in Science and Medicine between the Eighteenth and Twentieth Centuries*, Hemel Hempstead, Harvester Wheatsheaf, 1989, p. 52, and Klein, 'Gender and the public/private distinction' for a critique of Jordanova's position.

12 L.E. Klein, 'Gender, conversation and the public sphere', in J. Stills and M. Worton (eds), *Textuality and Sexuality: Reading Theories and Practices*, Manchester, Manchester University Press, 1992.

13 Jurgen Habermas, *The Structural Transformation of the Public Sphere*, Oxford, Polity Press, 1989, p. 30. See also Dena Goodman, 'Public sphere and private life: toward a synthesis of current historiographical approaches to the old regime', *History and Theory*, 31, no. 1, 1992, pp. 1–20.

14 *An Examen of Mr Sheridan's plan for the Improvement of Education in this Country*, London, 1784, p. 40.

15 What Klein calls the 'associative public sphere', a sphere of social, discursive and cultural production, ' 'Gender and the public/private distinction', p. 104.

16 See Klein, 'Gender and the public/private distinction'.

17 Fordyce, *Sermons*, I. p. 20; Sir John Fielding, *The Universal Mentor*, London, 1763, p. 250.

18 Burton, *Lectures*, vol. 1, p. 182.

19 I also refer to Hannah More's earlier *Essays*, which complements the *Strictures* and contains many of the same arguments.

20 For a discussion of the social classes represented in girls' boarding-schools in the eighteenth century, see P.J. Miller, 'Women's Education, 'Self-improvement' and social mobility – a late eighteenth-century debate', *British Journal of Educational Studies*, 20, 1972, pp. 302–314.

21 Fordyce, *Lectures*, vol. 1, pp. 87, 92, 95, 107–108, 111, 137–138, 178.

22 More, *Strictures*, vol. 1, pp. 73, 74; vol. 2, pp. 175–176. Men, on the contrary, 'are formed to the more public exhibitions on the grand theatre of human life. They derive no injury and lose no polish by being always exposed and engaged in constant commerce of the world. It is their proper element where they respire their natural air and exert their noblest powers'. *Essays*, p. 5.

23 More, *Essays*, p. 14.

24 More, *Strictures*, vol. 2, pp. 46–47, 66–67, 72.

25 See David Fordyce, *Dialogues*, James Fordyce, *Sermons*, Henry Home, *Loose Hints*.

26 For a discussion of 'the just or only phenomenon' in relation to girls' achievement today, see Rosie Walden and Valerie Walkerdine, 'Girls and Mathematics: the early years', *Bedford Way Papers*, 8, London, Institute of Education 1982. See also Valerie Walkerdine, 'Femininity

as performance' in Lynda Stone (ed.), *The Education Feminism Reader*, London, Routledge, 1994.

27 More, *Strictures*, vol. 2, pp. 6, 67, 69. More, *Essays*, p. 54.

28 More, *Strictures*, vol. 2, pp. 46–47, 66–67, 72.

29 More, *Strictures*, vol. 1, pp. 23, 150–151, vol. 2, pp. 70–71, 186–188.

30 See also the section on female education in Knox's *Liberal Education*.

31 More, *Strictures*, vol. 1, p. 106.

32 Maria Edgeworth, for example, did not share her objections, on the contrary. See her story *The Good Governess*; Nicholas Hans argues that 'almost every exiled aristocrat ... resorted to giving private lessons as a living'. *New Trends in Education in the Eighteenth Century*, London, Routledge & Kegan Paul, 1966, p. 188.

33 Throughout the century the English worried lest they might be taught the French of the servant class. See Abel Boyer, *The Compleat French Master for Ladies and Gentlemen*, London, 1694. James Fauchon, for example, exploited this anxiety and advertised the fact that he would teach the pronunciation of the polite. *The French Tongue*, Cambridge, 1751.

34 More, *Strictures*, vol. 1 pp. 106, 107. Whereas men could be improved or corrupted by travel to France, women could only be corrupted. See for instance Chesterfield, *The World*, no. 29, July 19, 1753.

35 Lewis Chambaud, *The Art of Speaking French*, Dublin, 1772, pp. xvi, xvii.

36 David Fordyce, *Dialogues*, vol. I, p. 146.

37 *The Early Diary of Fanny Burney 1768–1778*, Annie Raine Ellis (ed.), London, 1913, vol. 1, p. 102. It is ironic that she eventually married a Frenchman, Alexandre D'Arblay, an *émigré* from the French Revolution, in 1793.

38 *History of Sandford and Merton*, chap. 13, pp. 225–226, 227.

39 More, *Strictures*, vol. 1, p. 72, vol. 2, p. 164.

40 Burton, *Lectures*, vol. 2, p. 93.

41 Hester Chapone, *Letters on the Improvement of the Mind*, (1773), London, 1820, Letter viii, p. 144; Bennett, *Letters* vol. 2, pp. 6–7.

42 Chapone, *Letters*, p. 146; Bennett, *Letters*, vol. 2, pp. 7, 8; see also More: 'cultivate true politeness, for ... it is consistent with the gospel of Christ'. *Strictures*, vol. 2, pp. 101–102.

43 Bennett, *Letters*, vol. 2, p. 8.

44 This was integral to politeness, and its constant problematic. As Klein writes: 'politeness remained a phenomenon of the surface. It was permanently involved in conflicts between surface and depth, between exteriority and interiority'. L.E. Klein, 'The rise of "politeness" in England, 1660–1715', Ph.D thesis, Baltimore, Johns Hopkins University, 1984, p. 44.

45 Burton, *Lectures*, vol. 2, p. 91.

46 Burton, *Lectures*, vol. 2, pp. 95, 97; Bennett, *Letters*, vol. 2, pp. 6, 8.

47 L.E. Klein, 'Liberty, manners and politeness in early 18th-century England', *The Historical Journal*, 32, no. 3, 1989, p. 587.

48 Burton, *Lectures*, vol. 2, p. 93.

49 See Richard Hurd, *Dialogues on the Uses of Foreign Travel*, London,

1764, and Chapter 4 above.

50 Burton, *Lectures*, vol. 2, p. 83. Note that the eighteenth-century meaning of gentleness was 'good breeding'. *OED*.

51 Chapone, *Letters*, p. 144.

52 Bennett, *Letters*, vol. 2, p. 7; Burton, *Lectures*, vol. 2, pp. 93, 97, 98; More, *Strictures*, vol. 2, pp. 102–103.

53 Burton, *Lectures*, vol. 2, p. 91.

54 For example, *The Baboon à la Mode*, a satire against the French, London, 1704.

55 Bennett, *Letters*, vol. 2, p. 125.

56 Maria Edgeworth, *Patronage*, (1814), London, Pandora, 1986, p. 388.

57 See Chapter 4, n. 43.

58 Leonore Davidoff and Catherine Hall, *Family Fortunes: Men and Women of the English Middle Class, 1780–1850*, London, Hutchinson, 1987, p. 19.

59 John Andrews, *Remarks on the French and English Ladies*, London, 1783, pp. 49, 50. This observation was confirmed by French visitors to England, but the same trend was developing in France. See M.H. Darrow, 'French noblewomen and the new domesticity', *Feminist Studies*, 5, no. 1, Spring 1979, pp. 41–65; Marmontel, 'Contes Moraux', *Oeuvres Complètes*, Paris, Amable Costes et Cie., 1819; Grace Gill-Mark, *Mme du Boccage: une femme de lettres au XVIIIième siècle*, (1927), Geneva, Slatkine Reprints, 1976.

60 Andrews, *Remarks*, pp. 17, 18, 22, 51, 165, 184, 221, 242.

6 THE SEXED MIND

1 Hannah More, *Essays on Various Subjects Principally Designed for Young Ladies*, London, 1785, pp. 9–10.

2 James Fordyce, *Sermons To Young Women*, 2 vols, (1766), London 1770, pp. 206, 208.

3 More, *Essays*, pp. 4, 13.

4 Fordyce, *Sermons*, vol. 1, p. 206.

5 More, *Essays*; John Bennett, *Strictures on Female Education*, London, 1787 and J.L. Chirol, *An Enquiry into the Best System of Female Education*, London, 1809.

6 Bennett, *Strictures*, p. 107; Chirol, *Enquiry*, p. 8. Hannah More used nearly the same words: the female mind, she wrote, is not 'capable of attaining so high a degree of perfection in science as the male'. *Essays*, p. 6.

7 Bennett, *Strictures*, p. 105; Burton used the same observation to assert that there were no mental differences between boys and girls. His argument is not more benign than Bennett's, since it erases the difference which would mark girls' superiority. John Burton, *Lectures on Female Education and Manners*, London, 1793, vol. 1, p. 164.

8 Bennett, *Strictures*, p. 105–106.

9 Chirol, *Enquiry*, p. 16.

10 More, *Essays*, p. 6; Bennett, *Strictures*, p. 104. Chirol, *Enquiry*, pp. 4–5,

17. It should also be pointed out that in the early nineteenth century, the term 'science' also denoted the study of Latin grammar and classical literature.

11 Bennett, *Strictures*, pp. 138–139.

12 This attitude was by far the most common. See Chapter 5, note 2.

13 Chirol, *Enquiry*, pp. 15–16, 274; Bennett, *Strictures*, p. 104. One wonders which birds Bennett looked at since it is usually the male bird that displays the brilliant plumage. Ornella Moscucci points out how science and 'nature' were used to provide evidence for the allocation of gender roles in society, *The Science of Woman: Gynaecology and Gender in England, 1800–1929*, Cambridge, Cambridge University Press, 1990. See also Thomas Laqueur, *Making Sex: Body and Gender from the Greeks to Freud*, London, Harvard University Press, 1990.

14 Sheldon Rothblatt, *Tradition and Change in English Liberal Education: An Essay in History and Culture*, London, Faber and Faber, 1976, pp. 129–130.

15 On this point, see Lorraine Daston, 'The naturalized female intellect', *Science in Context*, vol. 5, no. 2, 1992, pp. 209–235.

16 More, *Essays* p. 5, Chirol, *Enquiry*, p. 15.

17 Frances Power Cobbe, 'Female education, and, how it would be affected by university examinations', Paper read at the Social Science Congress, London, 1862, pp. 8, 10.

18 Eric Hawkins, *Modern Languages in the Curriculum*, Cambridge, Cambridge University Press, 1981; L.G. Kelly, *25 Centuries of Language Teaching: 500BC–1969*, Rowley, MA, Newbury House, 1976; John Foster Watson, *The Beginnings of the Teaching of Modern Languages in England*, (1909), Wakefield, S.R. Publishers, 1971; W.F. Mackey, *Language Teaching Analysis*, London, Longman, 1965; Kathleen Lambley, *The Teaching and Cultivation of the French Language in England during Tudor and Stuart Times*, Manchester, Manchester University Press, 1920.

19 Watson, *Beginnings*

20 *An Essay in Defense of the Female Sex*, London, 1696, p. 37.

21 John Locke, *Some Thoughts Concerning Education*, (1693), J.W. and J.S. Yolton (eds), Oxford, Clarendon Press, 1989; Michèle Cohen, 'Sexism and French language teaching', M.A. diss., London, University of London, 1982.

22 E.R. Curtis, *Lady Sarah Lennox: an Irrepressible Stuart 1745–1826*, London, W.H. Allen, n.d., pp. 17, 18. See also S. Harcstark Myers, *The Bluestocking Circle: Women, Friendship, and the Life of the Mind in Eighteenth-Century England*, Oxford, Clarendon Press, 1990; Stella Tillyard, *Aristocrats*, London, Chatto and Windus, 1994.

23 R. Brimley Johnson (ed.), *Mrs Delany: At Court and Among the Wits*, London, Stanley Paul and Co., 1925, p. xx.

24 See Nicholas Hans, *New Trends in Education in the Eighteenth Century*, London, Routledge & Kegan Paul, 1966; Dorothy Gardiner, *English Girlhood at School*, Oxford, Oxford University Press, 1929; Josephine Kamm, *Hope Deferred: Girls' Education in English History*, London, Methuen, 1965.

25 David Lysons, *Collecteana*, London, n.d., vol. I, pp. 17, 19.
26 Hawkins distinguishes two language learning situations: 'The language lesson which is accompanied by use of the target language outside the classroom for everyday activities; and the language lesson which takes place in an otherwise English context and is the pupil's only experience of the target language ("gardening in a gale")'. *Modern Languages*, p. 99.
27 Bouton argues that this is the main reason why grammars of French began to be published in England in the sixteenth century, even when French was habitually spoken among the English nobility. C.P. Bouton, *Les Grammaires Françaises de Claude Mauger à l'usage des Anglais*, Paris, Klincksieck, 1972.
28 Lambley, *Teaching and Cultivation*, p. 124.
29 Abel Boyer, *The Compleat French Master for Ladies and Gentlemen*, (London, 1694), Edinburgh, 1767. Later on in the century, grammar and language tended to be published as separate texts. See, for example, Lewis Chambaud, *A Grammar of the French Tongue*, London, 1758 and *The Art of Speaking French*, Dublin, 1772.
30 Cheneau, *French Grammar*, London, 1685, p. 157.
31 French nouns were declined: for example, le roi, du roi, au roi.
32 Claude Mauger, *Mauger's French Grammar*, London, 1688, pp. 45–51.
33 The changes such as gender, number, case etc., to which words are subject. *OED*.
34 James Fauchon, *The French Tongue*, Cambridge, 1751, Dedication. This claim undoubtedly also served to advertise the efficacy of Fauchon's method.
35 V.G. Peyton, *The True Principles of the French Language*, London, 1757, p. iv.
36 George Picard, *A Grammatical Dictionary*, London, 1790; see also B. Calbris, *The Rational Guide to the French Tongue*, London, 1797; Abbé Jean Pons Victor Lecoutz de Lévizac, *L'Art de Parler et d'Ecrire Correctement la Langue Françoise*, London, 1797; Marc Antoine Porny [Antoine Pyron du Martre], *The Practical French Grammar*, Dublin, 1812. Porny was French master at Eton in the early nineteenth century.
37 John Murdoch, *The Pronunciation and Orthography of the French language rendered perfectly easy on a plan quite original*, London, 1788, p. 5; Chambaud, *Art of Speaking French*, p. xxiii.
38 'Quiconque a l'expérience avouera qu'il a été capable de traduire toute espèce de livres François surtout en prose, avant de pouvoir ou entendre ou tenir une conversation' [Anyone who has experienced it will confess that he has been able to translate all sorts of French books, especially prose, well before he was able either to understand or sustain a conversation]. Calbris, *The Rational Guide* p. 179. Chambaud, *Art of Speaking French*, p. xx.
39 For example, Boyer, *Compleat French Master*, Mauger, *Mauger's French Grammar*, Francis Cheneau, *French Grammar*, London, 1685, and *The True French Master*, London, 1723. Pierre de Lainé, *The Princely Way to the French Tongue*, London, 1677.
40 Calbris, *The Rational Guide*, Part III, 'A Treatise for Attaining

Idiomatical French Elegance, and Rules for Learning the Language without Disgust, and for Speaking it with Facility.'

41 Henri Gratte, *Nouvelle Grammaire Françoise à l'Usage de la Jeunesse Angloise*, London, 1791, p. viii. Vicesimus Knox used the same argument concerning boys learning Latin rules in Latin, *Liberal Education*, London, 1784, p. 49.

42 *Report of Her Majesty's Commissioners appointed to inquire into the revenues and management of certain colleges and schools and the studies pursued and instruction given therein*, 4 vols, London, 1864. *Report from the Commissioners, The Schools Inquiry Commission*, London, 1867–68, 23 vols. Both reports are often referred to by the name of their chairmen, Lord Clarendon and Lord Taunton respectively. See J.W. Adamson, *English Education 1789–1902*, Cambridge, Cambridge University Press, 1930; H.C. Barnard, *A History of English Education from 1760*, London, University of London Press, 1969. I will follow this convention, and they will henceforth be referred to as the Clarendon Commission and the Taunton Commission respectively.

43 Kamm, *Hope Deferred*, p. 214. The decision to investigate girls' schools was not initiated by the Taunton Commission, but by women, Emily Davies in particular, who sought to improve girls' education. Chapter 14 of *Hope Deferred* gives an account of how they fought and won.

44 'Over a quarter of the Cabinet from 1801 to 1924' were educated at Eton, writes T.W. Bamford, in *The Rise of the Public Schools: A Study of Boys' Public Boarding Schools in England and Wales from 1837 to the Present Day*, London, Nelson, 1967, p. 230.

45 Clarendon Commission, Eton evidence, vol. 3, Q.3740. As early as 1822, 'when the Prince and Princess of Denmark visited the school ... none of the three Fellows in residence could speak a word of French', Richard Ollard, *An English Education: A Perspective of Eton*, London, Collins, 1982, p. 51.

46 Clarendon Commission, Eton evidence, vol. 3, QQ. 3740, 7025.

47 Taunton Commission, vol. 5, Q.16,620.

48 Mr Tarver, the French master at Eton, reported that a number of boys had learned French at home with their sisters' governesses. This was the excuse Balston, Eton's headmaster, invoked for not including it in the curriculum: French was something one did at home, before coming to Eton. Clarendon Commission, Eton evidence, vol. 3.

49 Clarendon Commission, vol. 3, Q.9362.

50 Clarendon Commission, vol. 3, Q.382.

51 Mr Tarver said he tried to have 10 to 12 pupils every lesson but often had only two or three. Clarendon Commission, vol. 3, Q.6945.

52 Clarendon Commission, vol. 2, p. 216. My emphasis. Anyone who has tried knows that it is not possible to learn to speak a language 'in a short time' just because one has learned its grammar.

53 Clarendon Commission, vol. 2, p. 216.

54 Clarendon Commission, vol. 4, pp. 77, 120.

55 The division of schools into three grades was devised by the commissioners for their own guidance. It was based on the length of school life, and was therefore grounded in social distinctions. First

or higher grade schools retained their pupils to the age of eighteen or nineteen. The pupils in grade two and grade three schools completed their courses at the ages of sixteen and fourteen respectively. Adamson, *English Education*, p. 259.

56 The modern school, said an assistant commissioner, 'is rather an excrescence than an organic part of the school. It exists rather by sufferance than with strong approval,' Taunton Commission, vol 9. p. 169.

57 Leeds Grammar School, and Newcastle Grammar School in particular where boys were taught French 'precisely in the same way as the ancient languages'. Taunton Commission, vol. 8, p. 401.

58 Taunton Commission, vol. 5, Q.10,756; vol. 7, p. 201; vol. 9, pp. 644, 645.

59 Taunton Commission, vol. 9, p. 645–646.

60 Taunton Commission, vol. 7, pp. 392, 400; vol. 9, p. 646.

61 Fearon suggested that girls attached more importance to French, and that they were 'more anxious to learn' and less disposed to 'ridicule a foreigner'. Taunton Commission, vol. 7, p. 392; vol. 8, p. 481.

62 Such as the caricatures of Bunbury, Rowlandson, and Hogarth. See M. Duffy, *The Englishman and the Foreigner*, Cambridge, Chadwick-Healey, 1986. See also R. Leppert, *Music and Image: Domesticity, Ideology and Socio-cultural Formation in Eighteenth-Century England*, Cambridge, Cambridge University Press, 1988.

63 Taunton Commission, vol. 7, p. 403; vol. 9, p. 644.

64 Taunton Commission, vol. 7, p. 524.

65 Lévizac, *L'Art de Parler*; Gratte, *Nouvelle Grammaire Française*.

66 Taunton Commission, vol. 9, p. 297; assistant commissioner Stanton thought that girls would break the rule and lie about it, vol. 7, p. 71. See also vol. 7, p. 201; vol. 8, pp. 523, 524; vol. 9, p. 298.

67 Taunton Commission, vol. 9, p. 297.

68 Taunton Commission, vol. 9, p. 809. Assistant Commissioner Bryce, for example, found that they were better than boys in reading, spelling, geography and history. Taunton Commission, vol. 8, p. 49, vol. 9, pp. 291, 807, 811.

69 Assistant Commissioner Bompas referred to girls' 'natural aptitude' for languages and deplored the fact that fluency was more important than accuracy. Taunton Commission, vol. 8, pp. 49, 53, 54; vol. 9, pp. 91, 292. 'Aptitude' refers to skills, not intellectual ability.

70 Rosie Eynard and Valerie Walkerdine, *The Practice of Reason: Investigation into the Teaching and Learning of Mathematics*, vol. 2: 'Girls and Mathematics', Institute of Education, London, 1984, p. 4.

71 It was Wilhelm Vietor's book *Sprachunterrict muss umkehen* (1882), written while he was a lecturer in Liverpool, which provided the real impetus towards the reform movement. See Mark Gilbert, 'The origins of the reform movement in modern language teaching in England', Part I, *Research Review*, no. 4, September 1953, pp.1–9, Part II, *Research Review*, no. 5, September 1954, pp. 9–18, Part III, *Research Review*, no. 6, September 1955, pp. 1–10.

72 Walter Ripman, preface to the 5th edition of *Easy Free Composition*, (1905), London, J.M. Dent & Sons, 1925.

73 'The striking success of the "Reform School" in Germany ... has brought into prominence the right of French to receive a respectful hearing. This right rests upon a variety of considerations. There is no modern instrument of expression that can be more perfectly lucid, or more severely exacting in its demands on the logical faculty, if it is to be thoroughly understood and, still more, if it is to be tolerably well spoken or written ... Accurate knowledge implies accuracy of pronunciation'. Board of Education, *Memorandum on the Study of Languages*, London, 1907, pp. 4, 6. See also Vernon Mallinson, *Teaching a Modern Language*, London, Heinemann, 1953.

74 Alice Zimmern, *The Renaissance of Girls' Education in England*, London, A.D. Innes & Co., 1898, p. 74. See also Hawkins, *Modern Languages*.

75 For example, Taunton Commission, vol. 8, p. 53; Deborah Thom discusses a similar situation in the twentieth century, 'Better a teacher than a hairdresser? "A Mad Passion for Equality" or, keeping Molly and Betty down', in Felicity Hunt (ed.), *Lessons for Life: the Schooling of Girls and Women 1850–1950*, Oxford, Blackwell, 1987; see also Geoffrey Walford (ed.), *The Private Schooling of Girls: Past and Present*, London, The Woburn Press, 1993, where Walford summarizes the Commission's recommendations to redress the imbalance of funding of girls' schools.

76 Taunton Commission, vol. 9, pp. 644, 645; vol. 5, Q.10,756.

77 Taunton Commission, vol. 7, pp. 299–301.

78 Taunton Commission, vol. 7, pp. 403, 405.

79 Taunton Commission, vol. 7, pp. 401, 405.

80 Henry Sweet, *The Practical Study of Languages*, (1899), London, Oxford University Press, 1964, p. 299. Sweet is considered the 'chief founder of modern phonetics'. *DNB*.

81 Hawkins, *Modern Languages*.

82 See for instance Valerie Walkerdine, *Counting Girls Out*, London, Virago, 1989.

83 Locke, *Some Thoughts*, p. 218.

84 Richard Wakely, 'The history of French teaching in Britain: some remarks', *Association for French Language Studies Newsletter*, 20, Summer 1988 pp. 22–23.

85 My emphasis. Porny, *Practical French Grammar*, p. 316.

86 Porny, *Practical French Grammar*, p. 316.

87 For Peyton, it was the effect of having to learn rules without reasons or explanations; Chambaud maintained that it was the 'abuse' of forcing beginners to 'speak nothing but French among themselves'. Peyton, *True Principles of the French Language*; Chambaud, *Art of Speaking French*, 1772, p. xvi; see also Picard, *English Guide to the French Tongue*; Calbris, *Rational Guide to the French Tongue*.

88 Peyton, *True Principles of the French Language*, p. iv.

89 For evidence of the same strategy in the twentieth century, see C. Grant and N. Hodgson, *The Case for Co-Education*, London, Grant Richards, 1913 and R.R. Dale, *Mixed or Single-Sex School*, London, Routledge & Kegan Paul, 1971, vol. 2, especially chap. 13. See also Jenny Price, '"We're just here to make up the numbers really", The

experience of girls in boys' public schools', in Walford, (ed.), *Private Schooling of Girls*.

90 Walkerdine, *Counting Girls Out*, p. 98.

91 Porny, *Practical French Grammar*, p. 319.

92 See, for example, Brian Simon, *Studies in the History of Education 1780–1870*, London, Lawrence and Wishart, 1969.

93 Joan Scott, 'Gender: a useful category for historical analysis', *American Historical Review*, 91, November 1986, p. 1067.

94 See, for example, Alison Kelly, Judith Whyte and Barbara Smail, *Final Report of the Girls into Science and Technology Project*, (GIST), Manchester, Manchester University Press, 1984.

95 Thus, the psychologist Philip Vernon's explanation for *girls'* superior scores in intelligence and arithmetic group tests in the 1940–50 period was that 'boys were likely to have been more seriously affected by wartime relaxations of home discipline and upsets to schooling'. Quoted by Barbara Thom, 'Better a teacher than a hairdresser', pp. 134, 139. This issue is discussed in greater detail in Michèle Cohen, 'Is there a Space for the Achieving Girl'? in Patricia Murphy (ed.), *Effective Pedagogies? Educating Girls and Boys*, Basingstoke, Falmers Press, (forthcoming).

96 Bob Powell, *Boys, Girls and Languages in School*, London, CILT, 1986; Locke, *Some Thoughts*, p. 218.

97 Hawkins, *Modern Languages*, p. 221.

98 Powell, *Boys, Girls*, pp. 48, 62. Teachers he interviewed also said they were 'too easily impressed by the neatness and presentation of girls' work', p. 67.

7 TONGUES, MASCULINITY AND NATIONAL CHARACTER

1 See for example S. Prickett, *England and the French Revolution*, Basingstoke, Macmillan, 1989; M.J. Quinlan, *Victorian Prelude: A History of English Manners 1700–1830*, London, Cass, 1965; M.L. Bush, *The English Aristocracy: a Comparative Synthesis*, Manchester, Manchester University Press, 1984; J.V. Beckett, *The Aristocracy in England 1660–1914*, Oxford, Basil Blackwell, 1986.

2 Hevda Ben-Israel, *English Historians on the French Revolution*, Cambridge, Cambridge University Press, 1968. See also Ceri Crossly and Ian Small *The French Revolution and British Culture*, Oxford, Oxford University Press, 1989; H.T. Mason and W. Doyle, *The Impact of the French Revolution on European Consciousness*, Gloucester, Alan Sutton, 1989.

3 George Newman, *The Rise of English Nationalism: A Cultural History 1740–1830*, London, Weidenfeld & Nicolson, 1987, pp. 235–236. Hannah More, *Strictures on The Modern System of Female Education*, (1799), London, 1811, p. 110.

4 Olivia Smith, *The Politics of Language 1791–1819*, Oxford, Clarendon Press, 1984, p. 96.

5 This was possibly due to the influx of aristocratic *émigrés* who could give private French lessons. See Chapter 5 above, note 33.

6 G.T. Clapton and W. Stewart, *Les Etudes Françaises dans l'Enseignement en Grande Bretagne*, Paris, Les Belles Lettres, Linda Colley, 1929; *Britons: Forging the Nation 1707–1837*, London, Yale University Press, 1992, p. 165.

7 Frances Cobbe wrote that when travelling in Europe, English women were not only able to chatter 'on their own account' and use the local language, but to 'assist our countrymen out of the multitudinous dilemmas to which their ignorance (of modern languages) consigne[d] them'. 'Female education, and, how it would be affected by university examinations', Paper read at the Social Science Congress, London, 1862, p. 14.

8 *Report from the Commissioners, Schools Inquiry Commission*, also called Taunton Commission, 23 vols, London, 1867–1868, vol. 7, p. 298.

9 Taunton Commission, vol. 9, p. 647. The same attitude could be found in Public Schools, see *Report of Her Majesty's Commissioners Appointed to Inquire into Revenues and Management of Certain Colleges and Schools*, also known as the Clarendon Commission, 4 vols, London, 1864.

10 Nineteenth-century literature is full of references to this, from Jane Austen and Charlotte Brontë to J.H. Ewing's *Six to Sixteen* which was serialized in *Aunt Judy's Magazine*, published 1867–1874.

11 Most notably Eric Hawkins, *Modern Languages in the Curriculum*, Cambridge, Cambridge University Press, 1981 and L.G. Kelly, *25 Centuries of Language Teaching: 500 BC–1969*, Rowley, MA, Newbury House, 1976.

12 William Darrell, *A Gentleman Instructed in the Conduct of a Virtuous and Happy Life*, (1704), London, 1720, pp. 544–546; David Fordyce, *Dialogues Concerning Education*, 2 vols, London, 1745–48, vol. 2, p. 305.

13 See Chapter 4, n. 39. Richard Hurd, *Dialogues on the Uses of Foreign Travel Considered as a Part of an English Gentleman's Education: Between Lord Shaftesbury and Mr Locke*, London, 1764. Hurd uses *Locke*'s voice.

14 Hurd, *Dialogues*, p. 74.

15 D. Fordyce, *Dialogues*. See Chapter 3 above for a detailed description of his Plan of Education.

16 Colley, *Britons*, p. 172. Nor is there any evidence that domestic tourism developed instead of the Grand Tour. On the contrary, it was suggested in addition to the European tour or as preparation for it, even in the early eighteenth century. See Josiah Tucker, *Instructions for Foreign Travel*, Dublin, 1758; K.S. Dent, 'The informal education of the landed classes in the eighteenth century, with particular reference to reading', Ph.D. thesis, University of Birmingham, 1974.

17 Colley argues that the emergence of public schools was a crucial aspect of the 'cultural reconstruction of the British élite' as patriotic and nationalistic. *Britons*, pp. 167–168, 172.

18 Hurd, *Dialogues*, p. 66.

19 As against a private one which, throughout the century, had traditionally been 'finished' by the Grand Tour.

20 George Chapman, *A Treatise of Education*, (1773), London 1784, p. 46; John Moore, *A View of Society and Manners*, 2 vols, Dublin, 1797, vol. I, Letter XXXI, pp. 197, 201.
21 Colley, *Britons*, p. 167.
22 David Fordyce, *Dialogues*, II, 305 [my emphasis]. See also Michèle Cohen, 'The Grand Tour: constructing the English gentleman in eighteenth-century France', *History of Education*, vol. 21, no. 3, 1992, pp. 241–257.
23 Colley, *Britons*, p. 168. Author's emphasis.
24 S. Rothblatt, *Tradition and Change in English Liberal Education: an Essay in History and Culture*, London, Faber and Faber, 1976. It was not until Cyril Burt's note 'Faculty Psychology' in the Spens Report that this doctrine was officially laid to rest in England. Board of Education, *Report of the Consultative Committee on Secondary Education with special reference to Grammar Schools and Technical High Schools*, (Spens Report), London, 1938, Appendix IV.
25 John Locke, *Some Thoughts Concerning Education*, (1693), J.W. and J.S. Yolton (eds), Oxford, Clarendon Press, 1989, pp. 224–226.
26 John Clarke, *An Essay upon the Education of Youth in Grammar Schools*, London, 1720, p. 5; Locke, *Some Thoughts*, pp. 217–218.
27 Vicesimus Knox, *Liberal Education or, a Practical Treatise on the Methods of Acquiring Useful and Polite Learning*, London, 1784, p. 52. Lewis Chambaud, *A Grammar of the French Tongue*, London, 1758, and, *The Art of Speaking French*, Dublin, 1772.
28 See M. Stubbs, *Knowledge about Language: Grammar, Ignorance and Society*, London, University of London, Institute of Education, 1990. Anthony Grafton and Lisa Jardine give an illuminating account of the historical value ascribed to learning the minutiae of grammar, *From Humanism to the Humanities: Education and the Liberal Arts in Fifteenth- and Sixteenth-Century Europe*, London, Duckworth, 1986.
29 John Stuart Mill, 'Inaugural address at St Andrews', (1867) in F.A. Cavenagh, *James and John Stuart Mill on Education*, Cambridge, Cambridge University Press, 1931, pp. 150–151.
30 The level of success achieved was not very high, as even Eton Headmaster Balston admitted, Clarendon Commission, Eton evidence, vol. 3, Q.3550.
31 Taunton Commission, vol. 7, p. 260. This explains why they were not able to give an account of 'one of the most valuable parts of analysis', the 'relations of a subordinate to a principal clause'. Vol. 7, p. 400.
32 To get a sense of the shift that had taken place, compare with the comment made by the Bishop of Salisbury, in 1708: 'I have often thought it a great error to waste young gentlemen's years so long in learning Latin, by so tedious a grammar . . . Suppose a youth had . . . an incurable aversion to Latin, his education is not for that to be despaired of; there is so much noble learning to be had in the English and French languages. . .', quoted by Geoffrey Holmes, *Augustan England: Professions, State and Society 1680–1730*, London, George Allen and Unwin, 1982, p. 48.

33 Taunton Commission, vol. 5, p. 190, Q.10757, vol. 9, pp. 292–293; Clarendon Commission, Eton evidence, vol. 3.

34 Henry Home, *Loose Hints upon Education, Chiefly Concerning the Culture of the Heart*, Edinburgh, 1781, p. 135. Home probably borrowed this phrase from Rousseau's 'Emile'. See Jean-Jacques Rousseau, 'Emile', (1762), in *Oeuvres Complètes*, Paris, Gallimard, 1969, vol. IV, Book 5, p. 718.

35 More, *Strictures*, vol. 2, p. 59.

36 James Fordyce, *Sermons to Young Women*, (1766), London, 1770, vol. I p. 153.

37 More, *Essays on Various Subjects*, London, 1785, p. 135.

38 Thomas Wilson, *The Many Advantages of a Good Language to Any Nation*, London, 1729, p. 32.

39 Thomas Carlyle, *On Heroes, Hero Worship, and the Heroic in History*, (1840), London, 1940, p. 411; See also Norman Vance, *The Sinews of the Spirit: The Ideal of Christian Manliness in Victorian Literature and Religious Thought*, Cambridge, Cambridge University Press, 1985.

40 Like the effects of excessive venery. It also calls to mind the moral and medical panics starting in the late eighteenth century about the debilitating effects of male masturbation on the *mind*. See, for example, Ed Cohen, *Talk on the Wilde Side: Towards a Genealogy of Discourse on Male Sexualities*, London and New York, Routledge, 1993.

41 Henry Sweet, *The Practical Study of Languages*, (1899), London, Oxford University Press, 1964.

42 Clarendon Commission, Eton evidence, Q.5536. Thus too, when Lord Clarendon asked Balston, Eton Headmaster: 'Would it not be considered necessary for the authorities of Eton to render obligatory a thing which [parents] think ought to be a part of an English gentleman's education?', Balston replies: 'I should think not'. Clarendon Commission, vol. 3, p. 84.

43 Clarendon Commission, vol. 3, p. 91.

44 Taunton Commission, vol. 9, pp. 300, 826.

45 Taunton Commission, vol. 5, Q.11476, p. 254. It is interesting to read how Molly Hughes, who attended the school at that time, remembers those French classes: 'Of all the lessons French was the dullest ... hardly a word of French was spoken ... The bulk of the lesson consisted of so-called translation'. M. Vivian Hughes, *A London Family*, Oxford, Oxford University Press, 1946, p. 173.

46 *An Examen of Mr Sheridan's Plan for the Improvement of Education in this Country*, by a set of Gentlemen associated for that purpose, London, 1784.

47 St Evremont is reported to have said: 'Generally no Conversation would be more agreeable than that of the *French*, if they would talk a little less, and that of the *English*, if they would speak a little more than they do', [John Constable] *The Conversation of Gentlemen*, London, 1738, p. 90.

48 *Spectator*, no. 135; Thomas Wilson, *The Many Advantages of a Good Language*, London, 1729.

49 Abbé Trublet, *Essays Upon Several Subjects of Literature and Morality*, 3 vols, London, 1744, pp. 23, 306. Abbé Le Blanc, *Letters on the English and the French Nations*, 2 vols, Dublin, 1747, p. 26.

50 *Monthly Review*, vol. 8, Jan-June 1753, p. 257.

51 *Spectator*, no. 135; Swift, 'A Proposal for Correcting, Improving and Ascertaining the English Tongue', in T. Roscoe (ed.), *The Works of Jonathan D.D. Swift*, 2 vols, London, Geo. Bell & Sons, 1880.

52 Alexander Jardine, *Letters from Barbary, France, Portugal, etc.*, 2 vols, London, 1788, vol. 1, pp. 268, 360.

53 John Andrews, *Letters to a Young Gentleman on his Setting out for France*, London, 1784, p. 32, and *A Comparative View of the French and English Nations*, London, 1785, p. 318.

54 Jardine, *Letters*, vol. 1, p. 347.

55 Catherine Sinclair, *Modern Accomplishments or the March of Intellect*, Edinburgh, William Whyte & Co., 1836.

56 Susan Bayley, 'Modern languages as emerging curricular subjects in England 1864–1914', *History of Education Society*, Bulletin no. 47, Spring 1991, pp. 23–31.

57 Clarendon Commission, vol. 4, p. 77; Taunton Commission, vol. 5, QQ. 10756, 10760. During the 1880s, writes Eric Hawkins, 'oral French [was] despised as "nursery", "tea-party", "courier" or "bagman" French', *Modern Languages in the Curriculum*, Cambridge, Cambridge University Press, 1981, p. 121.

58 Jardine, *Letters*, vol. 1, p. 268.

59 See Michèle Cohen, 'Chauvinistic silence; patriotic conversation: nation, gender and the tongue in France and England', Paper given at the Department of History and Civilization, European University Institute, Florence, March 1995.

60 Jardine, *Letters*, vol. 1, p. 266.

61 Mary Wollstonecraft, *A Historical and Moral View of the Origin and Progress of the French Revolution and the effect it has produced in Europe*, London, 1794, Book V, Chap. IV, pp. 504–505.

62 William Alexander, *The History of Women from the Earliest Antiquity to the Present Time*, London, 1779, vol. 1, p. 314.

63 More, *Strictures;* Thomas Gisborne, *An Enquiry into the Duties of the Female Sex*, London, 1796, p. 58.

64 In the eighteenth century conversation referred to both verbal and sexual intercourse. Laqueur takes the 'demotion of the female orgasm' as central evidence for the new model of the body. 'Why', he asks, 'did sexual arousal and its fulfillment – specifically female sexual arousal – become irrelevant to an understanding of conception?'. Thomas Laqueur, *Making Sex: Body and Gender from the Greeks to Freud*, London, Harvard University Press, 1990, pp. 8,9. See also Roy Porter, 'English society in the eighteenth century revisited', in J. Black (ed.), *British Politics and Society from Walpole to Pitt 1742–1789*, Basingstoke, Macmillan, 1990; P.-G. Boucé, 'Some sexual beliefs and myths in eighteenth century Britain', in P.-G Boucé (ed.), *Sexuality in Eighteenth Century Britain*, Manchester, Manchester University Press, 1982; *The Ladies Dispensatory*, London, 1748.

BIBLIOGRAPHY

PRIMARY SOURCES

Alexander, William, *The History of Women from the Earliest Antiquity to the Present Time, giving some account of almost every interesting particular concerning that sex among all nations*, 2 vols, London, 1779.

[Allestree, Richard], *The Government of the Tongue*, Oxford, 1674. 'The Anatomy of a Woman's Tongue', (1638), in the *Harleian Miscellany*, vol. 1, London, 1744.

Andrews, John, *Remarks on the French and English Ladies*, London, 1783.

—— *Letters to a Young Gentleman on his Setting out for France*, London, 1784.

—— *A Comparative View of the French and English Nations in their Manners, Politics, and Literature*, London, 1785.

Angeloni, Battista, *Letters on the English Nation*, London, 1756.

Annual Register, A Periodical Paper, 1758–1791.

Arleville, Bridel, *Practical Accidence of the French Tongue; or Introduction to the French Syntax, upon a more Extensive and Easy Plan than any Extant*, London, 1798.

The Art of Speaking and Holding one's Tongue in and out of Doors, London, 1761.

Astell, Mary, *A Serious Proposal to the Ladies, for the Advancement of their True and Greatest Interest*, London, 1697.

Austen, Jane, *Mansfield Park*, (1814), New York, Bantam Press, 1964.

The Baboon à la Mode, London, 1704.

Bary, René, *Journal de conversation*, Paris, 1674.

[Bennett, Revd John], *Strictures on Female Education; Chiefly in Relation to the Culture of the Heart*, London, 1787.

—— *Letters to a Young Lady on Useful and Interesting Subjects Calculated to Improve the Heart, to Form the Manners, and Enlighten the Understanding*, 2 vols, Dublin, 1789.

Board of Education, *Memorandum on the Study of Languages*, London, 1907.

—— *Report of the Consultative Committee on the Differentiation of the Curriculum for Boys and Girls Respectively in Secondary Schools*, London, 1923.

Bordelon, Laurent, *La Langue*, Rotterdam, 1705, published in English as *The Management of the Tongue*, London, 1706.

Boswell, James, *The Life of Samuel Johnson*, (1791), A. Glover (ed.), 3 vols., London, J.M. Dent & Sons, 1925.

Bouhours, Dominique, *Entretiens d'Ariste et d'Eugène*, Amsterdam, 1671.

Boyer, Abel, *The Compleat French Master for Ladies and Gentlemen*, (London, 1694), Edinburgh, 1767.

Brown, John, *An Estimate of the Manners and Principles of the Times*, London, vol. 1, 1757, vol. 2, 1758.

Burgh, James, *Britain's Remembrancer: Or, The Danger is not Over*, London 1746.

—— *The Dignity of Human Nature*, London, 1754.

Burnet, Gilbert, *Thoughts on Education*, (1668), J. Clarke (ed.), London, 1761.

[Burney, Fanny], *The Early Diary of Fanny Burney 1768–1778*, 2 vols, Annie Raine Ellis (ed.), London, George Bell & Sons, 1913.

—— *Diary and Letters of Madame D'Arblay*, edited by her niece, 7 vols, London, Henry Colburn, 1854.

Burt, Cyril, 'Historical note on faculty psychology', in Board of Education, *Report of the Consultative Committee on Secondary Education with special reference to Grammar Schools and Technical High Schools*, (Spens Report), London, 1938, Appendix IV.

Burton, John, *Lectures on Female Education and Manners*, 2 vols, London, 1793.

Calbris, B., *The Rational Guide to the French Tongue*, London, 1797.

Carlyle, Thomas, *On Heroes, Hero Worship, and the Heroic in History*, (1840), London, 1940.

Castiglione, Baldassare, *The Book of the Courtier*, (1528), Eng. trans, Harmondsworth, Penguin, 1967.

Chambaud, Lewis, *Dialogues in French and English*, London, 1751.

—— *A Grammar of the French Tongue*, London, 1758.

—— *The Elements of the French Language*, London, 1762.

—— *The Art of Speaking French*, Dublin, 1772.

Chapman, George, *A Treatise of Education*, (1773), London 1784.

Chapone, Hester, *Letters on the Improvement of the Mind*, (1773), London, 1820.

Cheneau, Francis, *French Grammar*, London, 1685.

—— *The True French Master*, London, 1723.

Chesterfield, Stanhope Philip Dormer, Earl of, *Letters to His Son*, 1737–1768, (1774), London, W.W. Gibbings, 1890.

Chirol, J.L., *An Enquiry into the Best System of Female Education, or Boarding School or Home Education Attentively Considered*, London, 1809.

Clarke, John, *An Essay upon the Education of Youth in Grammar Schools*, London, 1720.

Cobbe, Frances Power, 'Female education, and, how it would be affected by university examinations', Paper read at the Social Science Congress, London, 1862.

Congreve, William, 'The Way of the World', (1700), in Edmund Gosse (ed.), *Restoration Plays*, London, J.M. Dent and Sons, 1968.

[Constable, John], *The Conversation of Gentlemen*, London, 1738.

Consultative Committee to the Board of Education, *Report on the Differentiation of the Curriculum for Boys and Girls Respectively in Secondary Schools*, London, 1923.

Corbet, John, *A Concise System of English Grammar*, Shrewsbury, 1784.

Costeker, J.L., *The Fine Gentleman or the Complete Education of a Young Nobleman*, London, 1732.

Cowley, Hannah, *The Belle's Stratagem*, Dublin, 1781.

Darrell, William, *A Gentleman Instructed in the Conduct of a Virtuous and Happy Life*, (1704), London, 1720.

Darwin, Erasmus, *A Plan for the Conduct of Female Education in Boarding Schools*, London, 1797.

Day, Thomas, *The History of Sandford and Merton*, (1783–1789), London, Ward & Lock, 1860.

Defoe, Daniel, *An Essay Upon Projects*, (1697), facsimile reprint, Menston, The Scolar Press, 1969.

—— *The Compleat Gentleman*, (c. 1728), K.D. Bulbring (ed.), London, David Nutt, 1890.

Dennis, John, 'A Defence of Sir Fopling Flutter', (1722), reprinted in E.A. Bloom and L.D. Bloom, *Addison and Steele: The Critical Heritage*, London, Routledge & Kegan Paul, 1980.

Department of Education and Science, *Curricular Differences for Boys and Girls*, Education Survey 21, London, HMSO, 1975.

—— *Boys and Modern Languages*, H.M.I. Inspection Report, London, HMSO, 1985.

Devisscher, Charles Antoine, *Grammaire de Lhomond or the Principles of the French Language*, London, 1816.

Du Bosc, Jacques, *L'Honneste Femme*, Lyon, 1665.

Du Mitand, Huguenin, *A New French Spelling Book*, London, 1784.

Edgeworth, Maria, *An Essay upon Education, Shewing how Latin, Greek and other Languages may be Learned more easily, quickly and Perfectly, than they commonly are*, London, 1811.

—— *Patronage*, (1814), London, Pandora, 1986.

—— *The Good Governess and other stories*, London, n.d.

—— and Richard Lovell, *Practical Education*, 2 vols, London 1798.

An Essay in Defense of the Female Sex, in which are inserted the characters of A Pedant, A Squire, A Beau, A Vertuoso, A Poetaster, A City-Critick, &c, London, 1696.

Essex, John, *The Young Ladies Conduct, or Rules for Education*, London, 1722.

Etheredge, Sir George, 'The Man of Mode', (1676), in E. Gosse (ed.), *Restoration Plays*, London, J.M. Dent and Sons, 1968.

[Evelyn, Mary], *Mundus Muliebris*, London, 1690.

An Examen of Mr Sheridan's Plan for the Improvement of Education in this Country, by a set of Gentlemen associated for that purpose, London, 1784.

Faret, Nicolas, *L'Art de plaire à la cour*, Paris, 1630.

Fauchon, James, *The French Tongue*, Cambridge, 1751.

Felton, Henry, *A Dissertation on Reading the Classics and Forming a Just Style*, London, 1723.

Fielding, Sir John, *The Universal Mentor*, London, 1763.

Foote, Samuel, 'The ENGLISHMAN return'd from Paris', (1756), in P.R. Backscheider and D. Howard (eds), *The Plays of SAMUEL FOOTE*, New York, Garland, 1983.

Fordyce, David, *Dialogues Concerning Education, or a plan laid down on that subject in several conversations of some philosophical gentlemen, for training up the youth of both sexes in learning and virtue*, 2 vols, London, 1745–48.

Fordyce, James, *Sermons to Young Women*, (1766), 2 vols, London, 1770.
—— *Addresses to Young Men*, 2 vols, London, 1777.

Fournel, V., (ed.), *Les Contemporains de Molière: recueil de Comédies rares ou peu connues jouées de 1650 à 1680*, 3 vols, Paris, Firmin Didot Frères, 1863.

Fournier, E., *Variétés Historiques et Littéraires*, 10 vols, Paris, 1859.

Gailhard, Jean, *The Compleat Gentleman or Directions for the Education of Youth as to their Breeding at Home, and Travelling Abroad*, 2 vols, London, 1678.

Gentleman's Magazine, April 1737.

Gérardot, Revd J.A.B., *Elements of French Grammar*, London, 1815.

Gildon, Charles and Brightland, John, *A Grammar of the English Tongue*, London, 1711.

Gisborne, Thomas, *An Enquiry into the Duties of the Female Sex*, London, 1796.

Goldsmith, Oliver, 'An Enquiry into the Present State of Polite Learning in Europe', (1756), in A. Friedman (ed.), *Collected Works of Oliver Goldsmith*, 5 vols, Oxford, Clarendon Press, 1966.

Gratte, Henri, *Nouvelle Grammaire Françoise à l'Usage de la Jeunesse Angloise*, London, 1791.

Greenwood, James, *An Essay Towards a Practical English Grammar*, London, 1711.

Grosley, P.J., *A Tour to London*, London, 1772.

Hall, Joseph, *QUO VADIS? a Just censure of Travel as it is commonly undertaken by the Gentlemen of our Nation*, London, 1617.

Home, Henry, *Loose Hints upon Education, Chiefly Concerning the Culture of the Heart*, Edinburgh, 1781.

Hooton, Henry, *A Bridle for the Tongue*, London, 1709.

Howell, James, *Instructions for Forreine Travel*, (1640), E. Arber (ed.), London, English Reprints no. 6, 1869.

Hughes, M. Vivian, *A London Family*, Oxford, Oxford University Press, 1946.

Hume, David, 'Of the Rise and Progress of the Arts and Sciences', in J.W Lenz (ed.), *Of the Standard of Taste and Other Essays by David Hume*, New York, 1965.

Hurd, Richard, *Dialogues on the Uses of Foreign Travel Considered as a Part of an English Gentleman's Education: Between Lord Shaftesbury and Mr Locke*, London, 1764.

Hyde, Edward, Earl of Clarendon, 'A dialogue concerning education', *A Collection of Several Tracts*, London, 1728.

Jardine, Captain Alexander, *Letters from Barbary, France, Portugal, etc.*, 2 vols, London, 1788.

Johnson, Samuel, *The Rambler*, a Periodical Paper, (1750–1752), London, 1824.

—— *A Dictionary of the English Language*, London, 1755.

Knox, Vicesimus, *Liberal Education or, a Practical Treatise on the Methods of Acquiring Useful and Polite Learning*, London, 1784.

La Bruyère, Jean de, *Les Caractères ou les moeurs de ce siècle*, (1688), Paris, Garnier Frères, 1962.

The Ladies' Catechism, London, 1703.

The Ladies Dispensatory, London, 1748.

Lainé, Pierre de, *The Princely Way to the French Tongue*, London, 1677.

Lane, A., *A Key to the Art of Letters or English as a Learned Language*, London, 1706.

La Rochefoucauld, François de, *Maximes et Réflexions*, (1662), Paris, Larousse, 1965.

Lassels, Richard, *The Voyage of Italy*, Paris, 1670.

Le Blanc, Jean Bernard, Abbé, *Letters on the English and the French Nations*, 2 vols, Dublin, 1747.

Le Breton, Philip, *Elémens de la Grammaire Françoise*, London, 1815.

Leigh, Edward, *Three Diatribes or Discourses*, London, 1671.

Lévizac, Abbé Jean Pons Victor Lecoutz de, *L'Art de Parler et d'Ecrire Correctement la Langue Françoise*, London, 1797.

Locke, John, *Some Thoughts Concerning Education*, (1693), J.W. and J.S. Yolton (eds), Oxford, Clarendon Press, 1989.

Lockitt, C.H., *The Relations of French and English Society*, London, Longmans & Co, 1920.

Lysons, David, *Collecteana*, London, n.d. vol. I.

The Macaroni Jester and Pantheon of Wit containing all that has lately transpired in the Regions of Politeness, Whim and Novelty, London, 1773.

Maittaire, Michael, *The English Grammar*, London, 1712.

Makin, Bathsua, *An Essay to Revive the Antient Education of Gentlewomen in Religion, Manners, Arts and Tongues, with an Answer to the Objections against this Education*, London, 1673.

Marmontel, 'Contes Moraux', *Oeuvres Complètes*, Paris, Amable Costes et Cie., 1819.

Masham, Lady Damaris, *Occasional Thoughts in Reference to a Virtuous or Christian Life*, London, 1705.

Mauger, Claude, *Mauger's French Grammar*, London, 1688.

—— and Festeau, Paul, *Nouvelle Double Grammaire Françoise-Angloise et Angloise-Françoise*, Brussels, 1696.

Méré, Antoine Gombauld, Chevalier de, *Oeuvres Complètes*, (1668–1677), C. Boudhors (ed.), 3 vols, Paris, Fernand Roches, 1930.

Miège, Guy, *The Grounds of the French Tongue*, London, 1687.

Mill, John Stuart, 'Inaugural address at St Andrews', in F.A. Cavenagh, *James and John Stuart Mill on Education*, Cambridge, Cambridge University Press, 1931.

Millar, John, *The Origin of the Distinction of Ranks*, London, 1779.

Misson, François Maximilien, *A New Voyage to Italy*, 2 vols, London, 1695.

[Moir, John], *Female Tuition, or an address to mothers*, London, 1784.

Molière, [Jean-Baptiste Poquelin], 'Les Précieuses Ridicules', (1662), in R. Jouanny (ed.), *Théâtre Complet*, 2 vols, Paris, Garnier, 1959.

—— 'Les Femmes Savantes', (1672), in R. Jouanny (ed.), *Théâtre Complet*, 2 vols, Paris, Garnier, 1959.

Moore, John, *A View of Society and Manners in France, Switzerland and Germany, with Anecdotes Relating to some Eminent Characters*, 2 vols, Dublin, 1797.

More, Hannah, *Essays on Various Subjects*, London, 1785.

—— *Strictures on The Modern System of Female Education, with a View of the Principles and Conduct Prevalent among Women of Rank*, 2 vols, (1799), London, 1811.

Morvan de Bellegarde, Jean-Baptiste, *Réflexions sur ce qui peut plaire ou déplaire dans le commerce du monde*, Paris, 1690.

—— *Modèles de conversation pour les personnes polies*, (1697), La Haye, 1719.

Muralt, B.N. de, *Lettres sur les Anglois et les François*, Cologne, 1727.

Murdoch, John, *The Pronunciation and Orthography of the French Language rendered perfectly easy on a plan quite original*, London, 1788.

Murray, Lindsay, *English Adapted to the Different Classes of Learners*, London, 1795.

Osborne, Francis, *Advice to a Son*, Oxford, 1656.

Parker, Samuel Sylva, *Letters Upon Occasional Subjects*, London, 1701.

Peacham, Henry, *The Complete Gentleman*, (1634), Virgil B. Heltzel (ed.), Ithaca, NY, Cornell University Press, 1962.

Perrin, John B., *The Elements of French Conversation*, London, 1774.

Peyton, V.J., *The True Principles of the French Language*, London, 1757.

Picard, George, *The English Guide to the French Tongue*, London, 1778.

—— *A Grammatical Dictionary*, London, 1790.

Pope, Alexander, 'The Dunciad', Book IV, in J. Butt (ed.), *The Poems of Alexander Pope*, London, Methuen, 1963.

Porny, Marc Antoine, [Antoine Pyron du Martre], *Grammatical Exercises, English and French*, Dublin, 1804.

—— *The Practical French Grammar*, Dublin, 1812.

Praval, Charles, *The Syntax of the French Tongue*, Dublin, 1779.

—— *The Rudiments of the French Tongue reduced to Question and Answer for the Use of Beginners*, Dublin, 1802.

Pure, Michel de, *La prétieuse ou le mystère des ruelles*, 2 vols, (1656–58), E. Magne (ed.), Paris, Droz, 1938.

Ramsay, William, *The Gentleman's Companion*, London, 1669.

Renaud, Antoine, *Manière de Parler*, Paris, 1697.

Report of Her Majesty's Commissioners Appointed to Inquire into Revenues and Management of Certain Colleges and Schools, (Clarendon Commission), 4 vols, London, 1864.

Report from the Commissioners, Schools Inquiry Commission, (Taunton Commission), 23 vols, London, 1867–1868.

Ripman, Walter, *Easy Free Composition*, (1905), London, J.M. Dent & Sons, 1925.

Rousseau, Jean-Jacques, 'Julie ou La Nouvelle Héloise', *Oeuvres Complètes*, Paris, Gallimard, 1964.

—— 'Emile', *Oeuvres Complètes*, Paris, Gallimard, 1969.

Scudéry, Madeleine de, *Clélie, Histoire Romaine*, Paris, 1658–1866.

—— *Célinte, Nouvelle Première*, (1661), A. Niderst (ed.), Paris, Nizet, 1979.

—— *Conversations sur Divers Sujets*, Amsterdam, 1686.

—— *Conversations Nouvelles*, Paris, 1688.

Sheridan, Thomas, *A Dissertation on the Causes of the Difficulties which Occur in Learning the English Tongue*, London, 1762.

—— *Dictionary*, London, 1780.

—— *A Rhetorical Grammar of the English Language*, (1781), facsimile reprint, Menston, The Scolar Press, 1969.

Sinclair, Catherine, *Modern Accomplishments or the March of Intellect*, Edinburgh, William Whyte & Co, 1836.

Smollett, Tobias, 'The Adventures of Roderick Random', (1748), George Saintsbury (ed.), *The Works of Tobias Smollett*, 12 vols, London, The Navarre Society, n.d.

Somaize, Antoine Baudeau de, *Le Grand Dictionnaire des précieuses ou la clef de la langue des ruelles*, Paris, Nizet, 1660.

—— *Dictionnaire Historique des Précieuses*, (1661), Charles-L. Livet (ed.), Paris, H. Welter, 1856.

—— 'Les Véritables Précieuses', (1660), in G. Mongrédien (ed.), *Comédies et Pamphlets sur Molière*, Paris, Nizet, 1986.

The *Spectator*, 1711–1714.

Spence, Joseph, *Letters from the GRAND TOUR 1730–1741*, S. Klima (ed.), London, McGill-Queen's University Press, 1975.

Stackhouse, Thomas, *Reflections on the Nature and Property of Languages in General and on the Advantages and Defects and Manner of Improving the English Tongue*, London, 1731.

Sterne, Laurence, 'Sermon on the Prodigal Son', Sermon XX, *The Works of Laurence Sterne*, London, Henry G. Bohn, 1857.

Swift, Jonathan, 'An Essay on Modern Education', in T. Roscoe (ed.), *The Works of Jonathan D.D. Swift*, 2 vols, London, Geo. Bell & Sons, 1880.

—— 'A Proposal for Correcting, Improving and Ascertaining the English Tongue', in *Works*.

—— 'Hints Toward an Essay on Conversation', in *Works*.

Tandon, J.E., *A New French Grammar*, London, 1745.

The *Tatler*, A Periodical Paper, London 1709–1711.

Trublet, Nicolas Charles Joseph, *Essays Upon Several Subjects of Literature and Morality*, 3 vols, London, 1744.

Tucker, Josiah, *Instructions for Foreign Travel*, Dublin, 1758

Vanbrugh, Sir John, 'The Relapse', (1697), in M. Cordner (ed.), *Sir John Vanbrugh: Four Comedies*, Harmondsworth, Penguin, 1989.

Vaugelas, Claude Favre de, *Remarques sur la Langue Française*, (1647), Paris, R. Lagane (ed.), Larousse, 1975.

Vaumorière, Pierre Ortigue, Sieur de, *L'Art de plaire dans la conversation*, Paris, 1690.

Walker, Obadiah, *Of Education*, (1673), facsimile reprint, Menston, The Scolar Press, 1970.

Wilson, Thomas, *The Many Advantages of a Good Language to Any Nation, with an examination of the present state of our own*, London, 1729.

Wollstonecraft, Mary, *Thoughts on the Education of Daughters*, London, 1787.

—— *A Historical and Moral View of the Origins and Progress of the French Revolution and the effect it has produced in Europe*, London, 1794.

The *World*, A Periodical Paper, London, 1753–1756.

Wraxall, Sir N. William, *Historical Memoirs of My Own Time*, 2 vols, London, 1815.

[Wray, Mary], *The Ladies Library*, published by Sir Richard Steele, London, 1722.

Wright, Thomas, *A Caricature History of the Georges or Annals of the House of Hanover, compiled from the Squibs, Broadsides, Pictures, Lampoons and Pictorial Caricatures of the Time*, London, John Camden Holten, 1868.

SECONDARY SOURCES

Adamson, J.W., *English Education 1789–1902*, Cambridge, Cambridge University Press, 1930.

Adler, K. and Pointon, M. (eds), *The Body Imaged: The Human Form of Visual Culture Since the Renaissance*, Cambridge, Cambridge University Press, 1993.

Alston, R.C., *A Bibliography of the English Language from the Invention of Printing to the Year 1800*, Leeds, E.J. Arnold & Sons, 1965.

—— *A Bibliography of the English Language*, vol. 12, Part I, The French Language Grammars: Miscellaneous Treatises, Dictionaries, Great Britain, 1985.

Armstrong, N., *Desire and Domestic Fiction: A Political History of the Novel*, Oxford, Oxford University Press, 1987.

Aronson, N., *Mademoiselle de Scudéry ou le voyage au Pays de Tendre*, Paris, Fayard, 1986.

Ashton, John, *Social Life in the Reign of Queen Anne*, London, Chatto and Windus, 1883.

Avery, G., *The Best Type of Girl: A History of Girls' Independent Schools*, London, Deutsch, 1991.

Avigdor, E., *Coquettes et Précieuses*, Paris, Nizet, 1982.

Ayres-Bennett, W., *Vaugelas and the Development of the French Language*, London, The Modern Humanities Research Association, 1987.

Ball, S.J., 'Introducing Monsieur Foucault', in S.J. Ball (ed.), *Foucault and Education: Disciplines and Knowledges*, London, Routledge, 1990.

Bamford, T.W., *Rise of the Public Schools: A Study of Boys' Public Schools in England and Wales from 1837 to the Present Day*, London, Nelson, 1967.

Barker-Benfield, G.H. *The Culture of Sensibility: Sex and Society in Eighteenth-Century Britain*, London, University of Chicago Press, 1992.

Barnard, H.C., *A History of English Education from 1760*, London, University of London Press, 1969.

Barrell, J., *English Literature in History 1730–1780: An Equal, Wide Survey*, London, Hutchinson, 1983.

—— '"The Dangerous Goddess": masculinity, prestige, and the aesthetic in early eighteenth-century Britain', in *The Birth of Pandora and the Division of Knowledge*, London, Macmillan, 1992.

Barthelémy, E. de, (ed.), *La Galerie des Portraits de Melle de Montpensier*, Paris, Didier, 1860.

Batters, J., 'Do boys really think languages are just girl-talk?', *Modern Languages*, vol. LXVII, 1986, pp. 75–79.

Battersby, C., *Gender and Genius: Towards a Feminist Aesthetics*, London, The Women's Press, 1994.

Baugh, A., *A History of the English Language*, London, Routledge & Kegan Paul, 1959; reprinted (revised) by Routledge, 1993.

Bayley, S., 'Modern languages as emerging curricular subjects in England 1864–1914', *History of Education Society*, Bulletin no. 47, Spring 1991, pp. 23–31.

Beckett, John V., *The Aristocracy in England 1660–1914*, Oxford, Basil Blackwell, 1986.

Ben-Israel, H., *English Historians on the French Revolution*, Cambridge, Cambridge University Press, 1968.

Benjamin, M., (ed.), *Science and Sensibility: Gender and Scientific Inquiry 1780–1945*, Oxford, Blackwell, 1991.

Bevis, P., Cohen, M. and Kendall, G., 'Archaeologizing genealogy: Michel Foucault and the economy of austerity', in M. Gane and T. Johnson (eds), *Foucault's New Domains*, London, Routledge, 1993.

Black, J., *The British and the Grand Tour*, London, Croom Helm, 1985.

Borsay, P., *The English Urban Renaissance: Culture and Society in the Provincial Town, 1660–1770*, Oxford, Clarendon Press, 1991.

Boucé, P.-G., 'Some sexual beliefs and myths in eighteenth-century Britain', in P.-G. Boucé (ed.), *Sexuality in Eighteenth-Century Britain*, Manchester, Manchester University Press, 1982.

Bouton, C.P., *Les Grammaires Françaises de Claude Mauger à l'Usage des Anglais*, Paris, Klincksieck, 1972.

Bouvier, M., 'Le Naturel', *XVIIe Siècle*, vol. 156, 3, July–September 1987.

Brauer, G.C., *The Education of a Gentleman: Theories of Gentlemanly Education in England, 1660–1775*, New York, Bookman Associates, 1959.

Bray, A., *Homosexuality in Renaissance England*, London, Gay Men's Press, 1982.

Bray, R., *La Préciosité et les Précieux*, Paris, Nizet, 1968.

Breward, C., *The Culture of Fashion: A New History of Fashionable Dress*, Manchester, Manchester University Press, 1995.

Brimley Johnson, R. (ed.), *Mrs Delany: At Court and Among the Wits*, London, Stanley Paul and Co., 1925.

Brittan, A., *Masculinity and Power*, Oxford, Basil Blackwell, 1989.

Browne, A., *The Eighteenth-Century Feminist Mind*, Brighton, The Harvester Press, 1987.

Bullough, V.L., and Bullough, B., *Cross-Dressing, Sex, and Gender*, Philadelphia, University of Pennsylvania Press, 1993.

Burgess, A. and Haskell, F., *The Age of the Grand Tour*, London, Paul Elek, 1967.

Burke, J., 'The Grand Tour and the rule of taste', in R.F. Brissenden (ed.), *Studies in the Eighteenth Century*, Canberra, Australian National University Press, 1968.

Burke, P., *The Art of Conversation*, Oxford, Polity Press, 1993.

Bush, M.L., *The English Aristocracy: A Comparative Synthesis*, Manchester, Manchester University Press, 1984.

Cannon, John, *Aristocratic Century: The Peerage of Eighteenth-Century England*, Cambridge, Cambridge University Press, 1984.

—— *Samuel Johnson and the Politics of Hanoverian England*, Oxford, Clarendon Press, 1994.

Castel, R., '"Problematization" as a Mode of Reading History', in Jan Goldstein, (ed.), *Foucault and the Writing of History*, Oxford, Basil Blackwell, 1994.

Castle, T., *Masquerade and Civilisation: The Carnivalesque in Eighteenth-Century Culture and Fiction*, Stanford, CA, Stanford University Press, 1986.

—— 'The culture of travesty', in G.S. Rousseau and R. Porter (eds), *Sexual Underworlds of the Enlightenment*, Manchester, Manchester University Press, 1987.

Chapman, R. and Rutherford, J. (eds), *Male Order: Unwrapping Masculinity*, London, Lawrence and Wishart, 1988.

Chard, C., 'Effeminacy, pleasure and the classical body', in G. Perry and M. Rossington (eds), *Femininity and Masculinity in Eighteenth-Century Art and Culture*, Manchester, Manchester University Press, 1994.

Clapton, G.T. and Stewart, W., *Les Etudes Françaises dans l'Enseignement en Grande-Bretagne*, Paris, Les Belles Lettres, 1929.

Cohen, E., *Talk on the Wilde Side: Towards a Genealogy of Discourse on Male Sexualities*, London and New York, Routledge, 1993.

Cohen, M., 'Sexism and French language teaching', unpublished M.A. diss., London, University of London, 1982.

—— 'The Grand Tour: constructing the English gentleman in eighteenth-century France', *History of Education*, vol. 21, no. 3, 1992, pp. 241–257.

—— 'The social space: a modest proposal for rethinking the boundaries of the private', paper presented at the Annual Conference of the Association for Eighteenth-Century Studies, Charleston, South Carolina, 1994.

—— 'Is there a space for the achieving girl'? in Patricia Murphy (ed.), *Effective Pedagogies? Educating Girls and Boys*, Basingstoke, Falmers Press, (forthcoming).

Colley, L., *Britons: Forging the Nation*, London, Yale University Press, 1992.

Connell, R.W., 'The big picture: masculinities in recent world history', *Theory and Society*, Special Issues: *Masculinities* vol. 22/5, October 1993, pp. 597–624.

Cottrell, S., 'The devil on two sticks: Franco-phobia in 1803', in Raphael Samuel (ed.), *Patriotism: the Making and Unmaking of British National Identity*, London, Routledge, 1989.

Cousin, V., *La Société Française au XVIIième Siècle, d'après Le Grand Cyrus de Melle de Scudéry*, Paris, Didier, 1858.

Cousins, A. and Hussain, A., *Michel Foucault*, London, Macmillan, 1985.

Craveri, B., *Madame Du Deffand and her World*, London, Peter Halban, 1994.

Cross, D. 'Sex Differences in Achievement', *System*, vol. 11, no. 2, 1982, pp. 159–162.

Crossley, C. and Small, I., (eds), *The French Revolution and British Culture*, Oxford, Oxford University Press, 1989.

Crow, T.E., *Painters and Public Life in Eighteenth-Century Paris*, London, Yale University Press, 1985.

Curtis, E.R., *Lady Sarah Lennox: An Irrepressible Stuart 1745–1826*, London, W.H. Allen, n.d.

Dale, R.R., *Mixed or Single-Sex School?* 2 vol., London, Routledge & Kegan Paul, 1971.

Dann, O. and Dinwiddy J., (eds), *Nationalism in the Age of the French Revolution*, London, The Hambledon Press, 1988.

Darrow, M.H., 'French noblewomen and the new domesticity', *Feminist Studies*, 5, no. 1, Spring 1979, pp. 41–65.

Daston, L., 'The naturalized female intellect', *Science in Context*, vol. 5, no. 2, 1992, pp. 209–235.

Davidoff, L. and Hall, C., *Family Fortunes: Men and Women of the English Middle Class, 1780–1850*, London, Hutchinson, 1987.

Deane, S., *The French Revolution and Enlightenment in England, 1789–1832*, London, Harvard University Press, 1988.

De Bolla, P., *Discourses of the Sublime: Readings in History, Aesthetics and the Subject*, Oxford, Basil Blackwell, 1989.

Dens, J-P., *L'Honnête Homme et la Critique du Goût: esthétique et société au XVIIe Siècle*, Lexington, KY, French Forum, 1981.

—— 'L'Art de la Conversation au Dix-Septième Siècle', *Les Lettres Romanes*, vol. 27, 1973, pp. 215–224.

Dent, K.S., 'The informal education of the landed classes in the eighteenth century, with particular reference to reading', Ph.D. thesis, University of Birmingham, 1974.

Diaconoff, S., 'Ambition, politics, and professionalism: two women painters', in Frederick M. Keener and Susan E. Lorsch (eds), *Eighteenth-Century Women and the Arts*, Contributions to Women's Studies, no. 98, London, Greenwood Press, 1988.

Duberman, M., Vicinus, M. and Chauncey, G. (eds), *Hidden from History: Reclaiming the Gay and Lesbian Past*, London, Penguin Books, 1989.

Duchêne, R., 'Honnêteté et Sexualité', in Y.-M. Bercé (ed.), *Destins et Enjeux du XVIIième Siècle*, Paris, Presses Universitaires de France, 1985.

Duffy, M., *The Englishman and the Foreigner*, Cambridge, Chadwick-Healey, 1986.

Dulong, C., *La Vie Quotidienne des Femmes au Grand Siècle*, Paris, Hachette, 1984.

Dwyer, J., *VIRTUOUS DISCOURSE: Sensibility and Community in Late Eighteenth-Century Scotland*, Edinburgh, John Donald, 1987.

— and Sher, R.B. (eds), *Sociability and Society in Eighteenth-Century Scotland*, Edinburgh, The Mercat Press, 1993.

Dyhouse, C., *Girls Growing Up in Late Victorian and Edwardian England*, London, Routledge & Kegan Paul, 1981.

Epstein, J. and Straub, K. (eds), *Body Guards: The Cultural Politics of Gender Ambiguity*, London, Routledge, 1991.

Eynard, R. and Walkerdine, V., *The Practice of Reason: Investigation into the Teaching and Learning of Mathematics*, vol. 2: 'Girls and Mathematics', London, University of London Press, 1984.

Feuillet de Conches, *Les salons de conversation au dix-huitième siècle*, Paris, Charavay Frères, 1882.

Fletcher, A., *Gender, Sex and Subordination in England 1500–1800*, London, Yale University Press, 1995.

Foucault, M., *Archaeology of Knowledge*, (1969), London, Tavistock, 1972.

— 'Nietzsche, Genealogy, History', in D.F. Bouchard (ed.), *Language, Counter-Memory, Practice*, Ithaca, Cornell University Press, 1977.

— 'The concern for truth', in L.D. Kritzman (ed.), *Michel Foucault, Politics, Philosophy, Culture: Interviews and Other Writings of Michel Foucault 1977–1984*, London, Routledge, 1988.

— 'Technologies of the self', in L.H. Martin, H. Gutman and P.H. Hutton (eds), *Technologies of the Self: A Seminar with Michel Foucault*, Amherst, University of Massachusetts Press, 1988.

Fournel, Victor (ed.), *Les Contemporains de Molière: recueil de comédies rares ou peu connues jouées de 1650 à 1680*, 3 vols, Paris, Firmin Didot Frères, 1863.

Fowler, J. and Cornforth, J., *English Decoration in the 18th Century*, London, Barrie and Jenkins, 1978.

France, P., *Politeness and its Discontents: Problems in French Classical Culture*, Cambridge, Cambridge University Press, 1992.

Friedli, L., '"Passing women": a study of gender boundaries in the eighteenth century', in G.S. Rousseau and R. Porter (eds), *Sexual Underworlds of the Enlightenment*, Manchester, Manchester University Press, 1987.

Fukui, Y., *Raffinement précieux dans la poésie Française du XVIIe Siècle*, Paris, Nizet, 1964.

Fumaroli, M., *Le Genre des Genres Littéraires Français: la Conversation*, The Zaharoff Lecture for 1990–91, Oxford, Clarendon Press, 1992.

— 'Animus et Anima: l'instance féminine dans l'apologétique de la langue Française au XVIIième siècle, *XVIIième Siècle*, no. 144, July–September 1984, pp. 233–240.

Garber, M., *Vested Interests: Cross Dressing and Cultural Anxiety*, London, Routledge, 1992.

Gardiner, D., *English Girlhood at School*, Oxford, Oxford University Press, 1929.

Genette, G., *Figures I*, Paris, Seuil, 1966.

Gilbert, M., 'The origins of the reform movement in modern language teaching in England', Part I, *Research Review*, no. 4, September 1953,

pp. 1–9
—— 'The origins of the reform movement in modern language teaching in England', Part II, *Research Review*, no. 5, September 1954, pp. 9–18.
—— 'The origins of modern language teaching in England', Part III, *Research Review*, no. 6, September 1955, pp. 1–10.
Gill-Mark, G., *Mme du Boccage: une femme de lettres au XVIIIième siècle*, (1927), Geneva, Slatkine Reprints, 1976.
Gilmore, D.D., *Manhood in the Making: Cultural Concepts of Masculinity*, London, Yale University Press, London, 1990.
Girouard, M., *Life in the English Country House*, London, Yale University Press, 1978.
Goldgar, A., *Impolite Learning in Conduct and Community in the Republic of Letters 1680–1750*, London, Yale University Press, 1995.
Goldsmith, E., *'Exclusive Conversations': The Art of Interaction in Seventeenth-Century France*, Philadelphia, University of Pennsylvania Press, 1988.
Goldsmith, M.M., '"The Treacherous Arts of Mankind": Bernard Mandeville and female virtue', *History of Political Thought*, vol. 7, no. 1, Spring 1986, pp. 94–114.
Goodman, D., 'Enlightenment salons: the convergence of female and philosophic ambitions', *Eighteenth Century Studies*, 22, Spring 1989, pp. 329–350.
—— 'Public sphere and private life: toward a synthesis of current historiographical approaches to the old regime', *History and Theory*, 31, no. 1, 1992, pp. 1–20.
Gordon, D., *Citizens Without Sovereignty: Equality and Sociability in French Thought, 1670–1789*, Princeton, NJ, Princeton University Press, 1994.
Grafton A. and Jardine, L., *From Humanism to the Humanities: Education and the Liberal Arts in Fifteenth- and Sixteenth-Century Europe*, London, Duckworth, 1986.
Grant, C. and Hodgson, N., *The Case for Co-education*, London, Grant Richards, 1913.
Greenblatt, S., *Renaissance Self-Fashioning: From More to Shakespeare*, London, University of Chicago Press, 1980.
Guest, H., 'A double lustre: femininity and sociable commerce, 1730–60', *Eighteenth-Century Studies*, vol. 23, no. 4, Summer 1990, pp. 479–501.
Habermas, J., *The Structural Transformation of the Public Sphere*, Oxford, Polity Press, 1989.
Halsall, E., 'Linguistic Aptitude', *Modern Languages*, vol. 50, no. 1, March 1969, pp. 18–23.
Hans, N., *New Trends in Education in the Eighteenth Century*, London, Routledge & Kegan Paul, 1966.
Harth, E., *Ideology and Culture in Seventeenth-Century France*, London, Cornell University Press, 1983.
—— *Cartesian Women: Versions and Subversions of Rational Discourse in the Old Régime*, London, Cornell University Press, 1992.
Hawkins, E., *Modern Languages in the Curriculum*, Cambridge, Cambridge University Press, 1981.

Hearn J., and Morgan, D. (eds), *Men, Masculinities & Social Theory*, London, Unwin Hyman, 1990.

Heath, S., *The Sexual Fix*, London, Macmillan, 1982.

Hekman S.J., *Gender and Knowledge: Elements of a Postmodern Feminism*, Oxford, Polity Press, 1990.

Heltzel, Virgil Barney, 'Chesterfield and the tradition of the ideal gentleman', Ph.D. thesis, University of Chicago, 1925.

Henriques, J., Holway, W., Urwin, C., Venn, C. and Walkerdine, V., *Changing the Subject: Psychology, Social Regulation and Subjectivity*, London, Methuen, 1984.

Heward C., *Making a Man of Him: Parents and their Sons' Education at an English Public School 1929–1950*, London, Routledge, 1988.

Holmes, G. *Augustan England: Professions, State and Society 1680–1730*, London, George Allen and Unwin, 1982.

Horowitz, L.K., *Love and Language: A Study of Classical French Moralist Writers*, Columbus, OH, Ohio State University Press, 1977.

Hunt, F. (ed.), *Lessons for Life: the Schooling of Girls and Women 1850–1950*.

Jardine, L., *Still Harping on Daughters: Women and Drama in the Age of Shakespeare*, Brighton, The Harvester Press, 1983.

Jarrett, D., *England in the Age of Hogarth*, London, Yale University Press, 1986.

Jones, A.R., 'Nets and bridles: early modern conduct books and sixteenth-century women's lyrics, in Nancy Armstrong and Leonard Tennenhouse (eds), *The Ideology of Conduct: Essays on Literature and the History of Sexuality*, London, Methuen, 1987.

—— and Stallybrass, P., 'Fetishizing gender: constructing the hermaphrodite in Renaissance Europe', in J. Epstein and K. Straub (eds), *Body Guards: The Cultural Politics of Gender Ambiguity*, London, Routledge, 1991.

Jordanova, L., *Sexual Visions: Images of Gender in Science and Medicine between the Eighteenth and Twentieth Centuries*, Hemel Hempstead, Harvester Wheatsheaf, 1989.

Kamm, J., *Hope Deferred: Girls' Education in English History*, London, Methuen, 1965.

Kelly, A., Whyte, J. and Smail, B., *Final Report of the Girls into Science and Technology Project, (GIST)*, Manchester, Manchester University Press, 1984.

Kelly, L.G., *25 Centuries of Language Teaching: 500 BC–1969*, Rowley, MA, Newbury House, 1976.

Kelso, R., *Doctrine for the Lady of the Renaissance*, Urbana, University of Illinois Press, 1956.

Kimmel, M.S., 'The contemporary "crisis" of masculinity in historical perspective', in H. Brod (ed.), *The Making of Masculinities*, London, Allen and Unwin, 1987.

Klein, L.E. 'The rise of "politeness" in England, 1660–1715', Ph.D. thesis, Baltimore, Johns Hopkins University, 1984.

—— 'Liberty, manners and politeness in early 18th-century England', *The Historical Journal*, 32, no. 3, 1989, pp. 583–605.

—— 'Gender, Conversation and the Public Sphere', in J. Stills and M.

Worton (eds), *Textuality and Sexuality: Reading Theories and Practices*, Manchester, Manchester University Press, 1992.

—— *Shaftesbury and the Culture of Politeness: Moral Discourse and Cultural Politics in Early Eighteenth-Century England*, Cambridge, Cambridge University Press, 1994.

—— 'Gender and the public/private distinction in the eighteenth century: some questions about evidence and analytic procedure', *Eighteenth-Century Studies*, vol. 29, no. 1, 1995, pp. 97–109.

Kowaleski-Wallace, B., '"Milton's Daughters": the education of eighteenth-century women writers', *Feminist Studies*, vol. 12, no. 2, Summer 1986, pp. 275–293.

Kuchta, D., 'The semiotics of masculinity in Renaissance England', in J. G. Turner (ed.), *Sexuality and Gender in Early Modern Europe: Institutions, Texts, Images*, Cambridge, Cambridge University Press, 1993.

Lambert, R.S. (ed.), *The Grand Tour – A Journey in the Tracts of the Age of Aristocracy*, London, Faber and Faber, 1935.

Lambley, K., *The Teaching and Cultivation of the French Language in England during Tudor and Stuart Times*, Manchester, Manchester University Press, 1920.

Langford, P., *A Polite and Commercial People: England, 1727–1783*, Oxford, Oxford University Press, 1989.

Laqueur, T., *Making Sex: Body and Gender from the Greeks to Freud*, London, Harvard University Press, 1990.

Lathuillère, R., *La préciosité: étude historique et linguistique*, Geneva, Droz, 1966.

Lees-Milne, J., *Earls of Creation*, London, Hamish Hamilton, 1962.

Leonard, S.A., *The Doctrine of Correctness in English Usage*, New York, Russell and Russell, 1962.

Leppert, R., *Music and Image: Domesticity, Ideology and Socio-Cultural Formation in Eighteenth-Century England*, Cambridge, Cambridge University Press, 1988.

Levine, P., *Victorian Feminism 1850–1900*, London, Hutchinson, 1987.

Littlewood, W.T., *Foreign and Second Language Learning: Language Acquisition Research and its Implications for the Classroom*, Cambridge, Cambridge University Press, 1984.

Livet, Charles-L., *Précieux et Précieuses: caractères et moeurs littéraires du XVIIième siècle*, Paris, H. Welter, 1895.

Lockitt, C.H., *The Relations of French and English Society*, London, Longmans, Green and Co., 1920.

Lougée, C., *Le Paradis des Femmes: Women, Salons and Social Stratification in Seventeenth-Century France*, Princeton, NJ, Princeton University Press, 1979.

Loulidi, R., 'Is language learning really a female business?', *Language Learning Journal*, no. 1, March 1990, pp. 40–43.

Lowe, Lucy, 'Modern Languages', in S.A. Burstall and M.A. Douglas (eds), *Public Schools for Girls*, London, Longmans, Green and Co., 1911.

Maccubin, R.P. (ed.), *'Tis Nature's Fault': Unauthorized Sexuality During the Enlightenment*, Cambridge, Cambridge University Press, 1987.

Mack, E.C., *Public Schools and British Opinion 1780 to 1860*, London, Methuen, 1938.

McKeon, M., 'Historicizing patriarchy: the emergence of gender difference in England, 1660–1760', *Eighteenth Century Studies*, vol. 28, no. 3, Spring 1995, pp. 295–322.

Mackey, W.F., *Language Teaching Analysis*, London, Longman, 1965.

Maclean, I., *Woman Triumphant: Feminism in French Literature 1610–1652*, Oxford, Clarendon Press, 1977.

Magendie, M., *La politesse mondaine et les théories de l'honnêteté en France de 1600 à 1660*, Paris, Presses Universitaires de France, 1925.

Mallinson, V., *Teaching a Foreign Language*, London, Heinemann, 1953.

Marshall, J.D., 'Foucault and educational research', in S.J. Ball (ed.), *Foucault and Education: Disciplines and Knowledges*, London, Routledge, 1990.

Mason, H.T. and Doyle, W., *The Impact of the French Revolution on European Consciousness*, Gloucester, Alan Sutton, 1989.

Maxwell, C., *The English Traveller in France 1698–1815*, London, George Routledge & Sons, 1932.

Mead, W.E., *The Grand Tour in the Eighteenth Century*, New York, Benjamin Bloom, 1914.

Miller, P.J., 'Women's education, "Self-improvement" and social mobility – a late eighteenth-century debate', *British Journal of Educational Studies*, 20, 1972, pp. 302–314.

Mingay, G.E., *English Landed Society in the Eighteenth Century*, London, Routledge & Kegan Paul, 1963.

Montandon, A., 'De l'urbanité: entre étiquette et politesse', in Alain Montandon (ed.), *Etiquette et Politesse*, Association des Publications de La Faculté des Lettres et Sciences Humaines de Clermont Ferrand, 1992.

Moore, S., 'Getting a bit of the other – the pimps of postmodernism', in R. Chapman and J. Rutherford (eds), *Male Order: Unwrapping Masculinity*, London, Lawrence and Wishart, 1988.

Moriarty, M., *Taste and Ideology in Seventeenth-Century France*, Cambridge, Cambridge University Press, 1988.

Moscucci, O., *The Science of Woman: Gynaecology and Gender in England, 1800–1929*, Cambridge, Cambridge University Press, 1990.

Mosse, G.L., *Nationalism and Sexuality: Respectability and Abnormal Sexuality in Modern Europe*, New York, Howard Fertig, 1985.

Motley, M.E., *Becoming an Aristocrat: the Education of the Court Nobility 1580–1715*, Princeton, NJ, Princeton University Press, 1990.

Muir, K., *The Comedy of Manners*, London, Hutchinson, 1970.

Myers, S.H., *The Bluestocking Circle: Women, Friendship, and the Life of the Mind in Eighteenth-Century England*, Oxford, Clarendon Press, 1990.

Newman, G., *The Rise of English Nationalism: A Cultural History 1740–1830*, London, Weidenfeld & Nicolson, 1987.

Nye, R.A., *Masculinity and Male Codes of Honour in Modern France*, Oxford, Oxford University Press, 1993.

Ober, W.B., 'Eighteenth-century spleen' in C. Fox (ed.), *Psychology and Literature in the Eighteenth Century*, New York, AMS Press, 1987.

O'Day, R., *Education and Society 1500–1800: The Social Foundations of Education in Early Modern Britain*, London, Longman, 1982.

Ollard, R., *An English Education: A Perspective of Eton*, London, Collins, 1982.

Ong, W.J., 'Latin language study as a Renaissance puberty rite', in W.J. Ong (ed.), *Rhetoric, Romance and Technology: Studies in the Interaction of Expression and Culture*, Ithaca, Cornell University Press, 1971.

Palmer, H., *The Scientific Study and Teaching of Languages*, (1917), Oxford, Oxford University Press, 1968.

Pardailhé-Galabrun, A., *La naissance de l'intime: 3000 foyers parisiens XVIIième-XVIIIième siècles*, Paris, Presses Universitaires de France, 1988.

Parker, P., 'On the tongue: cross gendering, effeminacy and the art of words', *Style*, vol. 23, no. 3, Fall 1989, pp. 445–465.

Parks, G.B., 'Travel as education', in R.F. Jones (ed.), *The Seventeenth Century: Studies in the History of English Thought and Literature from Bacon to Pope*, Stanford, Stanford University Press, 1951.

Pearson, N., *Society Sketches in the Eighteenth Century*, London, Edward Arnold, 1911.

Peers, E.A., *'New' Tongues*, London, Pitman, 1945.

Pelous, J.M., *Amour précieux, amour galant 1654–1675: essai sur la représentation de l'amour dans la littérature et la société mondaines*, Paris, Klincksieck, 1980.

Percival, A.C., *The English Miss To-day and Yesterday*, London, G.G. Harrap and Co., 1939.

Perry, Ruth, *The Celebrated Mary Astell: An Early English Feminist*, London, University of Chicago Press, 1986.

Phillips, P., *The Scientific Lady, A Social History of Woman's Scientific Interests 1520–1918*, London, Weidenfeld & Nicolson, 1990.

Pimlott, J.A.R., *The Englishman's Holiday: A Social History*, London, Faber and Faber, 1947.

Pointon, M., 'The case of the dirty beau', in K. Adler and M. Pointon (eds), *The Body Imaged: the Human Form of Visual Culture Since the Renaissance*, Cambridge, Cambridge University Press, 1993.

Porter, R., *The Enlightenment*, Basingstoke, Macmillan, 1990.

—— 'English society in the eighteenth century revisited', in J. Black (ed.), *British Politics and Society from Walpole to Pitt 1742–1789*, London, Macmillan, 1990.

Posner, R., *Sex and Reason*, London, Harvard University Press, 1992.

Potkay, A., 'Classical eloquence and polite style in the age of Hume', *Eighteenth-Century Studies*, vol. 25, Part 1, 1991, pp. 31–56.

Powell, B., *Boys, Girls and Languages in School*, London, CILT, 1986.

—— and Littlewood, P., 'Foreign Languages: The Avoidable Option', *The British Journal of Language Teaching*, vol. 20, no. 3, Winter 1982, pp. 153–160.

Price, J., '"We're just here to make up the numbers really", The experience of girls in boys' public schools', in G. Walford (ed.), *The Private Schooling of Girls: Past and Present*, London, The Woburn Press, 1993.

Prickett, S., *England and the French Revolution*, London, Macmillan, 1989.

Quinlan, M.J., *Victorian Prelude: A History of English Manners 1700–1830*, London, Cass, 1965.

Reed, J., 'Academically speaking, language and nationalism in seventeenth- and eighteenth-century England', Ph.D. thesis, University of California, Irvine, 1991.

Rogers, P. (ed.), *The Context of English Literature: The Eighteenth Century*, London, Methuen, 1978.

Rogoff, I. and Van Leer D., 'Afterthoughts ... A dossier on masculinities', *Theory and Society*, Special Issue: *Masculinities*, vol. 22/5, October 1993.

Roper, L., *Oedipus and the Devil: Witchcraft, Sexuality and Religion in Early Modern Europe*, London, Routledge, 1994.

Roper, R. and Tosh, J., 'Historians and the politics of masculinity', in M. Roper and J. Tosh (eds), *Manful Assertions: Masculinities in Britain since 1800*, London, Routledge, 1991.

Rothblatt, S., *Tradition and Change in English Liberal Education: An Essay in History and Culture*, London, Faber and Faber, 1976.

Rousseau, G.S., 'Sodomy – that utterly confused category', in R.P. Maccubin (ed.), *'Tis Nature's Fault': Unauthorized sexuality during the Enlightenment*, Cambridge, Cambridge University Press, 1987.

—— 'Towards a semiotic of the nerve: the social history of language in a new key', in P. Burke and R. Porter (eds), *Language, Self and Society: A Social History of Language*, Oxford, Polity Press, 1991.

Sambrook, J., *The Eighteenth Century: The Intellectual and Cultural Context of English Literature, 1700–1789*, London, Longman, 1986.

Saumarez-Smith, C., *Eighteenth-Century Decoration: Design and the Domestic Interior in England*, London, Weidenfeld & Nicolson, 1993.

Schiebinger, L., *The Mind Has No Sex?: Women in the Origins of Modern Science*, London, Harvard University Press, 1989.

Scott, J.W., 'Gender: a useful category for historical analysis', *American Historical Review*, 91, November 1986, pp. 1053–1075.

—— 'Deconstructing equality-versus difference: or, the uses of post-structuralist theory for feminism', *Feminist Studies*, 14, no. 1, Spring 1988, pp. 33–50.

Sekora, J., *Luxury: The Concept in Western Thought, from Eden to Smollett*, London, The Johns Hopkins University Press, 1977.

Shapiro, S., '"Yon Plumed Dandebrat": male "effeminacy" in English satire and criticism', *Review of English Studies New Series*, vol. XXXIX, No. 155, 1988, pp. 400–412.

Sharpe, J.A., *Early Modern England: A Social History 1550–1760*, London, Edward Arnold, 1987.

Sheridan, A., *Foucault: The Will to Truth*, London, Tavistock Publications, 1980.

Simon, B., *Studies in the History of Education 1780–1870*, London, Lawrence and Wishart, 1969.

Smith, D.G., 'French and the less able', *Modern Languages*, vol. 54, no. 4, September 1973, pp. 105–115.

Smith, O., *The Politics of Language 1791–1819*, Oxford, Clarendon Press, 1984.

Spolsky, B., *Conditions for Second Language Learning*, Oxford, Oxford University Press, 1989.

Stanton, D.A., *The Aristocrat as Art: A Study of the Honnête Homme and the Dandy in Seventeenth- and Nineteenth-Century Literature*, New York, Columbia University Press, 1980.

— 'The fiction of préciosité and the fear of women', *Yale French Studies*, vol. 62, 1981, pp. 107–134.

Staves, S., 'A Few Kind Words for the Fop', *Studies in English Literature*, vol. 22, no. 3, 1982, pp. 413–428.

Stephens, R.C., 'The courtly tradition in English education from Sir Thomas Elyot to John Locke', Ph.D. thesis, University of Belfast, 1955.

Stern, H.H., *Fundamental Concepts of Language Teaching*, Oxford, Oxford University Press, 1984.

Stoye, J.M., *English Travellers Abroad 1604–1667*, London, Jonathan Cape, 1952.

Strosetzki, C., *Rhétorique de la Conversation: sa dimension littéraire et linguistique dans la société française du XVIIe siècle*, Papers on French Literature, Biblio 17, Paris, 1984.

Stubbs, M., *Knowledge about Language: Grammar, Ignorance and Society*, London, University of London, Institute of Education, 1990.

Sweet, Henry, *The Practical Study of Languages*, (1899), London, Oxford University Press, 1964.

Thom, D., 'Better a teacher than a hairdresser? "A Mad Passion for Equality" or, keeping Molly and Betty Down', in Felicity Hunt (ed.), *Lessons for Life: the Schooling of Girls and Women 1850–1950*, Oxford, Blackwell, 1987.

Thornton, P., *Seventeenth-Century Interior Decoration in England, France and Holland*, London, Yale University Press, 1978.

Threadgold, T., and Cranny-Francis, A., *Feminine, Masculine and Representation*, London, Allen and Unwin, 1990.

Tickner, L., *The Spectacle of Women: Imagery of the Suffrage Campaign 1907–14*, London, Chatto and Windus, 1987.

Tillyard, S., *Aristocrats*, London, Chatto and Windus, 1994.

Tinker, C.B., *The Salon and English Letters*, New York, Macmillan and Co., 1915.

Tompson, R.S., *Classics or Charity? The Dilemma of the 18th-Century Grammar School*, Manchester, Manchester University Press, 1971.

Towner, J., 'The European Grand Tour, c. 1550–1840: a study of its role in the history of tourism,' Ph.D. thesis, University of Birmingham, 1984.

Traill, Henry D., (ed.), *Social England*, 6 vols, (1896), London, Cassell & Co, 1904.

Trumbach, T., 'The birth of the queen: sodomy and the emergence of gender equality in modern culture, 1660–1750', in M. Duberman, M. Vicinus, and G. Chauncey (eds), *Hidden from History: Reclaiming the Gay and Lesbian Past*, London, Penguin, 1989.

Vance, N., *The Sinews of the Spirit: The Ideal of Christian Manliness in Victorian Literature and Religious Thought*, Cambridge, Cambridge University Press, 1985.

Vincent, W.A.L., *The Grammar Schools: Their Continuing Tradition 1660–1714*, London, Murray, 1969.

Voitle, R., *The Third Earl of Shaftesbury*, London, Louisiana State University Press, 1984.

Wakely, R., 'The history of French teaching in Britain: some remarks', *Association for French Language Studies Newsletter*, 20, Summer 1988, pp. 22–23.

Walden, R. and Walkerdine, V., 'Girls and mathematics: the early years', *Bedford Way Papers*, 8, London, Institute of Education 1982.

Walford, G. (ed.), *The Private Schooling of Girls: Past and Present*, London, The Woburn Press, 1993.

Walkerdine, V., *Counting Girls Out*, London, Virago, 1989.

—— *Schoolgirl Fictions*, London, Verso, 1990.

—— 'Femininity as performance', in Lynda Stone (ed.), *The Education Feminism Reader*, London, Routledge, 1994.

Warner, M., *From the Beast to the Blonde: On Fairy Tales and Their Tellers*, London, Chatto and Windus, 1994.

Watson, J.F., *The Beginnings of the Teaching of Modern Languages in England*, (1909), Wakefield, S.R Publishers, 1971.

Weedon, C., *Feminist Practice and Poststructuralist Theory*, Oxford, Basil Blackwell, 1987.

Weeks, J., 'Foucault for historians', *History Workshop Journal*, 14, Autumn 1982, pp. 106–119.

White, R.J., 'The Grand Tour' in A. Natan (ed.), *The Silver Renaissance: Essays in Eighteenth-Century English History*, London, Macmillan, 1961.

Williams, C.D., *Pope, Homer, and Manliness: Some Aspects of Eighteenth-Century Classical Learning*, London, Routledge, 1993.

Wilson, K., *The Sense of the People: Politics, Culture and Imperialism in England, 1715–1785*, Cambridge, Cambridge University Press, 1995.

Wolfe, P.J. (ed.), *Choix de Conversations de Mademoiselle de Scudéry*, Ravenna, Longo, 1977.

Zimmern, Alice, *The Renaissance of Girls' Education in England*, London, A.D. Innes & Co., 1898.

INDEX

Académie Française 28, 38
accomplishments: defined 55–6,
    64–5; contrasted to 'solid'
    education 62; and display 65,
    71; and effeminacy 100; 'false'
    68–74; and France 38, 55, 60;
    in French language 71–3; and
    national character 61–2; in
    relation to social space 66, 108;
    'true' 76, 77
achievement 59, 93–7; boys
    perceived as potential 94;
    Schools Inquiry Commission
    on girls 91–2
Addison, Joseph: delight in
    silence 106; on Frenchified
    men 37, 38; improvement
    on English from Hebrew 39;
    light talkative tongue 3; on
    taciturnity of the English
    33–5, 106, 107; women's
    conversation improves men 4
Alexander, William 109–10
Allestree, Richard: tongue a
    'slippery member' 2
Andrews, John: A Comparative
    View of the English and French
    Nations 50; comparing French
    and English women 77; on
    Frenchmen's masculinity 77;
    French substitute politeness for
    truth 3; on learning foreign
    languages 62, 107; on manly
    national character 9

archaeology 10
Ashton, John 41

Barker-Benfield, George 5
Barrell, John 5, 9, 62–3;
    gentleman defined as empty
    potential 59, 94
Baugh, Albert: History of the
    English Language 28–9
Bennett, John 70–1, 73; mental
    differences between boys and
    girls 80; politeness compatible
    with Christianity 73; homage
    to domestic women 76;
    Strictures on Female Education
    80–8
Black, Jeremy 57
Body Guards (Epstein and Straub)
    7
Boyer, Abel: The Compleat French
    Master for Ladies and Gentlemen
    85
Brightland, John 31
British Broadcasting Corporation
    xi
Brown, John 6
Burgh, James 62; bewitching
    pleasure of French 6–7;
    distinguishing men of sense
    from fools 59–60
Burnet, Gilbert 57
Burney, Fanny 72
Burton, John: on 'false' politeness
    73, 75; on girls learning French

171

INDEX

Printed in the United Kingdom
by Lightning Source UK Ltd.
131465UK00004B/7/A